ROUTLEDGE LIBRARY EDITIONS:
COMMUNICATION STUDIES

Volume 9

RECEPTION AND RESPONSE

RECEPTION AND RESPONSE

Hearer Creativity and the Analysis of Spoken and Written Texts

Edited by
GRAHAM MCGREGOR AND R.S. WHITE

Routledge
Taylor & Francis Group
LONDON AND NEW YORK

First published in 1990 by Routledge

This edition first published in 2016
by Routledge
2 Park Square, Milton Park, Abingdon, Oxon OX14 4RN

and by Routledge
711 Third Avenue, New York, NY 10017

Routledge is an imprint of the Taylor & Francis Group, an informa business

British Library Cataloguing in Publication Data
A catalogue record for this book is available from the British Library

ISBN: 978-1-138-93903-5 (Set)
ISBN: 978-1-315-67052-2 (Set) (ebk)
ISBN: 978-1-138-94044-4 (Volume 9) (hbk)
ISBN: 978-1-315-67045-4 (Volume 9) (ebk)

Publisher's Note
The publisher has gone to great lengths to ensure the quality of this reprint but points out that some imperfections in the original copies may be apparent.

Disclaimer
The publisher has made every effort to trace copyright holders and would welcome correspondence from those they have been unable to trace.

Reception and Response

Hearer Creativity and the Analysis of Spoken and Written Texts

Edited by
Graham McGregor
R.S. White

Routledge
London and New York

First published 1990
by Routledge
11 New Fetter Lane, London EC4P 4EE

Simultaneously published in the USA and Canada by Routledge
a division of Routledge, Chapman and Hall, Inc.
29 West 35th Street, New York, NY 10001

Printed in Great Britain
by T.J. Press, Padstow, Cornwall

British Library Cataloguing in Publication Data
also available

Library of Congress Cataloging in Publication Data
Reception and response : hearer creativity and the analysis of spoken and written texts / edited by Graham McGregor, R.S. White.
p. cm.
Bibliography: p.
ISBN 0-415-01075-6
1. Listening. 2. Oral communication. 3. Hermeneutics.
4. Criticism. I. McGregor, Graham. II. White, R. S., 1948- .
P95.46.R44 1990 89-10491
302.2′42—dc20 CIP

Contents

Notes on the contributors

CHRISTINE CALLENDER has a degree in English and Education from Roehampton Institute, where she specialized in linguistics, with a particular interest in the language of the black community. She is a part-time youth worker and is currently training as a teacher.

DEBORAH CAMERON studied linguistics at the Universities of Newcastle upon Tyne and Oxford, and now teaches the subject at Roehampton Institute, London. She is author of *Feminism and Linguistic Theory* (London, Macmillan, 1985) and joint author with Talbot Taylor of *Analysing Conversation* (Oxford, Pergamon, 1987).

SUSAN CORDWELL taught young children and adults with acute learning difficulties, psychiatric patients, and prisoners before doing an MA in Women's Studies. She is now working full-time in primary school and teaching on gender issues in continuing and higher education in Sheffield.

MARK CORNER teaches Religious Studies at the University of Newcastle upon Tyne. He is interested in approaches to biblical interpretation, and is currently working on a book concerned with the use of the Bible in the theology of liberation.

JUSTINE COUPLAND is Research Associate at the University of Wales, Cardiff, Centre for Applied English Language Studies. She is co-editor of *Contexts of Accommodation: Developments in Applied Sociolinguistics* (forthcoming, Cambridge, Cambridge University Press). Other published work, in stylistics, discourse analysis, and gerontological sociolinguistics appears in *Language in Society*, *Language and Communication*, and *Textual Practice*.

NIKOLAS COUPLAND is Director of the Centre for Applied Language Studies at the University of Wales, Cardiff. He is author of *Dialect in Use: Sociolinguistic Variation in Cardiff English* (Cardiff, University of Wales Press, 1988), editor of *Styles of Discourse* (London, Routledge and Kegan Paul, 1988) and coeditor of three other books due to appear in the near future. His other published work is principally in the areas of sociolinguistic style, discourse variation, and gerontological sociolinguistics and appears in journals such as *Language in Society*, *International Journal of the Sociology of Language*, *Language and Communication* and *Journal of Language and Social Psychology*. With Howard Giles, he codirects an interdisciplinary ESRC research programme entitled 'Communication and the Elderly'.

CHRISTINE DEVONSHIRE taught English in Comprehensive Schools before doing an MA in the nineteenth- and twentieth-century novel at East Anglia University. She has taught EFL in Italy and established women's literature classes for the WEA and in the Department of Continuing Education, University of Sheffield while teaching part-time at Newcastle University. She has written articles on contemporary European women writers, contributed nineteenth-century entries for a forthcoming companion to women's writing in English and is completing doctoral research on the 'sensation' novelist Mary Elizabeth Braddon in Sheffield, where she lives with her daughter.

HOWARD GILES is Professor of Social Psychology and Director of the Centre of Communication and Social Relations at the University of Bristol. He is founding editor of both the *Journal of Language and Social Psychology* and a forthcoming annual on language and communication in the Pacific Rim as well as being general editor of three books series relating to social psychology and language. He has published widely in the areas of language attitudes, speech accommodation theory, and intercultural communication.

PETER GOODRICH is a lecturer in law at the University of Newcastle upon Tyne where he teaches jurisprudence. He gained his LLB from Sheffield University and PhD from the University of Edinburgh before teaching law at Liverpool Polytechnic. He has published two books – *Reading the Law* (Oxford, Blackwell, 1986) and *Legal Discourse* (London, Macmillan, 1987) as well as numerous articles, and is currently working on a book on the grammatology of the common law tradition for Weidenfeld & Nicolson.

KAREN HENWOOD graduated with a BSc in psychology from the University of Bristol in 1981 and gained a doctorate in social psychology from the same university in 1987. She has been a joint small research grant holder from the Nuffield Foundation with Howard Giles, investigating intergenerational stereotyping and speech accommodation. From 1985, she has been employed as Research Associate on the ESRC funded interdisciplinary (applied linguistics and social psychology) project on 'Communication and the Elderly', directed by Howard Giles and Nikolas Coupland.

DEBORAH HILLS is a graduate of the Roehampton Institute in London. She is now teaching English at Epsom College, Surrey.

IAN MASON is a senior lecturer in French at the University of Heriot Watt, where his major research interest is in translation theory. He undertook his undergraduate and doctoral research at the Queen Mary College in London. He is coauthor of two language teaching texts, *Français en Faculté* and *Lyon à la Une*, and currently working on similar material in Spanish for a multimedia course.

GRAHAM McGREGOR teaches sociolinguistics and English language at the University of Newcastle upon Tyne where he has been a lecturer since 1978. He is editor of *Language for Hearers* (Oxford, Pergamon, 1986) and coeditor with R.S. White of *The Art of Listening* (London, Croom Helm, 1986). He has published a number of papers on the theme of conversational inferencing by third-persons in journals such as *Language and Communication* and *Language and Speech*.

JOHN PELLOWE has taught linguistics at universities in England, Libya, and China. He is well known for his scholarly contributions to sociolinguistics and currently teaches DIY syntax at the National University of Singapore, where he is a senior lecturer.

RICHARD TEDESCHI received his BA in psychology from Syracuse University in 1972 and his PhD in clinical psychology from Ohio University in 1976. He served his clinical psychology internship at North Carolina Memorial Hospital in Chapel Hill from 1975 to 1976. Since then he has held a faculty position at the University of North Carolina at Charlotte where he is currently Associate Professor of Psychology. During 1987 he was Visiting Professor in the Department of Psychology at the University of Newcastle upon Tyne.

ROBERT SHARPE is Professor of Philosophy at St David's University College, University of Wales. He has particular interests in aesthetics, the aesthetics of music, and Freud, and is author of *Contemporary Aesthetics* (London, Harvester, 1986).

R.S. WHITE is Professor of English at the University of Western Australia. He grew up in Sydney and was educated at Adelaide (law and arts) and Balliol College, Oxford. He has held positions as Senior Lecturer in English Literature at the University of Newcastle upon Tyne and Visiting Research Fellow at the Australian National University. He has published many articles and four books on Shakespeare, the latest of which is *Keats as a Reader of Shakespeare* (London, Athlone, 1987).

Introduction

Graham McGregor and R.S. White

This collection reflects widespread interest in an idea that was first mooted in a previous volume for Croom Helm, McGregor, G. and White, R.S. (eds) *The Art of Listening* (1986), and in a more specifically linguistic context by McGregor, G. (ed.) *Language for Hearers* (1986). In essence, the idea is that the active and creative abilities of listeners and readers deserve as much attention as the skills of speakers and writers. As a result of both these projects, we became increasingly convinced of the wider implications of the idea, and its potential application, across and within different disciplinary contexts. Subsequent correspondence and discussion with individuals from widely differing subject backgrounds have not only reinforced our own conviction but also encouraged us to extend and develop the idea.

Each essay in the present collection builds upon a *recipient*- rather than a *production*-centred approach to the analysis of spoken and written texts. The notion of recipiency is inextricably tied to the notion of response since for us reception *is* response, and response *is* reception. In other words, we are not dealing here with discrete categories but simultaneous processes that are dynamically active as a consequence of individual creativity, selectivity and/or reactivity to *language use* in whatever medium or variety. We focus on the role of *hearers* and *readers* because it is they, as receiver–responders, who are the actual arbiters of what becomes meaningfully determinant in an interpretive sense. It is thus their achievements, their contributions, their skills which principally concern us here.

A corollary of the perspective adopted in the collection is that divisions between subject areas are at best artificial and at worst designed to promote concepts of elitist mystification of knowledge. Consequently, although a number of the contributions may be identified with particular subject areas, such as law, psychotherapy, discourse analysis and sociolinguistics, or within some newly-existing theoretical framework, like reception theory or reader-response criticism, individual authors have contributed to the general philosophy of the volume by *responding*, in their own ways, to issues and debates that we hope will be both comprehensible and stimulating for readers with widely differing interests. In order to accommodate these interests, the collection has been organized to reflect three major themes.

In Part one, **Contexts of responsiveness**, four essays consider the social significances of listening in quite disparate settings – the law court, the psychotherapeutic interview, and radio phone-in programmes. The theoretical and practical implications of recipiency in each setting are weighed by each of the authors, demonstrating the very narrow constraints of much of our listening practice.

Peter Goodrich argues in Chapter 1 that lay images of law are fostered by both the legal community and by the media. The perception of legal discourse as objective, rule-governed, and unequivocal is challenged in the light of different responses within the courtroom and particularly by juries, litigants, witnesses, and lay advocates. Detailed examination of particular cases is used in order to deconstruct the predominantly objectivist versions of legal argumentation.

In Chapter 2, Richard Tedeschi works from the basis that listening is at the very core of all therapeutic activities. He considers the contribution of important psychotherapists to the development of therapeutic listening and identifies three components of the listening process: the selective attention to particular aspects of the client's disclosures, the formulation of a therapeutic response, and the client's perception of that response as s/he listens to the therapist. The difficulties and pitfalls of therapeutic listening are confronted within this framework, and the activity compared to other types of listening practice.

Chapter 3, by Deborah Cameron and Deborah Hills, focuses on the medium of radio in terms of the virtually unique status it accords to the category of *listeners*. The genre of the 'phone-in' constitutes their primary interest because it entails a constant renegotiation of the roles of *speaker* and *listener* by presenters, callers, and studio guests, as well as being subject to various constraints that are a consequence of the existence of a mass of inaudible, yet ever-present listeners. Examination of the ways in which these negotiations are handled by presenters shows how relationships are managed both with actual callers and the generalized audience – the 'listeners out there'.

Finally in this section, John Pellowe explores the concept of 'context' itself. By detailed discussion of how the term has been used and continues to be used in a confused and confusing way, the essay confronts a problem that has perplexed scholars since modern linguistic study began, namely how to decide 'What is context?' or 'What is the context?' of some particular linguistic act. However, if we focus on the issue of recipiency, these questions need to be rephrased. Thus Pellowe explores the ramifications, for language study, of asking, '*Who* is context'? or '*Who* is the context?' of some communicative sequence.

Part two is titled **Listener response and communication**. It presents four essays which seek to analyse interpretive behaviour and strategies in social interactions ranging from everyday communicative events, intergenerational discourse, and the oral mode of translation, to Black Pentecostal church services.

Graham McGregor considers a special case of interpretive work in Chapter 5; that of third-party inferencing-making. This work is based on the ideas of Harvey Sacks and John Gumperz in particular, and responds to the need to provide a closer understanding of how linguistic and social knowledge interact in discourse interpretation. The research presented involves various studies of 'eavesdropping', that is, the means by which different third-person participant and non-participant judges make sense of tape-recorded extracts taken from everyday verbal exchanges. This method enables the exploration of communicative norms and processes that are not normally verbalized by participants in talk. Its methodological and theoretical implications are considered thereafter.

The experience of age and ageing in social encounters and between social groups is investigated in Chapter 6 by Nikolas Coupland *et al.* They show that the discourse of talk between different generations is more than descriptively interesting, since it can expose the interplay of generational wishes and needs, beliefs, stereotypes, and assumptions, fulfilment, and dissatisfactions. Their essay examines one complex of strategies – to do with the disclosure of 'painful', personal information – in intergenerational talk, realized in a corpus of video-taped interactions involving young and elderly women. These strategies are characterized through detailed discourse analyses, and set against attitudinal data based on a comparable young female population's reports of the elderly's and their own beliefs about self-disclosive talk. The implications of these intergenerational patterns (behavioural and cognitive) are discussed in terms of speech accommodation theory, and a model of psycho-socio-linguistic interaction is premissed on considerations of recipiency.

Ian Mason deals with the oral mode of translating, known more generally as simultaneous translation, in Chapter 7. This mode is compared to written translating, where the translator's response to a source text is subject to all kinds of modifications before it appears in the form of a target text and hence raises difficulties if one attempts to recover the translator's immediate response during the reading process. In the oral mode of simultaneous interpreting, however, the translator's response is immediate, can be heard directly if we tune into the translator's output, and is as a consequence presumably much closer to the actual listening process. Comparison of five trainee interpreters' output from the same source text provides striking evidence of differences in their 'text worlds' as listeners.

The fourth essay in this section, by Christine Callender and Deborah Cameron (Chapter 8), contests the view that preaching can be described in rather simple terms as a speech event where one active speaker dominates an essentially passive congregation. They analyse the conventions of Black Pentecostal worship at two London churches. Sermons in Pentecostal contexts are clearly interactive performances structured by the creative abilities and interventions of listening members of the congregation, and indeed by the preacher listening to his flock. Observations about the nature of these performances are linked to the work of Max Atkinson on the nature of political oratory, and to ethnographic studies of black verbal culture in general.

We complete the volume (Part three) with a change of medium from spoken to written language use, and in particular to the case of the **responsive reader**. The section opens with an essay by Robert Sharpe on the subject of reader response criticism. It begins by considering this approach in the context of other literary critical modes such as text-based criticism (New Criticism) and post-structuralist theory. The essay then traces the development of reader response theory and goes on to examine its relevance to critical practice. It is argued that some aspects of literature and, indeed, some literary styles can benefit from reader response theory but that, in general, it has limitations; namely, the limitations imposed by acceptable interpretation.

The antithesis to this approach is one of interpretative diversity and open-endedness. From limit setting, the following three chapters return to the theme of individual creative responsiveness, and the fertile possibilities of reader-oriented analysis. Thus in Chapter 10, Christine Devonshire and Susan Cordwell provide a comparison of how four very different groups (taught by themselves) responded to Nadine Gordimer's novel, *Burger's Daughter*. The book is essentially about the search for a personal voice, where the capacity to hear it is part of self-definition. By examining how far the expectations of teachers and students help to determine what is heard both in the text and in particular responses to it, the authors present a uniquely feminist perspective that offers much in the way of critical insight and challenge.

When the text happens to be the Bible, rather than a novel, the volume of its readership and the plurality of that readership's reading increases exponentially. Biblical criticism initially thought of its task as an historical one, as Mark Corner points out in Chapter 11. It would recover the intentions of the authors of Scripture, identifying their sources and placing them within the cultural context of the ancient world. New forms of biblical criticism associated with structuralism, literary critcism, and the theology of liberation have challenged the confidence of the 'historical' approach in its task, and have pointed to the importance of studying the context in which the Bible is read and heard today as well as that in which it was written. The author concludes that both aspects must be integrated into the process of interpretation. Hence, just as nineteenth-century biblical criticism drew upon an interest in history that affected the classical scholars of the time, so contemporary biblical criticism draws upon an interest in hermeneutics that has profound implications across many disciplines.

In the final essay of the volume, R.S. White proclaims 'the birth of the reader'. He does so by making it clear that neither traditional approaches to literary criticism, nor newer theoretical models, can justly define the limits of debate. If the author is dead, and the text neutral, then the reader is, and always has been, creatively active and very much alive. The contribution of individual knowledge and experience to reading practice is evaluated in the light of of a process that is not merely passive reception of finite material, but the art of selecting and creating personal sense.

In the process of compiling any collection such as this, there are all manner of readings and responses, re-readings, responses to outside readers' reports, letters to the publisher, letters to contributors, the exercise of patience and abandonment to impatience, conversations which can be excited or gloomy. A kind of closure comes only when an artefact exists which did not exist before, when it is ready for readers to take over. Then it appears to have a singleness or simplicity of existence that belies all the chaos from which it came. This kind of closure, however is an illusion, for when the book is plucked from a library shelf, a whole new process, an open-ended and limitless one, begins as ideas grow in unexpected ways.

Within such a book, seams may show between essays as a result of internal contradictions, holes in the logic, or disagreements in the content. However, it has not been our purpose as editors to try to conceal or to patch up for the sake of achieving cosmetic unity of material. This is partly because the subjects and individual responses of our contributors were too diverse to submit to homogenization, and more importantly because we believe that any 'statement', whether written or spoken, contains rifts that should be acknowledged as windows to new meanings rather than condemned as flaws. It is these that can potentially be the most creative aspects of the enterprise, giving readers unanswered questions, provisional answers ripe for re-opening, tantalizing hints in new directions, dark spaces illuminated.

Beneath all the editorial self-doubts and worries encountered along the way, what has emerged is a strengthening of our conviction in the timeliness and importance of developing theories of 'listening' that are sensitive to the creativity of receptive responsiveness. An almost universal mode of analysis in all fields of thought has underwritten and perpetuated the idea that our's is a civilization whose accomplishments are manifest in literary and verbal performance. A hungry, impatient media waits to cite the words of belligerent leaders, and is avid for 'news'. Debate is dominated by articulate and eloquent, if not necessarily moral forces. Advertising flourishes by the persuasiveness and relentlessness of its 'messages'. Consumer responsiveness is sought only in the name of profit. Self-appointed authorities express outrage in the name of safeguarding 'standards' of speaking and writing, public order and morality. The writers of words and images have their say, and are traditionally paid loving and relatively uncritical attention.

Where there is dogma and social injustice, there is also an inherent deafness to real need, and power is misappropriated where the desire to listen is effectively abandoned. The impulse behind this collection is to allow a backing away from such procedures of reasoning, to highlight their stark contradictions even at the risk of revealing our own, rather than pretending these can be glibly explained away or disguised in rhetoric. If there is to be social progress, it must come by listening in good faith, and this means without motive or prejudice, without manipulating the 'voice' of power in order to control.

Can there be such progress in the complex and difficult world in which we live? Yes, there can. But this requires us to unpick some of our deepest assumptions about the dangerously self-destructive environment human beings have created (however unwittingly) for themselves. We suggest that new beginnings will always be possible where, and when, reception *is* response.

Final words must go to all those who have contributed to the volume. The project owes its life to the receptiveness and responsiveness of our co-writers, and we offer sincere thanks for their unselfish sharing of ideas. Special thanks also to Alison Gallagher for typing the manuscript and to helping with the preparation of what was to be camera-ready-copy. Judy Baker wrote a special programme for laser printing, and though this too was unused we are grateful for her work and advice. For permission to quote from her work, we are grateful to Elizabeth Jolley; for permission to quote from A.F. Parker-Rhodes, we are grateful to his heir and executor Adam Parker-Rhodes.

Elaine and Jane have seen us through another volume with all that this implies; our appreciation of their love and suppport is immeasurable.

Part one

Contexts of responsiveness

Chapter one

Attending the hearing: listening in legal settings

Peter Goodrich

Introduction

The Queen Charlotte Islands form a small archipelago off the coast of mainland British Columbia. Lyell Island is the largest of the group and has been inhabited since before the Dutch and subsequent British discovery and colonization of western Canada, by the Haida Indians. The island is covered by primordial forest and its traditional economy is based upon woodcraft and fishing. In early 1985, and without consulting the inhabitants of the islands, the government of British Columbia granted a logging licence to an American company, Western Forest Products Ltd. to exploit the islands for lumber. By a variety of means, which included inserting metal spikes into the trunks of trees and a non-violent blockade, the Haida Indians prevented Western Forest Products Ltd. from commencing logging. On 6 November 1985, Western Forest Products Ltd. issued a writ naming the president of the Council of Haida nations, Chief Richardson, as defendant in an action for an injunction seeking to prevent any further interference with logging on the island. The case of *Western Forest Products Ltd. v. Richardson and Others*[1] came before the Supreme Court of British Columbia and was heard by Justice McKay in the following week.

At the preliminary hearing of the case, the Haida Indians appeared before the court unrepresented by lawyers and endeavoured to argue their preliminary case without legal assistance. During argument Justice McKay on several occasions attempted to persuade Chief Richardson to employ Counsel and eventually adjourned the case for three days during which time he urged the defendant to obtain representation. For the period of the recess, Chief Richardson persisted in refusing legal representation, partly on the ground of cost but primarily on the ground of not wishing to create an illusion of justice: 'the issue of our lands is too important to leave in the hands of lawyers who are unfamiliar with our people'. He was also reported as remarking that 'for whatever reason, [Justice McKay] does not want us to speak for ourselves'. It should also be noted in this context, first, that in Haida custom any dispute over land or the use of land was traditionally settled by consent, negotiation and participation rather than by adjudication, and, second, that logging of the islands threatened not simply the community and lifestyle of the Haida but their existence as a nation, insofar as its economic consequences would force large numbers of the community to leave the islands.

On the first day of the trial Chief Richardson appeared before the court in full ceremonial dress accompanied by eighteen elders of the Haida nations but without lawyers. The significance of the ceremonial dress, a button blanket, is that the embroidery on the blanket symbolically depicts both the status of the wearer within the Haida nation and also denotes the wearer's relationship to and rights over traditional lands. No comment was made as to the ceremonial dress nor was evidence allowed as to its significance. Despite subsequently expressed doubts, Justice McKay allowed Chief Richardson to speak to the court and to call witnesses. At the risk of vastly oversimplifying a court transcription that runs to over a thousand pages, the following sequence of arguments were heard – though arguably heard only in a notional sense – by the court. Draped in red and black button blankets, all witnesses called addressed the issue of the Haida's arrival in and occupation of the Queen Charlotte archipelago. Noting that the writ served on the Haida made reference, as was until recently the standard form for common law writs, to the 'grace of God', Chief Lightbrown and others retold at length the mythological history of the Haida arrival in the islands. God, whom they referred to as the 'Great Spirit and Creator', had granted the islands to the Haida at the beginning of time for their use and occupation. They had a right 'to stand on the islands' and to act as caretakers from that moment at the dawn of time when the first Indians had emerged, according to Haida legend, from a clamshell carried by a raven and dropped on the sands of the islands.

A series of further anecdotal narratives, mythologies and traditional poems were presented to the court as evidence of the ancestral claim of the Haida to the islands. Several Haida artists explained at length the character and symbolism of their art forms, of their totem poles, masks and carvings all of which also spoke to the integral relationship of the Haida to the land, of their love of it and respect for it. They had been there since time began, yet were threatened by a writ and a property right that ran only to a hundred or so years. After the island's forests had been reduced to stumps by the loggers, the intruders would leave but the Haida would remain to inhabit what was left of their destiny and their island. They would have nowhere else to go. Of the other anecdotes and histories presented the most striking occurs towards the end of the evidence, when one of the women elders sang traditional songs to the court for a full afternoon. The songs repeated ancestral legends and evidenced again that in Haida custom and art, inhabitant and nature were one; that as occupiers of the islands the Haida do not differentiate themselves from their environment but rather see their culture and community as being inextricably and intrinsically bound up in the land. She ended her songs weeping. Chief Richardson concluded his defence by appeal to natural justice, which he argued invested the Haida cause with a spirit of truth that pre-existed and would long survive any ruling as to law.

The testimony presented to the court was extremely novel in legal terms. It took the form of symbolic dress, mythologies, legends, stories, poems and songs together with more prosaic arguments as to Haida customary law of dispute settlement and land claims. Unreserved[2] judgment was given by the court the day after argument ended. Justice McKay observed that the court would not normally have allowed argument of the political kind heard but that, in view of the fact that the Haida had no other arena available to them, he had been prepared to listen and generously recommended that a record of the evidence presented should be kept for posterity. The judgment itself was extremely brief. The evidence presented as to the Haida title to and relationship with the islands was not legally relevant to the case being heard which simply concerned interference with a valid logging licence. In law he had no alternative but to grant an injunction and he proceeded to do so while absolving himself of any moral responsibility by remarking in time-honoured form that 'while people sometimes think that judges have the power to do what they want, they must in fact act according to law; they administrate the law but cannot make policy'. In short, although it was the only arena available to the Haida, the court was not prepared to countenance their arguments which related not to law but rather to those more intangible courts of politics, history and moral reason. In those arenas the Haida might well be vindicated and justice be seen to lie down on their side; but in the meantime the trees and their livelihood would have been prised from their lands and their nation dispersed.[3]

The apparently emotive example of legal deafness presented in *Western Forest Products Ltd. v. Richardson and Others* is in fact no more than a vivid illustration of the procedural peculiarities and stringent evidential rules of relevance and admissibility that pertain to all forms of legal dialogue. Routine hearings for rent arrears, repossession of goods bought on credit, unfair dismissal, maintenance, breach of the peace, social security appeals or incompletely performed contracts exhibit identical disparities between expectations of audience and the reality of routine processing of claims before tribunals and the lower courts. As is reasonably accurately articulated in popular presentations of the legal community, the law, both as an institution and as a profession, represents itself as an arcane and elite pursuit. Its image of a language is that of a peculiarly legal reasoning, that of the logic of rules, and its forms of utterance reflect the idiosyncracies and inaccessibility of a language that is 'learned' in both senses of the term. In the most obvious of senses, legal dialogue is exclusory in the same manner that medieval usage of Latin was exclusory, namely that the language of legal communication is not a vernacular usage but rather a closely-guarded and professionally-governed specialist register whose lexicon and syntax reflect the historical influence of two alien, and one obsolete, specifically legal dialects (Mellinkoff, 1963). Against the background of that history it should be born in mind that before any lawyer is equipped to 'estreat recognisances', 'escheat' property, pass 'fee simples', attend to '*res judicata*', counsel in '*voir dire*' or plead '*ex turpi causa non oritur actio*' they have applied in excess of six years to the acquisition of the language and techniques of the legal register. As the case of the Haida Indian land claim well illustrates, however powerful the arguments or cause, however justified the case in terms of natural justice or moral competence, it is unlikely to be to the advantage of the laity to speak for themselves in legal settings, they are unlikely to be heard. It is rather to their benefit to join the community of legal language and to place their civility and their fate in the hands of the profession.

It is to that profession and language, to the complex particularity of a legal audience, that the present essay will turn in endeavouring to outline certain of the more salient features of listening in legal settings. Throughout, my theme will be that irrespective of the aura of rationality and of specialism that surrounds legal hearings, they are best depicted not in terms of the law's own image, that of impartiality and the inexorable necessity of the application of pre-existent rules of statute and precedent, but rather in terms of the uneven exchange that characterizes the flawed dialogue or 'distorted communication' of most contemporary bureaucratic discourses. What underpins and prolongs the unilateral monologue of most legal auditoria is not the exquisite precision of scientific expression but is simply political expedience and the linguistic manifestation of the vested interest of economically and sexually dominant social groups.

Legal auditoria

The books of the law run to many volumes. If one includes the full panoply of historical and contemporary law in force, together with the synopses, commentaries, doctrinal and procedural writings, updates and treatises on method, it runs to many libraries. It is a literal impossibility to know the law, and even if one expended an entire existence in legal repositories, one could only ever know part of the law. While much law is available in literary form to those trained in the art of finding and reading it, it should also be observed that many decisions are not reported, and that many that are transcribed are not published but are only available in court libraries to which the judiciary alone have access. Even were one to accept for the sake of argument that the physical availability of law rendered the majority of legal rules accessible, in a broader sense the unequal distribution of legal knowledge gives the profession or community of lawyers an inevitable advantage or superiority in the forms and utility of legal discourse. In both linguistic and rhetorical senses dialogue before the law is likely to be heavily weighted in favour of legal actors, a point which I will pursue in terms of legal audience by examining first the pragmatic contexts of legal address, and second the specific linguistic forms of legal argumentation.

The image of law as a pre-eminently rational enterprise, as the inexorable application of axiomatic rules, is predicated in the main upon doctrinal systematizations of statutory law and the reported decisions of a very small number of higher courts. It is primarily upon the strength of textbook studies of a relatively small number of appeal court decisions – most notably those of the High Court, the Court of Appeal and the House of Lords – that notions of the certainty and completeness of legal regulation are derived. Invested with a high degree of public visibility and symbolic prominence, these courts inspire the mythology of legal certainty and of the mystery of legal presence, which textbooks reformulate for didactic educational purposes without ever evidencing either the necessity of the decisions reported, or their relevance to the preponderant domain of law's public presence. That presence of law as social discipline and authoritative regulation intersects with public life at a wholly different and largely unrelated level, that of enforcement agencies, tribunals and courts of first instance, within which arena those sitting in judgment are seldom legally trained, and in which those who 'come before' the system of justice are rarely if ever successful in their pleas. The conviction rates in 1978 were 84 per cent of English Crown Court cases (93 per cent of indictable offences, 95 per cent of non-indictable cases) in the magistrates' courts. It is the bureaucracy, in the form of the police, administrative agencies, and large corporate enterprises, that are overwhelmingly the victors in the adversarial process of trial. In criminal cases, for example, the majority of defendants are unrepresented, and statistically the vast bulk of them plead guilty as charged, sample studies indicating that 76–93 per cent of defendants in magistrates' courts and 57–75 per cent in higher courts enter guilty pleas (McBarnet, 1983). The defendant's day in court is seldom a voluble one; their hearing is brief and their processing swift.

Assuming that the process of justice, of receiving a hearing, is best understood in terms of that point at which law is created and applied to members of the public (that is, at the point at which it becomes law for them) then the image of legal rationality as a phenomenon of texts and rules has only the most indirect of relevances. The day in court is likely rather to be experienced in terms of confusion, ambiguity, incomprehension, panic and frustration and if justice is *seen* to be done it is so seen by outsiders to the process (Cain, 1985). Nor is justice likely to be *heard* to be done by participants in the trial. The visual metaphor of justice as something that must be visible and seen enacted has a striking poignance, in that it well captures the paramount symbolic presence of law as a facade, a drama that unrolls before the eyes of those subject to it. Any attempt to depict the nature of a legal hearing does well to begin by examining that visibility, the physical structure and architecture of a peculiar auditory space.

Legal dialogue, and particularly the verbal creation of law, occurs in very specific formal institutional settings (Atkinson and Drew, 1979). Although the architecture, the spatial arrangement, symmetries and positionings, of the contemporary courtroom are variable, certain general structural features can be singled out. By way of introduction we may observe briefly that the relationship between culture, communication and the built environment has not been the object of very extensive study (Preziosi, 1979, 1984). To the relatively obvious issue of acoustics, contemporary architectural studies have, however, added an impressive list of signifying dimensions to public spaces: buildings variously store information, hierarchically arrange communicational relations, separate and align visual axes, strategically facilitate the administration of their occupants and above all, in Foucault's terminology, construct and constitute 'enunciative modalities' (Foucault, 1981). The latter concept refers to the fashion in which social discourse or discursive formations are tied to particular sites and roles, bound to specific institutional settings within which specifically delimited subjects are socially authorized to present a qualified specialist speech. The enunciative modality determines both what can and should be said within a particular form, that of, for example, a lecture, a political speech, a sermon or a judgment, as well as delimiting the context and conditions of its reception and appropriation in, respectively, the lecture theatre, the hustings, the church or the courtroom. Intrinsic to such enunciative modalities is not simply an analytic space, but equally a physical architecture which both delimits and contributes to the symbolic effect of carefully-regulated genres of speech. The building hosts and echoes the semantic import of discourse, while also strategically facilitating and administrating its subjects (Hirst, 1985).

On the portals of the court buildings will be inscribed the royal motto, '*Dieu et mon Droit*', while in other regimes it would be '*Fiat Iustitia*' or some variant thereon. The windows to the buildings are likely either to be barred or to be somewhat higher and narrower than is usually the case. Access to the rear of the building will be likewise barred, and the entrance to the courts will be in some varying measure imposing, not simply by virtue of their size but also by dint of their elevation from the street. Whatever the form it takes, and the degree of emphasis or imposition is likely to vary according to the date of design and the status of the courts within the legal hierarchy, the threshold to the court building will be marked, and physical access to the seats of justice will involve both a visual and conceptual ascension from the quotidian street to ritualized space. That the situation and external structure of the courts signify a degree of distance from the everyday and from the mundane concerns of public space gains further emphasis upon entry into the ritualized internal spacing of the courts, of the judicial world secreted in the heart of the city and wrapped in an archaic and sacral atmosphere of special functions and the silent unravelling of other times.

Semioticians of architectural form have tended to distinguish usefully between the 'formal' and 'material' syntax of buildings (Preziosi, 1984). The formal syntax of buildings, as the linguistic metaphor suggests, is concerned with the study of the formal properties of the built environment, that is with the geometry of organization which may be reduced to (i) sets of items or formal properties of space; (ii) sets of relationships amongst these; and (iii) a set of rules or laws obeyed by the latter. In a necessarily simplified account, the fundamental issue involved in formal syntax is the study of the complexly ordered manner in which the built environment communicates through organizing visual relationships, symbolizing subject positions (placements) and controlling avenues of circulation and visibility according to generally functional criteria, be they those of devotion, (panoptic) surveillance, isolation, communion or some other alternately disciplinary or hedonistic design (Foucault, 1979). As an adjunct to formal syntax, material syntax concerns the study of a set of rather more accessory features to the surface of buildings, the materials used, textures, colours, scales, modulations and insignia that range from gargoyles to heraldic crests.

Summoned by writ, subpoena or condition of bail, even before arriving at court the subject of legal proceedings will already have had to traverse the linguistic complexities of what were until recently archaic and verbose standard legal forms of interpellation that variously invoked God and monarch, and threatened sanctions of fine or imprisonment. The subject is called and arrives in the ill-demarcated open hallway of the courts to an atmosphere of hushed routine efficiency of business, combined with a confusion engendered by a general absence of clear indicators, either of the order of proceedings or of where the relevant court is sitting. While lists are displayed, the order and place of proceedings will generally have to be explained, save in the case of defendants in custody who either arrive under police escort or are brought from the sparse environs of the court cells up to the lavishly-contrasting well of the court. At this point, generalization becomes difficult in view of the diversity of courts and of their arrangement. Viewing and listening positions will also vary markedly according to the role that is to be played within the proceedings. While there are significant procedural and architectural facets to the roles of juror and of witness – the latter, for instance, with the exception of expert witnesses, are not allowed into the court until they are called to give testimony – I will limit my remarks to defendants.

The strategic organizing principle of the courtroom is a didactic one. It is that of the visibility of justice rather than of its audibility. The ritual character of proceedings in court have, first, an obvious material character in the higher courts in the form of the ceremonial dress of legal participants, in judicial robes and wigs, barristerial gowns and wigs, the use of royal red and emblazoned royal arms on, and frequently also above, the judicial seat or throne. To the aged pomp of the furniture and scale of the courtroom can be added the not altogether incidental features of procedure and address. The 'court' is silent and rises to its feet upon the entry of the judge. The judge is never addressed by name but either in metonymic form as 'the court' or 'bench', or sacrally as 'your honour', 'your lordship' or 'your worship'. It is not humanity, in other words, that sits when the court returns to their seats but rather justice (*jus*) and law (*lex*) that take their place at the pinnacle of a strictly ordered hierarchical space and surrounded by a veritable debauch of symbols of majesty and order. That sitting is accompanied by a strictly-controlled order and tone of speech: speakers are called upon to speak and cannot do so volitionally, nor is it in general possible to interrupt that order and decorum. The court must remain silent and indeed obedient to procedure, with stringent sanctions attaching to the common-law offence of 'contempt in the face of the court' which punishes any who 'scandalize' the court *in praesentia*, while the powers enacted in the 1981 Contempt of Court Act not only create wide-ranging offences of strict liability, but have also on occasion been used to imprison observers or participants who have done no more than laugh in court.

In an interesting discussion of genres of discourse, Mikhail Bakhtin observes that where discourse performs as authoritative discourse it no longer performs as information, direction, rules, models and so forth, but rather strives to determine the very bases of our ideological interrelations with the world, the very basis of our behaviour. In this respect we encounter the authoritative word:

> with its authority already fused to it. The authoritative word is located in a distanced zone, organically connected with a past that is felt to be hierarchically higher. It is, so to speak, the word of the fathers. Its authority was already *acknowledged* in the past. It is a prior discourse. It is therefore not a question of choosing it from among other possible discourses that are its equal. It is given (it sounds) in lofty spheres, not those of familiar contact. (Bakhtin, 1981, 342–3)

The social distance and unfamiliarity of the courtroom within which justice 'sounds' (as opposed to conversing in any more vernacular manner) gains further emphasis in the formal syntax of the court.

While the judiciary are, in a nominal sense, the servants of the public, their position within the spatial organization of the courtroom is one of absolute separation, of elevation and of privilege. The judges or magistrates will appear in court by means of a special entrance to the rear of the bench and, formalities completed, will take their seat on the 'bench', from which elevated location they look down upon the court protected by a series of barriers (bars) in the older courts, and by court officials and stenographers in more modern architectural design. No-one approaches the bench except on request, and any exhibits or documents are passed up to the bench by the court clerk. The adversarial process of the trial unrolls below the bench, and its agonistic or gladiatorial character lends an atmosphere of the classical games in the amphitheatre in which the Emperor decided life or death from a situation above the arena and in the form of concession or donation. In less allusive terms, juridical space is a separate and obligatory space for its occupants; a space hierarchically organized in the image of the Law:

> It suspends, for an instant, all the habitual differences of rank between men, so as to substitute others. *It incarnates order, it creates order, it is order.* Within the imperfection of the world and the corruption of life, it realises a temporary and limited perfection. (Garapon, 1984, 45)

In the court below, in those designed for jury trials, a certain symmetry prevails in which the dock, itself an elevated and enclosed space, faces the bench, and to either side rise tiers of seats to accommodate the jury and on the other side reporters and other official court observers. Prosecution and defence counsel take their place on either side of the open well of the court, and conduct the combative game of trial directly in front of the bench. Witnesses, when called, will appear to the side of the court, and while the dock is visually a focal point from the public gallery at the front of the court, it is frequently at such a distance from proceedings, the exchange of arguments, that irrespective of whether or not the legal wrangling between counsel and bench could be understood, it is near impossible to hear:

> spatial arrangements, however, which might signify to the onlooker a guarantee of an orderly display of justice, are too often experienced by participants as being generative of a

> theatrical autism with all the actors talking past each other. (Carlen, 1976)

The defendant, *accused* of an act of law breaking, is set apart from other actors, and frequently distanced from proceedings in which his or her contribution will seldom be more than that of responding to formal questions and projecting answers concerning intimate details of their lives across the auditory gulf that separates the dock from the elevated pinnacle of the court, the bench (Harris, 1982).

The language of annexation and reformulation

The thematic unity of courtroom architecture is to be found in elements and relationships of visual display in which the defendant is an isolated and usually unfamiliar witness of archaic and formulaic proceedings. Much of the argument in court, where it concerns points of procedure, evidence or law will neither involve defendants nor be comprehensible to them. The language used will appear learned and technical and references will be to sources of law generally inaccessible to the public. Where defendants are called to speak, it is not so as to present their own narrative of events or of motives and causes, but rather to respond on cue to formal questioning which, while it may be less archaic in lexical terms, is concerned with legal categories of relevance and intention, is subject to interruption from the bench, and bears an apparently indirect relation to any perceived narrative of real events.

The principal linguistic task of legal speech is to translate and reformulate vernacular dialects into the apparently separate and unitary genre of legal discourse (Stewart, 1987). To analyse the linguistics of that process of reformulation and annexation would involve an account of the historical development and disciplinary techniques of legal textual culture, its use of foreign languages and its exemplary forms of rhetorical organization, that far exceed the boundaries of an account of legal auditions (Goodrich, 1987a). It remains true, however, that courtroom speech is underpinned by many of the more general and manifest inequalities of relationship that exist as between legal discourse and non-legal discourses within the developmennt of legal language as a whole. In terms of legal dialogue, the 'imagined community' of the legal genre as an administrative discourse evidences its discursive power through an explicit superiority of attitude towards the exclusion of other discourses and usages.

Authoritative (professional) languages demand, as was observed above, an allegiance on the part of their listeners which accepts the authority of the language as an inert and indissoluble whole, irrespective of its content. That authority is linked initially or at least most obviously to a specific political power – that of sanction, to an institution – the court, and to a person – the judge. In a less direct but easily apparent sense, linguistic authority is manifest in the imposed forms of dialogue and silence and in the irrefragable truth of legal definitions that variously annex, reformulate, appropriate or exclude competing usages:

> what is important [in relation to professional languages] is the intentional dimensions, that is, the denotative and expressive dimension of the 'shared' language's stratification. It is not in fact the neutral linguistic components of language being stratified and differentiated, but rather a situation in which the intentional possibilities of language are being expropriated. (Bakhtin, 1981, 289)

The intentional possibilities of utterance are annexed and reformulated in a particular direction, and with a particular content, that conforms to the specific objects, belief-systems, forms of expression and value judgments of the relevant profession. For the speakers of the language the reformulation involved is directly intentional, whereas, for less powerful outsiders to the given purview, the intentions permeating these languages become '*things*, limited in their meaning and expression; they attract to, or excise from, such a language a particular word – making it difficult for the word to be utilized in a directly intentional way, without any qualification' (Bakhtin, 1981, 290).

While it would be useful to present a comprehensive typology of the forms of definition, annexation and reformulation endemic to dialogue between legal and extra-legal genres, I will limit my discussion to a more manageable analysis of examples drawn from dialogue in the lower courts. The examples will be loosely arranged according to the order of proceedings. In each instance my concern will be with the explicit manifestation of an image of legal community and sovereignty at the expense of other usages, that is, with the subordination of the listener to an imposed form and to purportedly pre-established definitions. By way of introduction to the preponderant number of examples, drawn from defendant's responses in magistrates' courts, it should be noted that prior even to the initial courtroom scene of entering of a plea defendants have probably been subject to considerable pressure in relation to their plea, either in terms of informal plea bargaining or straightforward persuasion to plead guilty (McBarnet, 1983; Baldwin and McConville, 1977).

The initial stage of criminal trial takes the form of pleading, while in civil cases it generally takes the form of a statement of claim and counter-claim. In both cases, though markedly less so in civil proceedings, the initial speech in the proceedings will be legally formulated, and will concern neither the events nor the perceived wrong at issue, but a legal category and definition of offence or civil claim. The question posed will not concern issues of what was done, why it was done, or the contexts and motives of its doing, but simply the legal statement of charge to which the defendant must reply either guilty or not guilty. The discursively interesting aspect of this initial ritual of legal recognition is that the statement of charge or wrong may well appear so irrelevant to the actions concerned that the option of pleading guilty or not guilty is either perceived as peripheral or as coercive. Its function, however, is largely one of recognition and submission to the arena of trial, as the following examples from magistrates' courts well illustrate. The first case (Carlen, 1976, 115–16) involves a charge of trespassing with intent to steal:

Clerk: Do you plead guilty or not guilty?
Defendant: Well, yes and no.
Clerk: Do you plead guilty or not guilty?
Defendant: Yes – I was guilty of trespassing – and no – I wasn't intending to steal.
Clerk: So you plead not guilty?
Defendant: That's not what I said.
Clerk: Not guilty.

A not guilty plea was entered on the record. In another relatively obvious example of reformulation (Carlen, 1976), the defendant is concerned to ignore the specific wording required in view of a legally ulterior purpose to the discussion:

Clerk: Do you plead guilty or not guilty?
Defendant: Yes, I did it. I said I did it.
Clerk: Do you plead guilty or not guilty?
Defendant: Yes, I did it. I just want to get out of here . . .
Magistrate: Do you plead guilty or not guilty?
Defendant: Yes, I did it.
Magistrate: No. I'm asking whether you plead guilty or not guilty. You must use either the words 'not guilty' or 'guilty'.
Defendant: (looking towards probation officer) She said, 'Say guilty'.

Magistrate:	No. You must say what you *want* to say.
Defendant:	Yes, I'll say what you like. I did it.
Magistrate:	No. You must use the language of the court.

In broader terms the central issue of the case may well be that of what the legally formulated charge means either in commonsensical, political or moral terms. The question of who defines whether peace activists demonstrating are guilty as charged of behaviour likely to cause a breach of the peace or whether, in *R v. Ponting* (1985, Criminal Law Review, 318; Ponting, 1985), passing information to an unauthorized person constituted an offence under s. 2(1) of the Official Secrets Act 1911 which makes it an offence to 'communicate . . . information to any person, other than to a person to whom he is authorised to communicate it . . .' is hardly encompassed in the option of pleading guilty or not guilty. The point is well made in terms of the semantic ambiguity of the plea in a case from Lancaster Magistrates' Court (Thomas, 1985) where the defendant, who was unrepresented, was charged with resisting arrest and hitting a policeman. He admitted that he had hit the policeman but later claimed that the policeman had hit him first, in which case self-defence may legally be pleaded as a defence to the action:

Clerk:	How do you plead – guilty or not guilty?
Defendant:	(silence)
Clerk:	Did you do it or not?
Defendant:	Well, I did hit him, yes.
Clerk:	So that's 'guilty' then.
Defendant:	Yes, sir.

The control of dialogue by court officials, counsel and judge, is a significant feature of subsequent discursive sequences. While I will refer to that strategy of formulaic and definitional control in subsequent discussion, the principal discursive operator in courtroom dialogue is undoubtedly that of paraphrase-reformulation. Paraphrase, of course, may involve either a relation of equivalence or symmetrical substitution between elements (words, expressions, propositions) such that the elements *a* and *b* 'mean the same thing' in the relevant discourse, or a relation of implication or orientated substitutability such that the relation of substitution *a* – *b* is not the same as the relation *b* – *a* (Pêcheux, 1982, 112–27; Fuchs, 1982). It is the latter form of paraphrase that is of greatest discursive and ideological significance in two respects. First, the choice of implication will organize the meaning attributed to the given statement and second, the content of that implication is not explicit, but depends upon a pre-established discourse and meanings that are not necessarily equally available to both parties to the dialogue, nor are both parties always equally equipped to contest the pertinent implications.

The most explicitly and significantly orientated forms of paraphrase, tend to take the form of implicating the respondent's statement, by lexical or referential means, in legally and often also morally opprobrious results:

Prosecutor:	And you say this before us is not the proceeds of shoplifting?
Defendant:	No, not that stuff, no.
Prosecutor:	And the police have invented this case against you, it must follow, mustn't it?
Defendant:	Well I suppose so.
Prosecutor:	Well it's the only thing possible isn't it?
Defendant:	Yes . . .
Prosecutor:	You think that they created the whole case against you?
Defendant:	I am not calling them liars but that's what happened.
Prosecutor:	It's not good enough to say you are not calling them liars, because that is the only possibility if you are telling the truth.

The reformulation in the above example (McBarnet, 1983, 79) is legally an effective and frequent one. The implication adduced is by no means a necessary one, the positive assertion could equally imply mistake as to the identity of the goods, as to the identity of the accused, or as to certification of payment, and certainly makes no necessary attribution of motive with regard to the police evidence. The further implications of the reformulation also draw upon the moral credibility of the police as routine witnesses in courtroom dialogue, and the further legal implication that if the character of witnesses is attacked by the defence, the character of the defendant can then be placed in issue. The process of reformulation thus acts to control the topic of discourse and to particularize a generic account of behaviour in a damaging yet, for the unrepresented defendant, unforseeable manner. In the following example (Harris, 1982) the defendant has explained at length to the Arrears and Maintenance Court how, after two years' unemployment, he has recently found employment again:

Magistrate: In other words what you're really saying to us is that you started to wake up to the fact
Defendant: yeh
Magistrate: that uh you've got certain obligations to meet and it's vitally important that you should start to think about them – that's what you're saying I take it
Defendant: yeh
Clerk: you did – you do accept that you should be paying ten pounds a week?
Defendant: oh yeh
Defendant: yeh I do accept it
Clerk: uh – are you really asking that uh some of these arrears be remitted – is that what you're really asking?
Defendant: yeh

The defendant's simple description of two years' unemployment followed by a short period of self-employment is reformulated by the magistrate into a set of moral obligations and motives of legal relevance, which the clerk proceeds to translate into a further acceptance of a specified amount and period of remission of arrears.

Aligned to control of topic in the form of paraphrase and definition can be added a series of rules of relevance, prohibition of hearsay, and admissibility. The ability to negate or to challenge adverse paraphrase and damaging implications depends throughout upon knowledge of their relevance, their preconstructed force within the legal form of discourse, and also upon the status and credibility of the witness or respondent. An interesting contrast in status and the power to reformulate can be explicitly seen in the following examples. The first (Chambers and Miller, 1986, 123) is a rape trial:

Defence: When you first saw him he was in company with another man and you approached both of these men?
Complainer: No.
Defence: And talked to them?
Complainer: No.
Defence: And that was at your suggestion that in fact, you went up this close in the first place?
Complainer: That is ridiculous, utterly ridiculous . . . no.
Defence: Was it not the case that the man in the dock did talk to you at some point in the street and offer

	to walk to wherever it was you said you were going?
Complainer:	How could he possibly do that if he was in . . . Road?
Judge:	Don't argue with counsel; at the moment all we want you to do is to answer the question.
Complainer:	No.

A second example (McBarnet, 1982, 16) of an even stronger exclusionary power predicated upon an accusatorially conceived concept of relevance may be briefly elicited from proceedings in the magistrates' court. Two youths are accused of suspicious activities around cars. They claim, in defence, that they were in fact being arrested for nothing in order to be questioned about a stolen television, but were interrupted as follows:

Magistrate:	I'm sorry – I'm not prepared to listen to information about a television.
Accused:	But he said he didn't ask us about a TV and he did.
Magistrate:	It's irrelevant to the charge.

In dramatic contrast to the preceding instances of annexation, the final example involves a much greater degree of parity of paraphrase, as might be expected to be associated with the titled head of the civil service, Sir Robert Armstrong, giving evidence of government actions in *Her Majesty's Attorney General in and for the UK v. Heinemann and Wright* (Transcript Day 2). Counsel is cross-examining Sir Robert Armstrong as to a letter he had written to W. Armstrong of Sidgwick & Jackson requesting a copy of their book *Their Trade is Treachery*, so that the Prime Minister should be in a position to make a statement to the House of Commons, 'clearly she cannot do so until she has seen . . . the book itself':

Q: That conveys the very distinct suggestion, the explicit suggestion that she has not had access to the book before this letter, does it not?

A: I don't know whether she had access to the book itself at that stage, but that is beside the point. I did not wish to disclose that we had obtained a copy of the book.

Q: You misled Mr William Armstrong in order not to disclose the fact –

A: I did not disclose to Mr Armstrong the fact that a copy of the book had been obtained.

Q: You misled Mr William Armstrong, did you not?
A: If you put that interpretation on it. I was bound to do so, but I wished to protect the source.
Q: That letter *was calculated to mislead*. Was it not?
A: It was *calculated to ask for a copy* of the book on which we could take direct action.
Q: It was *calculated to mislead* Mr Armstrong as to whether the Government had a copy of the book or not?
A: It was *calculated not to disclose* to Mr Armstrong that the Government had obtained a copy of the book.
Q: It was *calculated to mislead* Mr Armstrong to believe that the Government did not have a copy of the book. Correct?
A: It was *calculated not to disclose* to Mr Armstrong that the Government had a copy of the book in order to protect the confidentiality of the source from which it came.
Q: And the Government did have a copy of the book?
A: The Government did have a copy of the book.

. . . .

Q: I put it to you that the letter contains an untruth. That is the question.
A: It does not say that we have already got a copy of the book, that is quite true.
Q: So it contains an untruth.
A: It does not contain that truth.

. . . .

Q: So it contains a lie?
A: It is a misleading impression, it does not contain a lie, I don't think.
Q: What is the difference between a misleading impression and a lie?
A: You are as good at English as I am.
Q: I am just trying to understand.
A: A lie is a straight untruth . . .
Q: What is a misleading impression – a sort of bent untruth?
A: As one person said, it is perhaps being economical with the truth.

Suffice it to observe that Sir Robert Armstrong's refusal to accept the proffered reformulation of the implications of the letter in question was dependent upon a confidence and knowledge as well as a tolerance from the bench that are rarely found in lower court criminal proceedings, a conclusion which is well born out by studies of witness credibility in relation to status carried out by O'Barr and others at Duke University (O'Barr, 1982).

Forms of closure

If it is correctly argued, as I believe it to be, that implicative or orientated paraphrase at both semantic and lexico-referential levels is the most common form of argumentative manipulation, then the ability to challenge the legal control of topic and terms is primarily a matter of contesting the discursive preconstruction of questions. In general that ability will depend upon access to the 'shared knowledge' which acts as the pre-condition of the propositional content of the statement. In legal settings it also depends upon a knowledge of procedure and conversational forms as well as a more general capacity of confidence that will allow the respondent both to question or oppose legal dialect (the community of legal language) and to risk, as may be the case, the possibility of sanction.

The question of the accessibility of legal preconstructions to those without the linguistic community of lawyers is amenable to a relatively swift answer. At its most general level the discourse of law is that of an authoritative prior discourse which for the bulk of its history has been encoded in either an alien language or in an archaic register of the vernacular. While the function of that restricted coding is primarily that of authorizing particular speakers or enunciative modalities – irrespective of the specific content of their speech, as is most obviously the case with a lay magistrature who are forced to rely upon legally-qualified court clerks for esoteric points of law – a few comments may also be passed on the general semantic features of law as prior discourse. Restricting the discussion somewhat, the overwhelming empirical evidence is to the effect that the language of statute, precedent, jury instructions and argument on points of law is inaccessible even to those non-lawyers with several years' experience of higher education. The available tests of comprehension are by no means precise but the CLOZE test, to take one example, is considered an adequate measure of comprehension for commercial, educational and publishing purposes. The test simply involves the deletion of every fifth word of a text which then has to be completed by the respondent. In tests conducted at Loyola University, Los Angeles, by Professor Robert Benson (Benson,

1984–5; Charrow and Charrow, 1979), codified jury instructions and a Federal labour relations statute were amongst the documents used on a group of highly educated non-lawyers, 90 per cent of whom had attended higher education, 28 per cent of whom had done some post-graduate work. The CLOZE criterion of minimum adequate comprehension is a 55 per cent score. The jury instructions scored 48.6 per cent, the Federal Statute 39.2 per cent. Translated onto the rather more vivid Flesch scale, an educational test based upon word and syllable counts, legal documents fared even worse. The Flesch criterion of minimum adequate comprehension is a score of plus 40. Amongst the documents tested, the trust clause from a 1983 federal case scored minus 55, a 1982 Vocational Educational Act scored minus 83, a 1982 Social Security Act scored minus 132 while the winning score of minus 219 went, not entirely inappropriately, to a 1978 Ethics in Government Act.

Whatever the variations in reliability of the tests used, the general conclusion is that legal documentation, as a reservoir or lexicon of pre-established meanings within the discourse of law, are satisfactorily proven to annul ordinary discourse – in the case of a score of minus 219, they do so to the point of absurdity. In considering the significance of such data for the analysis of legal dialogue, and specifically of audience, two further observations pointing in a contrary direction are pertinent. The first is that tests of comprehension are generally based upon lexical and syntactic features of discourse and do not directly test comprehension in terms of 'gist' or effect. In that respect it is interesting that when Charrow and Charrow tested jury comprehension of formally drafted instructions in Maryland by means of a paraphrase test, the fact that they scored between 45 per cent and 54 per cent did not preclude the conclusion that in the overwhelming majority of cases, even where the instructions were clearly not understood, the jurors, inventing their own meaning for the instructions, acted (unwittingly) within the spirit of the formally drafted instructions. The point is an interesting one in terms of the assumptions to be made with regard to listening or viewing positions more generally. The second qualification of the results summarized above concerns the degree of acquiescence that is to be imputed to audiences. Recent important studies of audience reception (Richardson and Corner, 1986; Morley, 1980) clearly indicate that even where programmes are very clearly framed to present a particular ideological bias, audiences are frequently competent to view such presentations in a 'mediated' or 'oppositional' manner which takes full account of the framing or structured preferences or presentation.

In the context of legal dialogue it should not, therefore, be assumed that the annexation of non-legal dialects is universally successful or unopposed. In an example again drawn from Arrears and Maintenance (Harris, 1987) the defendant recognizes yet ironically challenges the assumptions of the court:

M: Well if you flatly refuse to accept the order of the court there's only one alternative – then you'll go to prison
D: yeh
M: is that what you're saying
D: yes
M: will you fetch a policeman [to the usher]
D: you can't do it now . . . I'm still uh under psychiatric treatment
M: you can receive that in prison Mr A
D: oh thank you
M: you can't tell – you can't refuse to do something and tell us what we can do at the same time you know
D: that's the system isn't it

The magistrate makes explicit that the defendant has broken the rules of courtroom discourse in challenging the power of the court to use force. An underlying assumption of the court is called into question and elicits a coercive response. In general the contestation of legal preconstructions does not and for obvious reasons cannot take the form of a response to the details of what is implied in the legal evaluation of behaviour. It tends rather to hinge upon generically expressed dissatisfaction with the fairness of justice or decisions in which, as in matters of legal meaning, the magistrature are arbiters of moral rectitude as it impinges upon legal obligations:

M: do you think it is a reasonable thing that a wife and child shall be without your support whilst you still enjoy the additional pleasure of colour television in your home . . . does that seem a reasonable thing to do?
D: depends on which way you look at it don't it
M: well looking at it from any reasonable point of view – is it reasonable for anybody to have the pleasure and the luxury of a colour television when a wife and child could be going without food . . . whichever way you look at it is that reasonable?
D: well I don't know because if I didn't have a colour telly I'd just spend my time – in the pubs then wouldn't I?

M: well you're not forced to do it – I don't have a colour television and I don't spend my time in the pubs – there's no compulsion to make you go to the pub because you don't have a colour television . . .

. . . .

D: no I don't agree with you

In formal terms counter-questioning by means of tags endeavours, ineffectively, to challenge the preconstructed meaning of the possession of a television and to draw the magistrate into agreeing with the proposition expressed in the declarative part of the utterance. In the circumstances of the case, as reported by Sandra Harris, the defendant wished (justifiably or not) to introduce evidence of the wife's current, relatively affluent, circumstances as relevant to the question of reasonableness. In its magnificent generality, however, the question of reasonableness is pre-eminently a matter for the closely-guarded confines of specifically legal discourse, which means in effect that whatever the mundane moral content of the discourse of the law, it is pronounced *ex cathedra* and as a consequence of its judicial source cannot be challenged, even though the definition of 'fairness', 'reasonableness' or 'commonsense' would not seem to be an exclusively legal skill. The recent case of *Masterton and another v. Holden* (1986, 3, All England Reports, 39) constitutes an interesting and fairly typical example of moral valuation dressed up as legal knowledge. Under s. 54 (13) of the Metropolitan Police Act 1839, 'Every person shall be liable to a penalty . . . who shall use any threatening, abusive, or insulting Words or Behaviour with Intent to provoke a Breach of the Peace, or whereby a Breach of the Peace may be occasioned'. What is to be constructed as behaviour intended to occasion a breach of the peace is pre-eminently a matter of value judgment concerned with norms of interaction, the justification of behaviour, the reasonableness of responses and the semantic import of an 'insult'. In the case in question two men, 'cuddling each other and kissing each other' in Oxford Street at 1.55 a.m. were found guilty of the offence of insulting behaviour intended to provoke a breach of the peace and were bound over to keep the peace. On appeal to the Divisional Court of the Queen's Bench Division before Justice Glidewell the decision at first instance was upheld on the strength of the legally-sanctioned reasonableness of the reaction of two other couples:

> Two couples were walking along the south footway of Oxford Street. First there were two young men about twenty-one years

> of age [AB] and second two young women of about twenty . . . The case finds that the two young men appeared not to notice them [the defendants] but the two young women stopped opposite the defendants and one of them raised a hand to her mouth and both of them ran up to the two young men [AB]. After a short conversation one of the girls pointed at the defendants who were still cuddling . . . Both of the young men [AB] then walked towards the defendants and one of them shouted: 'You filthy sods. How dare you in front of our girls?'. (*Masterson and another v. Holden* (1986, 3, All England Reports, 40)

While the issues involved in *Masterton* were pre-eminently political and moral, doctrine has always sought to separate such issues from the putatively normative sphere of legal argument. Although the predominant categories of legal argument and judgment concern broadly drawn and necessarily changing notions of reason, fairness, and justice as the criteria of interpretation of legal rules, and despite the didactic epithets of approval and disapproval that ground the majority of judgments, challenges to that legal pedagogy of forms of behaviour and lifestyle must take the form of extra-legal, political protest and lobbying. To be heard in court, arguments must be reformulated in the abstract legal terms of the case, presented on cue and subject to the potentially censorious intervention of the court. By way of conclusion, I would note that resistance to the legal imposition of order and forms of argument in court is generally disadvantageous. There is, however, an occasional yet interesting history of lay participants in trials disregarding legal forms.

That history centres around the changing role and presence of the jury in the common-law tradition. In its earliest form the jury was chosen from amongst the peer group of the accused and was arbiter of both fact and law (generally custom). More recently its role has been restricted to that of fact finding, but on occasions where the law to be applied has appeared too out of keeping with contemporary mores or the sentences likely to be passed are felt to be too draconian, the jury still retains a right to find the accused not guilty, irrespective of the legal direction that they have received from the judge. One such instance would be the earlier mentioned case of *R v. Ponting* where the judge had at one point in the trial threatened to stop proceedings on the ground that no legally relevant defence had been presented to the charge laid under the Official Secrets Act. In the event the jury acquitted Ponting in the face of a judicial summing up that had made it quite clear that in law the defence presented had to be disregarded. In the more recent American case of *State of Massachusetts v. Allain, Carter, Clay and Others* (Transcript, 1987, April, 14–15) a defence of necessity was pleaded to a charge of disorderly conduct and trespass. Students were charged in relation to demonstrations at the University of Massachusetts which had attempted to draw attention to and protest against Central Intelligence Agency recruitment techniques on American campuses. The defence of necessity involved arguing that the misdemeanours committed were justified on moral grounds as being necessary to prevent the commission of graver crimes by the CIA. Evidence was brought by the defence of subversion, political murder, terrorism and other illegal acts committed by the CIA in the course of 'intelligence-gathering' worldwide. Although it was made plain in summing up that the CIA were not a party to the case and that much of the defence argument was in consequence irrelevant, the jury acquitted. The case is interesting in that it represents the first reported occasion on which the defence of necessity, which has been regularly ruled out in nuclear weapons protest cases, has been allowed. It is unlikely that its admission in a first instance case in Massachusetts will greatly alter its status in common law, nor is it likely that rare occasions of what are generally legally regarded as 'perverse verdicts' will do anything to radicalize the structural constraints within which the overwhelming majority of cases receive their momentary legal audition.

Notes

1. The case was not reported in the Supreme Court of British Columbia law reports and the only available record is the trial transcript which is available for personal inspection but cannot be copied or removed from the Supreme Court building.
2. In legal terms the case simply concerned the formal validity of the logging licence and there was, in consequence, no need to take time to consider judgment.
3. The Haida continued to protest and to blockade the island and in a subsequent action for contempt of court several protesters received custodial sentences. Subsequent political protest ended in July 1987 when the southern part of Lyell Island was declared a National Park. For some of the background to the case, see Johnston and Jones (1987).

References

Atkinson, M. and Drew, P. (1979) *Order in Court*, London, Macmillan.
Bakhtin, M. (1981) *The Dialogic Imagination*, Texas, Texas University Press.
Baldwin, J. and McConville, M. (1977) *Negotiated Justice*, Oxford, Martin Robertson.
Bankowski, Z. and Mungham, G. (1976) *Images of Law*, London, Routledge and Kegan Paul.
Benson, R. (1984–85) 'The End of Legalese', *Review of Law and Social Change* 13, 519.
Cain, M. (1985) 'The General Practice Lawyer and the Client' in R. Dingwall and P. Lewis (eds), *The Sociology of the Professions*, London, Macmillan.
Carlen, P. (1976) *Magistrates' Justice*, Oxford, Martin Robertson.
Chambers and Miller (1986) *Prosecuting Sexual Assault*, Edinburgh, HMSO.
Charrow and Charrow (1979) 'Making Legal Language Understandable: A Psycholinguistic Study of Jury Instructions', *Columbia Law Review* 79, 1306.
Corner, J. and Richardson, K. (1986) 'The Documentary Viewer and the Discourse of Interpretation' in J. Corner (ed.), *Documentary and the Mass Media*, London, Arnold.
Fairclough, N. (1985) 'Critical and Descriptive Goals in Discourse Analysis', *Journal of Pragmatics* 9, 739.
Forrester, J. (1985) (ed.), *Critical Theory and Public Life*, Cambridge, Massachusetts, M.I.T.
Foucault, M. (1979) *Discipline and Punish*, London, Peregrine.
Foucault, M. (1981) *The Archaeology of Knowledge*, New York, Pantheon.
Fuchs, C. (1982) *La Paraphrase*, Paris, Presses Universitaires de France.
Garapon, A. (1984) *L'Ane Portant des Reliques*, Paris, Centurion.
Garfinkel, H. (1956) 'Conditions of Successful Degradation Ceremonies', *American Journal of Sociology* 64, 420.
Goodrich, P. (1986) *Reading the Law*, Oxford, Blackwell.
Goodrich, P. (1987a) *Legal Discourse*, London, Macmillan.
Goodrich, P. (1987b) 'The Politics of Literacy and the Languages of the Early Common Law', *Journal of Law and Society* 14, 422.
Harris, S. (1982) 'Language, Power and Control in Court', *Crosscurrents* 3, 35–53.
Harris, S. (1987) 'Defendant Resistance to Power and Control in Court' in H. Coleman (ed.), *Working with Languages*, The Hague, Mouton.
Hirst, P. (1985) 'Constructed Space and the Subject' in R. Fardon (ed.), *Power and Knowledge*, Edinburgh, Scottish Academic Press.
Johnston, M. and Jones, D. (1987) 'Queen Charlotte Islands, Homeland of the Haida', *National Geographic* p. 102.
Legendre, P. (1976) *Jouir de Pouvoir*, Paris, Seuil.
Lenoble, J. and Ost, Fr. (1981) *Droit, Mythe et Raïson*, Brussels, Presses Universitaire de Saint Louis.
Lerman, G. (1983) 'Dominant Discourse' in H. Davis and P. Walton

(eds), *Language, Image, Media*, Oxford, Blackwell.
Lind, A. and O'Barr, W. (1979) 'The Social Significance of Speech in the Courtroom' in H. Giles and R. St. Clair (eds), *Language and Social Psychology*, Oxford, Blackwell.
Mathieson, T. (1980) *Law, Society and Political Action*, London, Academic Press.
McBarnet, D. (1983) *Conviction*, London, Macmillan.
Mellinkoff, D. (1963) *The Language of Law*, Boston, Little Brown.
Morley, D. (1980) *The Nationwide Audience*, London, BFI.
Morley, D. (1981) 'The Nationwide Audience: A Critical Postscript', *Screen Education* 39.
O'Barr, W. (1982) *Linguistic Evidence*, New York, Academic Press.
Pêcheux, M. (1982) *Language, Semantics and Ideology*, London, Macmillan.
Ponting, C. (1985) *The Right to Know*, London, Sphere.
Preziosi, D. (1979) *The Semiotics of the Built Environment*, Bloomington, Indiana University Press.
Preziosi, D. (1984) 'Environmental and Linguistic Structure' in R. Fawcett *et al.* (eds), *Semiotics of Language and Culture*, London, Pinter.
Richardson, K. and Corner, J. (1986) 'Reading Reception', *Media, Culture and Society* 8, 458.
Stewart, I. (1987) 'Law and Closure', *Modern Law Review* 50, 908.
Thomas, J. (1985) 'The Language of Power', *Journal of Pragmatics* 9, 765.

Chapter two

Therapeutic listening

Richard G. Tedeschi

Introduction

Psychotherapy is much like other human interactions in that it is a situation established by persons who seek to exert influence over each other. In psychotherapy, however, the client presents himself to a psychotherapist in order to gain relief from some unpleasantness in his life through obtaining liking and information from the psychotherapist. This appears to be an inherently paradoxical situation for the client since he wishes to manage his impression in order to be liked and this involves demonstrations of competence, confidence and self-awareness. Yet at the same time by coming to psychotherapy the client admits inadequacy and must disclose details of this inadequacy in order to fulfill the role of the client and make progress in achieving a more fulfilling life.

The psychotherapist is aware of these general motives of the client and attempts to discover by listening to the client's self-presentation the specific ways in which the client tries to achieve these apparently contradictory aims. Clinical wisdom has it that clients never really seek to pay the price of changing but wish instead to find the easiest path to happiness by becoming better at their usual ways of operating. Therefore, while listening to the client tell his tale and showing concern, liking, and acceptance, the psychotherapist also listens for the deceptions which obstruct the process of change and must at some time be challenged. Psychoanalysts first described these deceptions as 'defense mechanisms' which allow people to control anxiety by balancing the wish to gratify impulses with the need to avoid punishment and guilt. Other deceptions are more conscious, such as the decisions to mention or avoid talking about certain events, thoughts or feelings. The psychotherapist therefore listens for various deceptions which take the form of hidden motives and missing pieces of information. These range from conscious, planned client strategies to influence the therapist to actions, thoughts and feelings whose motives are partially known, to the client's failure to recall significant aspects of their own story. The psychotherapist listens and notes what is missing, what doesn't make sense, what is contradictory and what alternative explanations there might be. Listening for a psychotherapist therefore becomes a complicated process of observing and remembering details, developing hypotheses about what is occurring both in the client's life outside the consulting room and in the therapeutic interaction, and planning a strategy for the next therapeutic manoeuvre.

If one reads a few books on psychotherapy, listens to a discussion between two psychotherapists or attends a case conference, it rapidly becomes clear that psychotherapists often hold widely divergent views on what is the important content of a client's presentation. How is it that these experts hear such different things? Psychotherapists' expertise and potential inaccuracy in understanding clients' talk is based on what they add, i.e. reframe and place within the context of a theory which produces new inferences, and subtract, i.e. discount as deceptive, defensive or irrelevant. But there is so much variability among psychotherapists in their processes of addition and subtraction that it remains unclear who is listening accurately, and how accuracy in therapeutic listening may be recognized and achieved. These issues will be addressed in the following discussion by considering the components of therapeutic listening from a number of different perspectives which are influential in this field.

Components of therapeutic listening

A psychotherapist is constantly engaged during a therapy session in a listening process which may be considered to have three components:

(1) attention to the client;
(2) attention to the therapist's own personal experience and his reactions to the client;
(3) use of theoretical information and similar sources of knowledge.

These components of therapeutic listening represent the cognitive activity of the psychotherapist and function more or less simultaneously, though one component is sometimes emphasized more than the others momentarily or consistently during a particular phase of treatment.

Attention to the client

In classical psychoanalysis, the analyst is seated behind the recumbent client, a position which encourages the process of free association and also permits the analyst to maintain the 'evenly suspended attention' recommended by Freud (1912). Virtually all contemporary psychotherapists use a face-to-face arrangement, necessitating careful use by the psychotherapist of listening microskills. These microskills are the fundamentals of maintaining attention and have been thoroughly described by Ivey and his colleagues (e.g. Ivey and Gluckstern, 1984). Listening microskills include facing the client in a relaxed fashion demonstrating that attention is focused on him. A posture which demonstrates this is often described as being 'open' without crossed legs or arms which might signal defensiveness to the client. Also recommended is consistent but not constant eye contact and leaning toward and away from the client according to the course of the conversation and how much closeness is appropriate. These microskills are utilized throughout psychotherapy in a natural way, but are especially crucial during the initial phase in order to demonstrate to the client that they may safely disclose to this psychotherapist who is attentive and concerned. These microskills are also important in orientating the psychotherapist toward the client physically and psychologically so that the therapist is in a position to hear the important elements of the client's story and observe his approach to the psychotherapist. Contained in these observations are the subtle signals of the client's inner life.

> The minutest movements accompany every process of thought; muscular twitchings in face or hands and movements of the eyes speak to us as well as words. No small power of communication is contained in a glance, a person's bearing, a bodily movement, a special way of breathing. Signals of subterranean motions and impulses are being sent silently to the region of everyday speech, gesture, and movement. (Reik, 1948, 135)

Many of the masters of psychotherapy have agreed that a psychotherapist with a non-selective, open mind is the ideal for gathering information from the client. Freud (1912) suggested that listening with evenly suspended attention is therefore the rule for the analyst which is the counterpart to the rule of free association, and together the analyst and patient who abide by these rules will eventually recognize the meaning of what is revealed. This approach to psychotherapeutic listening requires that the psychotherapist be tolerant of ambiguity which allows for more listening, less structuring and a willingness to withhold responses to client statements until a careful weighing of their import has been done (Pietrofesa, Leonard and Van Hoose, 1978). Probing beneath the words to the client's emotional life is what the psychotherapist means to accomplish. Bandler and Grinder (1975) have suggested that the seemingly magical therapeutic effects of great psychotherapists are related to an ability to see beyond the structures of language to the underlying emotional experiences of the client. Bugental's existential psychotherapy illustrates this. 'The great bulk of my attention to work during the hour is directed to the processes of the client's activity rather than to the content' (Bugental, 1978, 106). Bugental assesses the degree to which the client is accessing the inner stream of awareness, the therapist must listen rather than talk. Rogers (1961) recommends a similar approach, with the psychotherapist acting as a psychotherapeutic galvanometer in order to be sensitive to any ways the client may perceive him as a threat. Only when freed from such threats can the client begin to experience his internal threats. George Kelly describes a way to achieve this sensitivity.

> Often a beginning therapist finds it helpful to close his cerebral dictionary and listen primarily to the subcortical sounds and themes that run through his client's talk. Stop wondering what the words literally mean. Try to recall, instead, what it is they sound like. Disregard content for the moment; attend to theme. Remember that a client can abruptly change content – thus throwing a literal-minded therapist completely off the scent – but he rarely changes the theme so easily. Or think of these vocal sounds, not as words, but as preverbal outcries, impulsive sound gestures, stylized oral grimaces, or hopelessly mumbled questions. (1969, 229)

In his work with schizophrenic patients, Silvano Arieti gathers information in a similar way. He points out that listening for a long time without directly intervening will yield a surprising comprehension of psychotic word-salad:

> The therapist will detect that some themes recur often and that the patient's talk follows certain patterns. Finally, some preoccupations of the patient with certain topics will become

> evident and will offer important clues. The therapist will grasp the general feeling tone of what the patient says even if he does not grasp the content. The general frame of reference or the 'cosmology' of the patient will be indented. (1974, 551)

Attention to the psychotherapist's inner self

Some psychotherapists have suggested that listening is enhanced by the therapist's use of his own inner, perhaps unconscious processes, producing recognition of more subtle and deeply buried themes in the client's talk. Theodor Reik in his famous description of 'listening with the third ear' stated that the first step in this process

> leads from the conscious or potentially conscious perception of the subject matter to the point where it dives down into the unconscious mind of the psychologist. The second would then represent the unconscious assimilation of the observed material. The third stretches from the re-emergence into consciousness of the data so assimilated to the point of their description or formulation. (1948, 131)

Reik considers this communication between two unconscious minds telepathic in the sense that minute stimuli are perceived below the threshold of awareness, bypassing the ordinary mind's way of working and communicating instead with archaic processes. The effect is delicate, and the psychotherapist must consider the instinctive reactions that take place within him as he listens, since 'the only way of penetrating into the secret of this language is by looking into oneself, understanding one's own reactions to it' (1948, 147). The meanings of the client's messages are most accurately and richly decoded by the psychotherapist's unconscious since the most important elements of the messages are the deep ones, not the surface ones. Langs suggests that 'the therapist should operate as if writing a novel or a play – think of scenes, images, human emotions, human conflict and struggle. In substance, this is the language of unconscious expression and communication' (Freeman, 1984, 48).

Much of this unconscious communication has been discussed in the psychoanalytic literature as an aspect of countertransference. As Kernberg (1965) has pointed out, there are essentially two conceptions of countertransference:

(1) that it is the psychotherapist's emotional reaction, conscious

and unconscious, to all the needs of both the patient and himself;

(2) that it is the psychotherapist's unconscious reaction to the patient's transference, essentially a classical Freudian stance.

This classical conception treats countertransference as a detriment to psychotherapy while the other position treats it as an asset in that it provides information which is crucial to understanding the client. The problem for the psychotherapist is that this information sometimes comes in the form of highly disturbing reactions in the therapist. This is especially the case when working with psychotics who can produce menacing feelings which Arieti (1974) describes as threats that there is no content in what is heard or that it carries a meaning which is not grasped.

Pitfalls in the use of the inner self

As the psychotherapist uses himself, especially his inner emotional life as an aid in the identification of a client's messages, he runs certain risks of distorting these messages as well. Egan (1986) describes bias arising from cultural influences, judgements, and sympathies strongly held by the psychotherapist which act as filters of which he may not be aware. An especially commonplace filter found among psychotherapists is the tendency to perceive relatively innocuous behaviour as psychopathological within the context of psychotherapy.

To prevent this distortion of the client's messages the psychotherapist must make it a practice to question his motives and reactions, both within therapy sessions and without. While training analysis was designed to minimize the distorting effects of countertransference, every psychotherapist must sharpen his awareness of the messages of clients by challenging himself throughout his professional career to discover the source of the unconscious messages from within. Clients act as the psychotherapists in this regard, providing feedback to the therapist about the correctness of interpretations of messages. Malan (1979) describes this feedback as a 'deepening of rapport' so that there is an enhanced emotional contact between the client and the psychotherapist. Langs (1978) also sees the client in the role of validator of the psychotherapist's interventions and builds his theory of the listening process around the exchange of these conscious and unconscious messages between clients and their psychotherapists. Furthermore, the psychotherapist must maintain himself and his own frame of reference rather than becoming so close to the client that the new frame of reference is unavailable when the client needs it (Benjamin, 1981). Yet closeness must be maintained in order to produce trust in the empathy of the therapist and the power of the therapeutic relationship. The difficulty in maintaining this delicate balance is further reason for psychotherapists to monitor their actions and their internal lives in order to develop their abilities to decode messages.

Despite the recommendations in favour of listening for thematic and affective elements of client's presentations, at times it is crucial to understand as precisely as possible the exact meaning of the client's words. Kelly (1969) recommends this, especially when attempting to define personal constructs the client uses to understand his world. A psychotherapist describing Harry Stack Sullivan's approach to interviewing stated that the therapist must 'be always trying to be in a position where you are attempting to get at or help the patient define what he means without making any assumptions' (Kvarnes and Parloff, 1976, 84). This demands an awareness that words may have different connotations to clients as opposed to psychotherapists. Wachtel (1977) describes a similar 'naive' approach to the client's talk which involves the therapist assuming only that he does not know to what fairly simple statements refer, and then asking about them. Therefore in trying to achieve a precise understanding of the client's language, the psychotherapist maintains a listening stance which is untainted by preconceptions.

Use of theory in listening

Although there is an emphasis in some quarters on eschewing theory in developing an understanding of the client (Langs, 1978; Wile, 1984), most psychotherapists rely on theory in the gathering and integration of information. Wachtel (1977) draws an analogy to an informed spectator's understanding of a football game to illustrate the importance of theory.

> Consider what happens to our perception as we learn specific plays used by each team. Then, as we are alerted to expect and look for certain other actions by other men on the team and, if these occur also, to have still firmer expectations of what all of them will do in the ensuing moments of action . . . the likelihood of a correct guess is greatly enhanced by possession of these probabilistic concepts. (1977, 138)

Each of the theoretical frameworks available to the psychotherapist defines some aspect of the client's presentation which is important as the focus for the therapist's information-gathering and integration. Although this focus varies with each theory, certain general content categories are evident in most forms of psychotherapy. An elementary four-fold categorization includes experiences, behaviours, thoughts, and affect. When clients describe experiences, they are talking about what has happened to them, what others have done which has affected them, and the environment to which they are exposed. As clients describe their experiences therapists consider who are the important figures in the client's life and what kinds of interactions the client had with these people and the aspects of life the client assigns most importance: work life, friends, recreation, family. It is enlightening to listen for victimization of the client and the degree to which the client assigns him or herself little control over this difficult environment. Another issue frequently discussed in the psychotherapeutic literature is the degree to which social supports – friends, family, community organizations – provide care and help which plays a role in mitigating the effects of trauma.

Given the experiences through which the client has lived, the psychotherapist listens for how the client had behaved in these situations, especially patterns of rigidly inappropriate self-defeating behaviour. A usually complex series of interpersonal expectations and communications produces a pattern of living which includes failure in some area of life to achieve the rewards most persons wish to find. This failure may be due to some combination of the client's inability to recognize when rewards are available, a lack of knowledge of how to obtain these rewards by behaving in the appropriate fashion, and a tendency to avoid potential rewards due to anxiety or guilt. Behaviourists have developed a system of analysing the relationship between the environment and the behaviours of the client in it. They listen for links between environmental conditions and particular behaviours which produce new conditions which either encourage the future performance of similar behaviour or suppress it. Attempts are made to understand the behaviour regulation of a client by listening for the circumstances under which problem behaviours are performed, or appropriate behaviours are not. By listening to the client's reports and observing the client in therapy, the psychotherapist determines which skills the client may have and what in the client's experience maintains inappropriate behaviour or punishes appropriate behaviour. Clients are often poor reporters of their own behaviour, so that the psychotherapist attempting to understand may rely on direct observation in therapy rather than these reports.

The third content category to which psychotherapists attend in their use of theory is thinking. Psychoanalysts listen for associations which lead to fundamental truths about a client's motives relatively undistorted by defense mechanisms. In fact, the process of following the free associations or uncensored thoughts of the client is the basic strategy employed in psychoanalysis, and listening to this stream of consciousness represents an enormous proportion of the analyst's work. Hypotheses drawn from this material form the basis for interpretive comments which become more commonplace as treatment progresses. A variety of other psychotherapists, including humanists and cognitive behaviourists, listen for statements about felt competence, self-esteem and worth. Cognitive behaviourists theorize that judgements of competence mediate the relationship between available rewards and skilled performance of behaviour which enables the client to obtain rewards. Judging oneself to be incompetent produces a vicious cycle of inadequate performances or giving up, leading to lack of reward, judgement that the environment is uncontrollable and further confirmation of inadequacy.

Similar thoughts are of concern to humanistic psychotherapists (e.g. Rogers, 1951). These therapists listen for client statements of low self-esteem which tend to be associated with a lack of trust in one's own judgement and a rejection of the value of certain aspects of one's own perception. Such perceptions are then distorted in conscious awareness so that they conform to the client's notion of others' judgements of acceptability. The psychotherapist attends closely to statements by clients that they don't know their own mind or need others to tell them what to do.

Rational-emotive therapists (Ellis, 1962) also focus on the thinking processes of clients, with the psychotherapist listening for statements which reflect belief in any of a number of irrational propositions related to psychological problems. In a similar vein, Kelly's (1955) personal construct theory also provides for a primary focus on the system of anticipatory thoughts which allow for accurate prediction and understanding of interpersonal events.

The fourth content category to which psychotherapists attend is affect, or emotional expression. Perhaps there is greatest variation among psychotherapists of different theoretical persuasions in the degree to which they listen carefully for affect. Psychoanalysts are concerned with affect since it is associated with impulses seeking expression. They especially listen for signs of anxiety (Sullivan, 1954) which may be revealed in subtle ways, which indicates the presence of psychological defenses and some degree of debilitation. Among humanistic psychotherapists, Carl Rogers is a good example of an advocate for attention to affect. He emphasizes the necessity of empathic understanding of the affective life of the client more than any other aspect of the client's world. Affective content is important in Rogers' theory since the emotional life is most likely to be distorted by attempts to preserve self-esteem. Listening which is accurately empathic can produce a powerful effect on the client by clarifying the emotions felt, reassuring the client of the reality of the emotional experience, reducing any sense of aloneness which is based on feeling these emotions, and allowing further exploration of the emotional life without risking a blow to self-esteem since the therapist is clearly understanding. Although a psychotherapist utilizing such an approach is aware of the supporting theory, Rogers (1951) recommends that the focus on affect is the spontaneous emotional reaction of a therapist who is sharing the affective life of a client.

Use of theory in the stages of psychotherapy

In the first stage of psychotherapy, the therapist listens to the client's story carefully in order to demonstrate his capacity to understand and care for the client. The psychotherapist also listens in order to develop a parallel understanding of the client's story in which the details of the content categories of experiences, behaviours, thinking and affect are fitted into a theoretical framework which is used in order to direct the therapeutic manoeuvres which are a large part of the second stage of therapy.

During the second stage, the focus of the psychotherapist's attention shifts to observation of the client's reactions to therapeutic manoeuvres. Strong and Claiborn (1982) describe two manoeuvres which are at the heart of virtually all psychotherapies, regardless of theoretical basis: reframing and directives. Reframing involves providing feedback to clients which violate their expectations in such a way which makes their problems more solvable. Although each system of therapy specifies content on which reframing is based (e.g. psychoanalysts interpret defenses and traumatic events while rational-emotive therapists challenge particular beliefs), the content of the reframing may not be as significant as the client's belief in this new system of thinking (Frank, 1961) or the behaviour changes implied by the alternative perception of the world (Kelly, 1955). By listening to the reactions of the client to reframing, the psychotherapist judges the impact on the psychotherapeutic relationship and likelihood of behaviour change. Sullivan (1954) attended to the client's anxiety level in making this judgement, Langs (1978) considers the client's image of the therapist, and Malan (1979) listens for deepening of rapport.

Directives issued by the psychotherapist which produce movement toward therapeutic goals similarly generate feedback from clients which psychotherapists must consider. Therapists use directives in ways which promote change which is perceived by clients as resulting from internal forces, rather than simple compliance with the advice of the psychotherapist. Therefore the therapist listens for indications that the client attributes positive changes in life satisfaction to the learning achieved in psychotherapy and new behavioural choices. Taking personal responsibility for the choices and the change bodes well for a lasting therapeutic effect.

In the third and final stage of psychotherapy, the therapist listens for indications that the client is ready for termination. These indications take the form of summarizing the course of the therapy, description of its benefits, and justification of its termination. The psychotherapist also considers how well the benefits reported by the client fit with his theoretical conceptions of the proper goals of the therapy.

Pitfalls in the use of theory

Freud (1912) recognized that in selecting information, the psychotherapist runs the risk of following his expectations and discovering only what he already knows. Yet the enormous amount of information gathered during psychotherapy must inevitably be summarized by the therapist into a smaller number of concepts. This process is necessary because human beings have a limited capacity to process information in short-term memory compared to the amount of information available from long-term memory. This processing is often referred to as social inference (Fiske and Taylor, 1984) and is subject to many pitfalls to which the psychotherapist is not immune. The pitfalls include the following:

1 New material which is discounted is likely to be categorized on the basis of the fit with emerging formulations (Watts, 1983), and these formulations are usually based in turn on a pre-existing theory. This is disturbing in the light of the possibility that psychotherapists arrive at a stable image of their clients as early as the second session (Meehl, 1973).

2 Psychotherapists are exposed to small and biased samples of

populations in their clinical work which may lead them to develop inferences which are poor estimates of the characteristics of the population. For example, Freud's conception of psychological development is based on material gathered from psychoanalytic sessions with clients who may not be representative of other people.

3 Vivid, specific examples may be over-utilized in formulating an understanding of a person, although the overall picture of the person is quite different.

4 Psychotherapists may be prone to predict unlikely extreme behaviours to be performed by clients far more often than is warranted. This can be due to a misunderstanding of the process of combining probabilities of specific aspects of the behaviours in question. The likelihood of any behaviour cannot be greater than the probability of any specific aspect of the event occurring alone (Fiske and Taylor, 1984). Furthermore, psychotherapists may judge a false positive to be a safer error than a false negative (e.g. in the case of suicidal threats).

5 Determining and consistently applying weights to pieces of information in order to draw accurate conclusions is something better done by a computer than a person. A psychotherapist may be using a process of inference that could be computer-modelled, but he applies it in a less explicit and exact form due to the time constraints under which he works (Meehl, 1973).

If a psychotherapist is in a headlong rush to formulate an understanding of a client it may be because of the difficulty he has in tolerating ambiguity for any length of time. As Watts (1983) has pointed out, a psychotherapist enjoys novel but coherent stories (perhaps coherent in light of a favourite theory) but is unhappy with the apparently incoherent. To reduce anxiety which may be aroused in such circumstances, the therapist may prefer a bad formulation to none at all (Kelly, 1955). The psychotherapist arrives at the formulation, which is a rapid simplification of complex information, in a manner which involves a series of shortcuts which can be full of inaccuracies as described above. Fiske and Taylor (1984) are pessimistic about the possibility of improving this process. But they make several encouraging remarks about this process of special concern for psychotherapists. First, intuitive inferential strategies which consider content, context and change may be powerful in comparison to apparently 'ideal' strategies which emphasize correct ways of gathering and combining information. Second, many errors can be corrected through communication. If a psychotherapist is especially good at seeking validation from the client in the ways described above and testing disconfirmation of strongly held theoretical notions, the dangers of inadequate inferences can be minimized and corrections made. Third, speed in reaching decisions may be necessary during psychotherapy sessions, and sacrificing thoroughness may sometimes be a price worth paying.

The ideal therapeutic listener

So many of the difficulties confronted in therapeutic listening are due to the limitations of human capacities to attend to, remember and integrate the amount of information presented by a client. These processes are made even more difficult when much of the information is a kind which challenges the emotional life of the psychotherapist. Furthermore, theories utilized by therapists for attending to and integrating information are biased toward selection of certain content, leaving blind spots for the psychotherapists who use them.

The ideal therapeutic listener would be a psychotherapist who is conversant with his own inner life and not frightened by its contents. He also has the discipline and patience to tolerate the ambiguity of a client's unconscious messages. The ideal therapeutic listener has a working knowledge of a number of theoretical frameworks in order to shift comfortably among various content categories. Such knowledge would also allow the therapist to avoid feeling that it is necessary to fit new information into one available framework. Instead, various theories would suggest hypotheses on which the therapist could draw in order to guide therapeutic strategy. In reaching an understanding of a particular client, the ideal therapeutic listener would to some extent develop a new version of theory modified according to information about the client discovered by the 'third ear'. Finally, the ideal therapeutic listener would be constantly aware of the pitfalls of the social inference process operating in psychotherapy and apply the process appropriately in clinical work. These processes will continue to be important in psychotherapy to the extent available theories are inexact and psychotherapy remains an art.

References

Arieti, S. (1974), 2nd edn, *Interpretation of Schizophrenia*, New York, Basic Books.

Bandler, R. and Grinder, J. (1975) *The Structure of Magic*, Palo Alto, Science & Behavior Books.
Benjamin, A. (1981), 3rd edn, *The Helping Interview*, Boston, Houghton Mifflin.
Bugental, J.F.T. (1978) *Psychotherapy and Process: The Fundamentals of an Existential-Humanistic Approach*, Reading (Massachusetts), Addison-Wesley.
Egan, G. (1986), 3rd edn, *The Skilled Helper*, Monterey, Brooks/Cole.
Ellis, A. (1962) *Reason and Emotion in Psychotherapy*, New York, Lyle Stuart.
Fiske, S.T. and Taylor, S.E. (1984) *Social Cognition*, New York, Random House.
Frank, J.D. (1961) *Persuasion and Healing*, Baltimore, Johns Hopkins.
Freeman, L. (1984) *Listening to the Inner Self*, New York, Jason Aronson.
Freud, S. (1912/1957) 'Recommendations to Physicians Practicing Psycho-Analysis', *The Standard Edition of the Complete Psychological Works of Sigmund Freud*, vol. 12, London, Hogarth Press, 109–20.
Ivey, A. and Gluckstern, N. (1984), 2nd edn, *Basic Influencing Skills*, Amherst, Microtraining Associates.
Kelly, G. (1955) *The Psychology of Personal Constructs*, New York, Norton.
Kelly, G. (1969) 'Personal Construct Theory and the Psychotherapeutic Interview' in B. Maher (ed.) *Clinical Psychology and Personality: The Selected Papers of George Kelly*, New York, John Wiley and Sons, 224–64.
Kernberg, O. (1965) 'Notes on Countertransference', *Journal of the American Psychoanalytic Association* 13, 38–56.
Kvarnes, R.G. and Parloff, G.H. (1976) (eds) *A Harry Stack Sullivan Case Seminar: Treatment of a Young Male Schizophrenic*, New York, Norton.
Langs, R. (1978) *The Listening Process*, New York, Jason Aronson.
Malan, D.H. (1979) *Individual Psychotherapy and the Science of Psychodynamics*, London, Butterworths.
Meehl, P.E. (1973) *Psychodiagnosis: Selected Papers*, Minneapolis, University of Minnesota.
Pietrofesa, J.J., Leonard, G.E. and Van Hoose, W. (1978), 2nd edn., *The Authentic Counselor*, Chicago, Rand McNally.
Reik, T. (1948) *Listening with the Third Ear*, New York, Farrar, Straus & Co.
Rogers, C. (1951) *Client-Centred Therapy*, Boston, Houghton Mifflin.
Rogers, C. (1961) *On Becoming a Person: A Therapist's View of Psychotherapy*, Boston, Houghton Mifflin.
Strong, S.R. and Claiborn, C.D. (1982) *Change Through Interaction: Social Psychological Processes of Counseling and Psychotherapy*, New York, John Wiley & Sons.
Sullivan, H.S. (1954) *The Psychiatric Interview*, New York, Norton.
Wachtel, P.L. (1977) *Psychoanalysis and Behavior Therapy: Toward an Integration*, New York, Basic Books.

Watts, F.N. (1983) 'Strategies of Clinical Listening', *British Journal of Medical Psychology* 56, 113–23.
Wile, D.B. (1984) 'Kohut, Kernberg and Accusatory Interpretations', *Psychotherapy* 3, 353–64.

Chapter three

'Listening in': negotiating relationships between listeners and presenters on radio phone-in programmes[1]

Deborah Cameron and Deborah Hills

Introduction

Of all the mass media, radio is the one which most explicitly recognizes the category of 'listeners'. It is therefore an excellent source of material for researchers with an interest in what listeners do and how the role of the listener is negotiated in talk.

This is not just a trivial semantic point (i.e. that radio has 'listeners' where television has 'viewers' and printed media have 'readers'). Forty years ago, radio held a position in peoples' lives analogous to that of television today, but the advent of television has had far-reaching effects on our perception of radio. As J. Fred MacDonald (1980, 88) puts it, 'Radio has become a companion to the individual instead of remaining a focal point of family entertainment. An intimacy has developed between the radio and the individual.'

One consequence of this 'intimacy' – and indeed one marker of it – is the highly listener-oriented style of discourse to be found in many types of radio broadcast. Radio talk is shaped by broadcasters' awareness of and relationship with listeners to a very high degree. Many radio 'genres' encourage active participation from listeners in the form of letters, requests, on-air quizzes and so on. A peak of this listener involvement is reached in the phone-in programme, where interaction between radio presenters and listeners is the substance of what is broadcast.

The massive expansion that has taken place in phone-in programmes over the last two decades or so has been discussed in terms of economic, sociological and psychological factors. One relevant point is that local radio has expanded, with its allotted role as a community service; phone-ins provide, at low cost to the station, a forum for debate on the issues of the day, and increasingly a sort of informal social service to which people can turn for expert advice, information and reassurance. It has also been suggested (Brown, 1978; Losito, 1978) that in fulfilling this social duty phone-ins may incidentally meet the more personal needs of some individual listeners. They provide an opportunity to interact with a wide range of other people, an opportunity for public 'confession' or self-disclosure which is nonetheless relatively safe and anonymous, or simply an opportunity to hear one's own voice in public.

But although the phone-in has been examined from these sociological and psychological perspectives, we are aware of little or no research on it as a specifically linguistic event, despite the recent growth of interest in 'broadcast talk'.[2] In our view, research on the language of the phone-in offers insights into several areas which have been extensively discussed by discourse analysts and students of the media.

First, phone-in talk displays a variant form of the systematic organization that has been shown to be typical of both face-to-face interaction and telephone calls. It is essentially a form of telephone conversation, but with several unusual features: an ambiguous relationship between the parties, which has to be negotiated; a content and duration which are subject to control; and above all, a context in which the entire conversation is designed to be *overheard*. For in a phone-in we have two different levels of listener: there is the individual who is actually calling, and the collectivity of listeners 'out there'. We will argue that *both* types of listener make a significant contribution to the organization of phone-in talk. The presenter is responsible for balancing what he takes to be the claims of each; sometimes, as we shall see, their rather different needs are played off against each other.

A second area where research on phone-in talk might prove illuminating is the study of so-called *asymmetrical discourse*, that is, talk where one party has more power than others to control the discourse. In the case of the phone-in, as we have mentioned already, the presenter is responsible for the conduct of calls, the organization of available time and – a point of particular interest to researchers in media studies – the maintenance of a consensus which excludes 'unacceptable' views from the airwaves.

Data

The data for this study come from the output of LBC Radio, London's 'all talk' station. Fifty calls were recorded and transcribed; twenty-five came from general 'open line' phone-ins where presenters and callers discussed current affairs, and a further twenty-five were drawn from a selection of expert advice phone-ins on topics ranging from medical problems to gardening. The 'advice-line' programmes featured three-way conversation between a presenter, a guest expert and the caller. We chose to sample both open-line and expert advice programmes because these are both common types of phone-in. We also expected them to raise slightly different issues in analysis, an expectation which proved to be correct.

Transcription symbols

Most of the symbols we use are in line with the conventions used by conversation analysts in the tradition of Harvey Sacks. For the purposes of this paper, the most important symbols are as follows:

P = Presenter, C = Caller, E = Expert.
[Point of overlap onset
] Point at which an utterance or utterance part terminates *vis-à-vis* another
= Indicates one utterance following another with no gap
(20) Length of pause or silence in seconds.

Phone-in talk: opening the line

According to Schegloff (1972), the opening of a telephone call normally displays a highly specific and predictable pattern, as in the following example (adapted from Coulthard 1977, 85):

A: Makes telephone ring at B's location
(T1)B: Hello
(T2)A: Hi
(T3)B: Oh hi

What is specific to the telephone channel here is that the first spoken turn, T1, is not an initiation, but the 'second pair-part' of an 'adjacency pair'. It is the answer to a *summons* represented by the ringing of the phone. Calls begin, that is, with a summons-answer (SA) sequence rather than with greetings, as in many face-to-face encounters. The greetings follow in T2 and T3 (that B returns A's greeting in T3 illustrates that *hello* was an answer and not a greeting). The next slot, T4, is normally allocated to the summoner, A, to provide an initial reason for the call. Alternatively, the greeting sequence may be followed by a further 'phatic' exchange, e.g. polite enquiries after health, comments about the weather, etc. Eventually, however, the summoner will be obliged to introduce the 'business' of the call.

Phone-ins follow a slightly different pattern, because the roles of summoner and summoned are initially reversed. Normally, the person who answers the phone does not know who is calling until the summoner declares her/himself; but phone-in presenters do know who is calling, because callers have already given their name, location and a brief synopsis of what they want to say to station personnel. They are then summoned to speak at an appropriate moment by the presenter himself. The summons usually takes the form of mentioning NAME + LOCATION, as in these examples:

Brian from Southgate
Beatrice is on the line now in Mitcham
And Pam is first in Leytonstone
From Stanmore now to Shepherds Bush and Rita is on the line

This summons from the presenter puts the caller in the position of answerer. Sometimes the call proceeds exactly as in the example we quoted above, i.e. summons-answer-greeting-greeting:

P: Maria on the line now in [Sudbury
C: [Hello
P: Hello Maria
C: Good evening Mike

At other times, however, the caller moves straight into a greeting, but precedes it with the token *oh* or *yes* to mark acknowledgement of the summons:

P: John in Holloway
C: **Yes** morning Ed
P: morning

P: Let's try Marie in Edgware
C: **Oh** good morning to you Ed
P: good morning

This 'collapsing' of two turns is common in phone-in openings. It shows that callers continue to orient to 'ordinary' rules of telephone talk, but are also aware of the norms of the phone-in, where time-consuming and uninteresting exchanges must be kept to a minimum. In addition, the 'collapsing' strategy is used by callers to re-establish their status as summoner after the original reversal. This is necessary, because the business of the call must be introduced by the caller and not the presenter. By collapsing the end of the SA sequence with the beginning of the greeting sequence, a 'competent' caller ensures that the next turn after the greeting sequence ends will be theirs rather than the presenter's, and thus available for introducing the chosen topic:

P: John in Holloway
C: Yes morning Ed
P: Morning
C: about the recent (mm) the recent activities there in Moscow . . . etc.

Sometimes presenters pre-empt this move by immediately reminding the caller of her/his status as summoner with a question or eliciting move:

P: Celia in Epsom. What do you want to talk about?
P: Ken is next in Battersea. What do you want to say?

The presenter in examples like this is attempting to cut off the usual greeting sequence and get straight down to the 'meat' of the call. Greetings are necessary in ordinary phone calls for establishing friendly relations between the parties; but in phone-ins, which take place in a restricted time-slot and are designed to be overheard by a large audience, 'phatic' elements, like greetings and enquiries after health, are perceived by presenters as redundant.

Interestingly, however, the 'cut-off' strategy rarely succeeds in preventing callers from offering greetings and other phatic moves, nor indeed from briefly acknowledging the summons with *oh* or *yes*. For instance:

P: Celia in Epsom. What do you want to talk about?
C: Oh! Hello! I want to talk about . . . etc.

P: Brian's next from Tooting. What do you want to say?
C: Ah! Good morning. m-m-morning. Yes I want to make two points . . . etc.

Why do callers resist the efforts of presenters to hurry them on to the business of the call? One possible reason is that callers find it difficult to collect their thoughts on air without the initial exchanges. This seems somewhat unlikely, though, as calls are carefully planned and the first point at least is 'rehearsed' in the preliminary conversation with station staff. Another possibility is that callers tend to orient to everyday norms of politeness: to 'miss out' greetings goes against the grain. A third possibility, and one which strikes us as particularly intriguing, is that callers are determined to pursue a 'personal' relationship with the presenter by engaging him in phatic exchanges even though these delay the introduction of what 'listeners out there' have tuned in to hear.

At this point we must return to something we mentioned earlier, namely the ambiguous relation between presenters and callers. Although the presenter has certain personal details about each caller – name, address, etc. – s/he is unlikely to have any previous acquaintance, or interest in such acquaintance, with the individual listener. The presenter is simply doing a job in talking to members of the public, and each particular caller is simply one of many. But the person who calls may feel rather differently about it. S/he is probably a regular listener to the programme and may feel s/he knows the presenter quite well. In the LBC data, a number of callers deliberately voice their concern for the presenter as a person.

P: Joan is on the line in Westminster. Hello Joan.
C: Hello good morning. How are you?
P: Fine er yourself?

A few callers even took the opportunity to compliment the presenter:

C: How are you?
P: w-well I'm fine how are you?
[are you w-w-w
C: [now you are a very fair man and I and all
the time that you have been on LBC I have never been
able to tell your political line whether you are
Labour Tory conserv whatever
P: How kind of you to say
so

In this sort of situation the presenter is obliged to return personal enquiries and thank the caller in order to conform to minimal norms of politeness, but such moves among LBC presenters were always characterized by embarrassment (marked by hesitation phenomena) or a 'jokey' tone (as in the utterance 'how kind of you to say so'). The presenters appeared to view such exchanges as a deviation from the 'professional' mode and contradictory to their interests and those of the 'listeners out there'. For whereas an individual caller may wish to prolong their time on the air and pursue a satisfying personal relationship with the radio personality, presenters wish to get to the point as quickly as possible, in order to fit in as many callers as they can and to provide the maximum entertainment value. This is one example where the two kinds of listener are seen to have different interests which the presenter must resolve.

Managing closings

A similar conflict of interest arises in relation to the closing of phone-in calls. Schegloff and Sacks (1973, 244–5) observe that the problem in most talk is: 'How to organise the simultaneous arrival of the co-conversationalists at a point where one speaker's completion will not occasion another speaker's talk, and that will not be heard as some speaker's silence.'

They suggest that the problem is usually solved by the parties first 'bounding' the existing topic (i.e. agreeing they have nothing further to say about it, for instance by one party summing up and the other agreeing), after which one party produces a 'possible pre-closing' by 'passing' on the introduction of a further topic (for instance by saying something like *OK then* or *right*). At this juncture, the other person can do the same and 'pass' – in which case a closing (e.g. a sequence of goodbyes) can follow – or else s/he can raise what analysts have called 'unmentioned mentionables', i.e. introduce a new topic, as in this example from Schegloff and Sacks (1973, 320):

Caller: OK thank you
Crandall: OK dear
Caller: Oh by the way, I'd just like to say that . . . etc.

Closings pose problems for phone-in conversation. Even when successful – that is, when a possible pre-closing elicits no unmentioned mentionables and proceeds to an actual closing sequence – closings are notoriously lengthy. And if a caller chooses to exploit the opportunity provided by a possible pre-closing for raising new topics, this too can extend the length of a call unacceptably, as well as taking it into irrelevant or possibly dangerous terrain.

How, then, is the problem solved? From our data it appears that listeners accept, or are obliged to accept, closing strategies from presenters which would elsewhere be flagrant breaches of politeness. The presenter is the arbiter of when enough has been said on a particular topic, either because time has run out or because the caller is becoming repetitive and tedious for the listeners 'out there'.

This problem does not seem to be so marked in the 'expert advice' phone-ins we recorded. Since these deal usually with one specific problem from each caller, it is not surprising to find that closing is accomplished without much difficulty. Of the 46 per cent of calls which followed the pattern identified by Schegloff and Sacks, almost all were 'expert advice line' calls.

The majority of calls, however – 54 per cent – did deviate from the 'normal' pattern, and these were overwhelmingly 'open line' calls. In 34 per cent of calls the presenter either unilaterally bounded the topic and then closed the conversation without giving the caller an opportunity to mention unmentioned mentionables, or alternatively the caller was given this opportunity but was ignored if s/he tried to take advantage of it. Consider, for instance, this call about ethnic monitoring on American marriage licenses:

P: well I think I mean you know nei-neither you nor I have to suffer from this
C: No but
P: because it isn't on the British marriage certificate and I would advise anyone who feels strongly about it to leave it blank [further 114 words of comment]. Thanks Sally. Brian's next from Tooting.

The caller's *no but* indicates an unmentioned mentionable, or at least a lack of acquiescence in the bounding of this topic. The presenter is apparently not worried about time here – witness his very lengthy comment – but he has apparently decided that the caller's further remarks should not be aired. It will also be noted that in this case (and indeed most of the 'deviant' 54 per cent), no opportunity is offered for the caller to participate in a terminal exchange of goodbyes.

In cases where an abrupt closing was occasioned by lack of time, this was usually made explicit:

P: OK Alan er I'm afraid we've run out of time. Thank you very much indeed for your advice.

Listeners are aware that the presenter is constrained not only by the need to deal with as many calls as possible, but also, on LBC at least, by quarter-hourly breaks for news and sport, traffic bulletins, weather reports and commercials.

In calls where the problem is a lack of entertainment value, repeated attempts may have to be made at closing and the presenter may feel the need for a more than perfunctory apology.

C: It is that kind of behaviour =
P: = all right

C: that fires the type of sexual action which can lead
to AIDS and I think myself that (FADE)
P: Eddie! Eddie! I think I've got your general drift
[summarizes] let's leave (mm) let's leave it there I'm
sorry I'm not meaning to (mm) denigrate your remarks
at all (mm). Lets leave it there and move on to
Celia in Epsom.

The apology is occasioned by the fact that the presenter has attempted to interrupt the caller and has then faded him in order to give himself space to bound the topic and close the call.

So far we have left unexamined 20 per cent of the 'deviant' closings. This is because they illustrate the operation of a rather different constraint: not lack of time or lack of entertainment value, but lack of conformity to the station's norms of acceptability. We will deal with the challenge these calls represent in a separate section.

Extreme, outrageous and offensive calls: achieving consensus through phone-in programmes

Radio, like other media, upholds certain standards concerning what it is acceptable to say on the air. These standards are often justified as reflecting a public consensus on the limits of decency and reasonable debate, but as many commentators have pointed out, the practice of the media is actually very important in fixing such a consensus. The LBC data show how certain views which are in fact *typical* of public opinion are nevertheless defined as outside legitimate public discourse through 'containment strategies' which presenters use.

On LBC and other 'open line' radio phone-ins, would-be callers are vetted by station staff before they reach the airwaves, and some are eliminated on the grounds that they are drunk or otherwise incoherent, or because they are obvious 'cranks'. LBC also operates a further safeguard: a ten-second delay in transmission to allow bleeping or deletion of obscenities. But even with vetting and delayed transmission, a certain number of callers get through whose opinions turn out to be, in LBC's terms, politically extreme, overtly offensive to particular groups, or just embarrassingly ludicrous and bizarre. The presenter has the job of 'containing' these calls.

The containment strategies employed by presenters are interesting for the way notions of the 'listeners' and the station's responsibility to them are used to define and maintain a consensus, particularly on controversial topics. At some points the presenter adopts the stance of a representative of the listening public, while at others he poses as their educator or protector. He may in addition set out to entertain listeners by making the 'deviant' caller the butt of ridicule. Or he may make use of two, or all of these strategies simultaneously.

The presenter here treads a very fine line between containing offensiveness and being offensive himself. The personality of a phone-in host is supposed to have a certain provocative quality, especially on the general 'open line' type programme. It is no good having someone universally bland and tolerant when the whole idea is to produce an atmosphere of lively debate. But the presenter is also supposed to refrain from partiality and abuse of the caller. Sanctions are available if he oversteps the mark, as happened recently in the case of a host on Lancashire Red Rose Radio:

> Banned Red Rose Radio presenter Allan Beswick has been censured by the Independent Broadcasting Authority for making offensive remarks to a caller on his phone-in show. . . . The IBA is taking an extremely serious view of this lapse. (*West Lancs Evening Gazette*, 21 April 1987)

It is very interesting, however, that Beswick's show was popular with listeners for its 'outrageousness' in this respect. In the USA, similarly, there are reports of a new genre of phone-ins whose whole *raison d'être* is for the presenter to pour abuse on those who call. These programmes attract large audiences and queues of would-be callers wanting to take the presenter on. Such phone-ins cater to what Losito (1978) terms 'the exhibitionist call', and there are demands to ban them as they become more and more outrageous.

On LBC outrage is kept within bounds by the use of the 'containment strategies' mentioned above. We may now look more closely at what these strategies actually entail. Although we make no great claims for the following categories as being either exhaustive or discrete, there seem to be three main types of containment strategy: 'stating a common-sense cliché', 'defusing with humour' and 'expressing strong disapproval'.

Stating a common-sense cliché

Here is an extract from a call about the Soviet Union:

C: Whether they're humble or not they have a roof over their head and the rents are cheap (2.0) now you can't say that particularly in London
P: No you can't say that particularly in London but you

> would create one vacancy Ken if you upped sticks and went to the Soviet Union if it's so good (mm). Some would say – I don't – but some would say, why don't you?

In this extract the presenter has marked the pro-USSR stance of the caller as 'extreme', that is, outside the political consensus with which the British media operate. His response is to adopt what he takes to be a common 'man on the Clapham omnibus' position, i.e. if the Soviet Union is so wonderful, why don't you go to Russia? He is careful to put this in displaced form however, attributing it to others and distancing himself from it. 'Some would say – I don't, but some would say . . .' He then cuts the caller off. This strategy implicitly appeals to a knowledge of what 'ordinary people' think and identifies the presenter with the moderation of 'listeners out there' instead of the extremism of this particular listener.

Another example of this strategy comes in a discussion of the Middle East. In this case it is used not to define the caller as deviant but to smoothe over the fact that he is becoming very emotional and allow the closing of the call:

> C: well what have we done? What has happened to six million Jews? Have we been able to accommodate that group of people? Dachau, Auschwitz, Majdenek, whose technology created that? Were there any Arabs there? Not as far as I know. I saw the pictures there myself. You have a look at them as well. And as for the richness of Arabs figures are available. They're always misrepresented. There are countries like Saudi Arabia and Kuwait who are rich on a per head basis all other are extremely poor especially Syria for example. Especially Yemen absolutely at the bottom of the pile even in terms of the third world also Egypt.
>
> P: Peter I just want to say one thing and that's it's a comment really on all the calls we've had or certainly the first call and yours. People feel very strongly about this from opposing sides of the fence . . . I know that may sound a trite thing to say. It's not meant to be but it's all I can we're not going to solve it on this progran programme unfortunately. Eddie's next from Hendon . . . etc.

Here the presenter copes with a discussion which threatens to get into very deep water by appealing to 'trite' common sense notions about the problem being insoluble since it arises mainly from the fact that people 'feel very strongly'. What this has in common with the previous example is that the presenter again takes on a 'plain man' persona and states a piece of political folk-wisdom in order to re-establish the boundaries of consensus on a controversial topic. This also has the effect of providing a reason why the caller will not be allowed to go on with his line of argument – that is, because such strongly-felt sentiments are 'not going to solve it'.

It is interesting to note that Schegloff and Sacks (1973) cite clichés and aphorisms as common topic-bounding mechanisms. In the conversations Schegloff and Sacks are discussing, clichés can function in this way because they form part of a stock of shared or agreed wisdom. In phone-ins they tend to be imposed by the more powerful party, the presenter; but they are still appealed to in a way that suggests they are shared – assented to, in fact, by the 'listeners out there'.

Defusing with humour

C: Now Eddie, do you know there is a general election in the offing =
P: = I do know there's a general election in the offing
C: now could this [i.e. Mark Thatcher's wedding] be a show piece for the =
P: = oh come on Sam. No no you're going over the top. Calm down. Have a glass of water, drink some fresh air. It'll be all right on the night. Now honestly this this this this this is, you're you're getting carried away and I'm in danger of getting carried away too and I can't afford to be cause I'm here till one o'clock. Let's have a quick word from Casey over in Hendon.

Here the presenter finds the caller's point – that Mark Thatcher's wedding is a piece of carefully orchestrated Tory propaganda – extreme and ridiculous. He defuses it using humour – 'drink some fresh air' – and also by alluding humorously to his own situation 'I'm in danger of getting carried away too and I can't afford to cause I'm here till one o'clock'. This allusion also reminds the caller of the norms of the phone-in, that one should not 'get carried away' or 'go over the top'.

An interesting variant on the 'defusing with humour' strategy is for the presenter to imply that the caller 'must be joking'. The strategy works on several levels: its major aim is to lessen the impact of points which skirt the margin of acceptability by implying they are not serious, or that if they are they shouldn't be, but it also has a double function with regard to the caller. On one hand it denigrates the point s/he is making, with the possible implication that the caller is a fool; but on the other hand it saves the caller's face by interpreting the point as a deliberate joke or 'wind-up'. In fact it is usually clear to all concerned that the caller *is* serious. Take the following example:

C: I think the most dangerous man in our society today
. . . is the bisexual. Now he is the man who can to
use an English phrase = = he can pull a bird
P: = or woman =
C: far quicker than a red blooded a red blooded
man can and I would like to warn all young females if
they ever come across a guy with a feminine face
to watch out for him because he is the guy who can
really transfer the AIDS from the homosexual into the
heterosexual point of
P: well I don't quite know how you
spot a bisexual coming but I I I I take your point as
far as it is seriously delivered, thank you. Let's
hear from Joe in Chingford quickly

The presenter takes a fairly jocular tone throughout this rather bizarre contribution. His remark 'I don't quite know how you spot a bisexual coming' underlines the point that the caller's argument is ludicrous, while the qualified statement 'I take your point *as far as it is seriously delivered*' charitably suggests that the caller cannot mean him to take it seriously.

Expressing strong disapproval

In both the containment strategies dealt with so far, the presenter has used his authority to define a caller as 'extreme' or 'over the top', either by counterposing a common-sense cliché to the caller's view or suggesting it is nonserious or making a joke of it. The third strategy is more direct and more emphatic: it defines the caller as completely 'out of order' and takes him or her quite explicitly to task.

The 'expressing strong disapproval' strategy is reserved for callers who express opinions that in the current climate are completely taboo, outrageously prejudiced and/or utterly stupid. In our data, almost all instances of it occur in discussions of a single topic: AIDS. Presenters apparently feel a strong obligation to be active and unambiguous in their definition of the boundaries of acceptable discourse on this topic; callers cannot be allowed the same latitude as they would be on less explosive subjects. Thus presenters feel no inhibitions about severely censuring callers who disseminate what 'responsible people' have now decided are ignorant, bigoted and generally unhelpful views.

For instance, a caller who rings up to air her unusual ideas about the possible transmission of AIDS by inadequately washed pub glasses gets fairly short shrift:

C: With regard to the transfer of AIDS I wonder if anybody has considered the possibility of the connexion between gingivitis which you know is the bleeding of gums being transferred by cups and glasses in pubs.
P: I suppose they've considered it but why? Have you got reason to believe that that that is a way in which people transmit AIDS?
C: Yes yes I do I think that's a distinct possibility and I =
P: = no no hold on I didn't ask whether you thought it was a distinct possibility I was asking whether you had reason to believe
C: none except I consider it to be a possibility
P: well I suppose there are all kinds of vague possibilities . . . do you often see blood on glasses in pubs?
C: I don't use pubs. I honestly think that =
P: = well well this is all a little bit Alice in Wonderland Jean. I think there are far more serious aspects to deal with when we're discussing AIDS than desperately looking round for vague possibilities as to the means of transmitting the disease. It's too serious for that. Frank good morning . . .

The presenter is more critical here than is usual. He challenges the caller ('no no hold on I didn't ask . . .') and calls her idea 'vague'; but the really strong disapproval comes at the end of the call where he comments dismissively 'this is all a little bit Alice in Wonderland'. After upbraiding the caller for irresponsible triviality ('I think there are more serious aspects' . . . 'it's too serious for that') he cuts her off without giving her any opportunity to reply.

An even more extreme example of this strategy is the following:

P: Now George good morning
C: Oh good morning Brian oh (mm)
Some people might think it's silly but =
P: = I beg your
pardon =
C: = I said I'm sorry some people might think
it's silly but (mm) I think AIDS is nature's way of
getting back at the exploding world population
P: oh
do you. What a silly thing to say. Dave you're
calling from Romford . . .

The abruptness with which the call is terminated together with the unambiguous 'what a silly thing to say' leave us in no doubt that this view of AIDS is effectively 'beyond the pale'.

Unsuccessful containment: the caller strikes back

There is one example in the LBC data where the caller effectively thwarts the presenter's attempts to contain his offensive views on AIDS and the gay community. It is worth reproducing in full.

C: I object to the gay people coming on the radio and
expecting to be s– treated like ordinary people =
P: = why?
C: Why? I'm just about to tell you why. They
have introduced a hub of disease into the rest of humanity
= [what what]
P: = oh rhu [barb. I mean] there i-i-i there
you know there is some evidence that that I'm sorry
but rhubarb. We don't know what the origin of AIDS
is
C: well we know who is spreading it put it that
way
P: come on
C: is [that] a fact or not
P: [y–y] I think there is
a danger there is certainly a statistical danger at
the moment that it is spreading faster in the
homosexual community than it it is in the
heterosexual community but it is spreading into
the heterosexual community =
= it certainly is. One

of our nurses in the paper this morning got it from a needle after treating one of these people. What what are that girl's prospects?

P: Och you cannot solve a problem like this by simply revealing your prejudices against people who have not got the same sexual mores or habits you do =

C: =

well we don't we're not spreading it (mm) well I won't enlighten you any further on that one. I know you might be (mm) you might be a little bit (mm) in agreement with gays' point of view but the other thing is . . . etc.

The reason this caller succeeds in going on with his call to the point where he, and not the presenter, feels enough has been said is that the caller here appropriates for himself all the linguistic prerogatives which normally are reserved for the presenter. First, the caller interrupts the presenter twice. In previous examples most interruptions have been made by the presenter. He is also quick to come in wherever the opportunity offers (e.g. when the presenter says 'it is spreading into the heterosexual community' the caller immediately picks up with 'it certainly is'). Second, the caller reverses the usual order of things by asking the presenter questions ('is that a fact or not?' 'what are that girl's prospects?'). Note, too, that these are hardly invitations to the presenter to provide information or even opinion; they are rhetorical questions of a highly conducive form. On the other hand, when the presenter asks the caller a question – in this case, one that does ask for more information, 'why?' the caller contrives to imply that the presenter has unnecessarily and illegitimately interrupted him ('why? I'm just about to tell you why').

But the *coup de grâce* is delivered when the caller usurps the presenter's right to engage in topic bounding and closes the discussion, moving on immediately to another topic: 'well I won't enlighten you any further on that one . . . the other thing is . . .'. The caller even manages to challenge the presenter's impartiality in passing: 'I know you might be a little bit in agreement with gays' point of view'. Where other callers have had their remarks interrupted and cut short in their prime, this caller manages to imply that the presenter is being tiresome and that he, the caller, must change the subject!

Eventually the presenter does regain control, interrupting and then terminating what looks set to be an even more appalling diatribe on the subject of the Jews in the Soviet Union. But the caller, by seizing opportunities to define, evaluate and control the interaction himself, has successfully avoided for an exceptionally long time the usual fate of the phone-in 'extremist'.

Conclusion

Radio phone-ins are speech events in which relationships between individual listeners, a notion of the 'listening public' and the station as personified in the professional presenter are carefully negotiated. Although it is the presenter who has ultimate control in the encounter – a control he may legitimate in terms of the interests of the 'listeners out there', their right to be entertained and to be protected from offensive views – the listeners who call in may challenge the norms he lays down in various ways, from dogged pursuit of a 'personal relationship' with the presenter to equally dogged resistance to the 'containment strategies' presenters employ. Listeners, like presenters, are *aware* of the linguistic and social norms which structure acceptable phone-in talk; yet they are capable of ignoring or subverting these and of attempting to renegotiate the rules of the game.

Notes

1. All data collection and transcription was carried out by Deborah Hills; the analysis is a collaborative effort.
2. See, however, the work of Higgins and Moss (1981) and Moss and Higgins (1984).

References

Brown, R. (1978) *Characteristics of Local Media Audiences*, London, Saxon House.

Coulthard, M. (1977) *An Introduction to Discourse Analysis*, London, Longman.

Higgins, C.S. and Moss, P.D. (1981) 'A Discourse Analysis of Talk-Back Radio: Some Cultural Implications', *Australia Review of Applied Linguistics* 4, 32–48.

Losito, J. (1978) 'La "nuova" radio ed il pubblico', *RAI Informazione Radio TVI*.

Macdonald, J. Fred (1980) *Don't Touch That Dial*, New York, Nelson Hall.

Moss, P.D. and Higgins, C.S. (1984) 'Radio Voices', *Media, Culture and Society* 6, 353–75.

Schegloff, E. A. (1972) 'Sequencing in Conversational Openings' in J. Gumperz and D. Hymes (eds), *Directions in Sociolinguistics: The Ethnography of Speaking*, New York, Holt, Rinehart and Winston.

Schegloff, E.A. and Sacks, H. (1973) 'Opening up Closings', *Semiotica* 7.4, 289–327.

Chapter four

Who is context?[1]

John Pellowe

Introduction

Parker-Rhodes (1978) suggests that context can be thought of as another 'text', parallel to the spoken or written one, which itself *could* be spoken or written by a person whose context it is. He also suggests that one of the functions of dialogue is to create (or celebrate the prior existence of) convergence between the contexts of the participants. In this chapter, I try to expose and explore my confusion in the face of these suggestions.[2]

The notion of context

Context is the ground of its own figure. Stripping like Moebius, it laughs reclothed. It is difficult, slipperily Escheresque. And like those wonders, it teases the techniques and assumptions of our minds just below the level of self enquiry.

Difficult, because it is constantly self-referring, self-generating, self-focusing and self-dissolving. Self-contradictory because self-renewing. Inconstantly permanent; permanently inconstant.

All meanings which are made, whether by humans or others, whether verbal, perceptual, genetic, temporal, spiritual or others – all meanings are created against and in and through some context.

As a technical notion context is immensely powerful, and yet, it seems to me, it is a notion whose use always just misses the opportunity of tapping this power. This eluding quality of context has its source in the factors of its ubiquity, abstractness and changeability, but it is only made apparent by problems of definition and presumption. Though defining and presuming are as indissociably intimate as the velocity and mass of an electron, I must, for the moment, write as if they were not.

I shall not be concerned here with the epistemological question as to the theoretical level upon which the tool of context should best be used. As Lyons points out (1977), Katz and Fodor (1963) argue for a descriptive semantics which is contextless, whereas Firth (1957) uses the technique of context to build his whole semantic theory – which includes phonetic and phonological, as well as syntactic, considerations. Whether matters of context are thought of as comprising a separate *kind* of competence from that governing the well-formedness of strings (Hymes, 1972), or as being inextricably compounded with all levels of linguistic organization and realization (Firth, 1957; Wittgenstein, 1967), are ones which do not affect the outcome of an enquiry into the nature of the pre-theoretical notion of context itself. Here then I am only concerned with an ontological question. What *is* context?

Regardless, then, of the uses to which their theoretical constructs are to be put, let me examine different definitions of 'context' (and commentaries upon them).

Hurford and Heasley give the following definition:

> the context of an utterance is a small subpart of the universe of discourse shared by speaker and hearer, and includes facts about the topic of the conversation in which the utterance occurs, and also facts about the situation in which the conversation takes place. (1983, 68)

In their comment they say that exact contexts can never be specified with any certainty, and that the notion is flexible if not vague. A subsequent comment says:

> Contexts are constructed continuously during the course of a conversation . . . [new] items . . . become part of the context . . . perhaps things mentioned . . . previously . . . 'fade out' of the context. (1983, 70)

The points I wish to extract from comparing these remarks are as follows (and we shall see that they recur in other writers):

1 The assumption of a single, unique context for an *utterance* ('*the* context of an utterance . . .'). I shall refer to this as the Uniqueness Problem;
2 Though it is only weakly inferrable from this definition, context seems to be *static* for the period of the utterance: I shall refer to this as the Stasis Problem;
3 This unique context is *shared* by the participants – the Sharedness Problem;
4 Nevertheless, contexts are *constructed*, probably by the parti-

cipants (but possibly by themselves 'items become part of . . . things fade out of the context') – the Agent Problem;

5 And they are constructed *continuously*, but not necessarily cumulatively – the Dynamism Problem.

Generally speaking, as a matter of logical coherence, one might expect two general *types* of definition of context: (a) those which focused upon uniqueness, or stasis, or sharedness, would also tend to embrace one, or both, of the other two; (b) those which focused upon agent, or dynamism, might refer to the other. In any case, the factors under (a) and those under (b) seem to be incompatible, which at least lends retrospective context to the first seven sentences above, and may, in addition, indicate that the pre-theoretical and theoretical uses of context cannot be brought into correspondence.

Lyons writes:

> Context . . . is a theoretical construct, in the postulation of which the linguist abstracts from the actual situation and establishes as contextual all the factors which, by virtue of their influence upon the participants in the language event, systematically determine the form, the appropriateness, or the meaning of utterances. (1977, 572)

This definition certainly embodies the Uniqueness Problem (UP) ('abstracts all [and only] the factors which determine *the* meaning of utterances'), the Stasis Problem (StP) ('the factors *systematically* determine . . .'), the Sharedness Problem (ShP) ('their influence upon the participants'), and the Agent Problem (AP) ('the linguist abstracts . . .'). The AP is made more complex by Lyons' view that:

> Contextualization [is both] the process whereby the native speaker of a language produces contextually appropriate and internally coherent utterances . . . [and] the process which the linguist carries out in his description of particular languages . . . [Given the need for descriptive adequacy] there must be some correspondence between these two kinds of contextualization (1977, 610).

Here also we see an embodiment of the Dynamism Problem (DP) ('the process whereby one participant produces appropriate utterances'), though in much weaker form than it occurs in the definition of Hurford and Heasley.

For Firth (1957), contextualization, of various types and levels, provides the technique, par excellence, for the analysis and categorization of meanings at all levels of linguistic structure from the phonetic to the semantic. And perhaps because there are so many types of context (but equally, perhaps, because it is his preferred way of writing) Firth does not simply, in any one place, define generic 'context'. Hints and allusions abound throughout his work; and so, working in the other direction, I shall make a quotational collage to relate to the views cited above.

> 'Context of situation' is best used as a schematic construct to apply to linguistic events . . . it is a group of related categories at a different level from grammatical categories, but rather of the same abstract nature . . . it brings into relation the following: A. The relevant features of participants . . . their verbal and non-verbal action, B. The relevant objects, C. The effect of the verbal action . . . (1957, 32)
>
> the technique . . . is an empirical rather than a theoretical analysis of meaning . . . a serial contextualization of our facts, context within context, each one being a function, an organ of the bigger context and all contexts finding a place in what may be called the context of culture . . . (1957, 195)
>
> we must take our facts from speech sequences . . . in contexts of situation which are typical, recurrent and repeatedly observable . . . (1957, 35)
>
> contextual meaning is the functional relation of the sentence to the processes of context of situation . . . (1957, 195)
>
> [in] the context of situation . . . whole stretches of personal biography and cultural history are involved and . . . past, present and future all meet . . . (1957, 18)
>
> the central concept of . . . semantics . . . is the context of situation [in which we may include] the contexts of experience of the participants. Every man carries his culture and . . . his social reality . . . wherever he goes . . . it is this situational and experiential study that I would [call] 'semantics' . . . (1957, 27)
>
> if I . . . turn to you, on this occasion, with the question *bAWd?* [i.e. a word which could be bawd, board, bored] you may possible reply 'not really' or just 'no' with a rising intonation, or 'go on', and in the several cases furnish contextual relations which determine the meaning [of *bAWd*]. In such a context of situation you have . . . *semantic function* . . . (1957, 27)
>
> just as contexts for a word multiply indefinitely, so also situations are infinitely various . . . (1957, 28)

> each word when used in a new context is a new word . . .
> (1957, 190)

It is fairly clear from these fragments, I hope, that Firth, no less than the other writers I have so briefly cited, variably and *without apparently noticing the problem* makes use of the two incompatible sets of factors labelled (a) and (b) above.

How is it possible that such problems go undetected? It seems to me that the answer lies in presumptions of distinction, or of difference, or of knowledge, which are certainly wanting. The presumptions all come togther at a single point, namely that it is legitimate to attempt precisely to determine the meanings of linguistic events in terms of a notion whose difficulty of definition is at least alluded to by the definers themselves. In such a situation a tidy semantics can be established on the basis of a background knowledge context, but as Lakatos (1976, 45) warns us 'background knowledge is where we assume that we know everything but in fact know nothing'.

The persistence and depth of this difficulty indicates to me that we are confronted by what Bateson (1972, 486ff.) calls a pathology of epistemology, that is, an erroneous proposition, or series of propositions, concerning the nature and manner of our knowing something about the universe. It is not obvious to me that the meanings of linguistic events *can* be precisely determined. And surely the exact differences between 'the meanings of linguistic events' and 'contexts' – if there are differences – need to be determined before the one can be used to specify the other?

Bateson points out that the persistence of such errors and their resistance to change is largely due to their apparent correctness on many occasions – an epistemically false premise is not refuted by the circumstances of its use, otherwise it would not persist as an epistemically false premise. And of the more general problem, Raine writes:

> It is difficult for us to realize wherein our own unspoken assumptions, the foundations upon which we build our world, differ from those of others; for this assumed ground is the very thing we cannot discuss, for we may not know what it is, still less what it might be; we cannot imagine how the world might appear if we do not possess the groundwork of knowledge which we do possess; nor can we in the nature of things imagine how reality would appear in the light of knowledge which we do not possess. Yet we continue to assume that whatever theories we may construct upon it the primary experience of the world is the same for everyone; even when in

> theory we would admit that this cannot be so, we continue to imagine that we all live in the same apparent world through the sheer inability to imagine otherwise. From time to time we receive a shock, when we are compelled to realize the immense divergence not of deductions and conclusions, but of premises, the basic assumptions upon which these rest, and thus even of the primary experience itself, inseparable from the attitude of the consciousness which receives it. (1985, 105)

In the face of the impossibility of one's position as indicated by Raine, it might prove beneficial to espouse the divine Principle of Ignorance, to feel the connnectedness without the construction (or the constriction). Da Free John (1980a, 35–9) asks:

> Do you know what anything *is*? . . . what is *is*, not what it looks like, not how you can experience it, not what it can do. . . . You can enter into play with it and think *about* it, but you never know what it *is*. . . . You do not even know what you are. . . . The only thing you know about anything is still *about* it. . . . Ignorance is the Principle of existence. . . . The summarization of our existence is Mystery, absolute, unqualified confrontation with what we cannot know. . . . No one will ever know what anything *is*. That is the Truth. Becoming submitted to that Truth is spiritual life.

Similarly from their different perspectives many other thinkers have emphasized the Principle of Ignorance. Bateson (1985, 35) says 'we shall never be able to claim final knowledge of anything whatsoever'; Capra says

> the crucial feature of quantum theory is that the . . . electron does not *have* properties independent of my mind . . . the split between mind and matter, between I and the world, is no longer valid. We can never speak about nature without, at the same time, speaking about ourselves (NB. *about*) (1982, 132);

and Laing:

> The I that I am is not the me that I know, but the wherewith and the whereby the *me* is known. But if this I that is the wherewith and whereby is not anything that is known, then it is no thing – nothing. Click – sluice gates open – body guts outside in. (1967, 147)

Sacks (1985; 1986) shows both of his patients and of himself, with great sympathy and some awe-fulness, the falsity of our 'common-sense' belief that each of us knows not only 'this is my hand' (cf. Moore, 1939), but also what that sentence means. These 'cases' of Sacks are strikingly living examples of Bateson's epistemological pathology.

There thus seem to be persuasive internal arguments from many different areas of thinking and feeling, in favour of constantly keeping before us the Principle of Ignorance. Persisting in this way, I shall proceed to ask what I do not know rather than what I do know.

Meaning and context

If meanings are determinable from contexts, then one way of focusing upon our ignorance about context would be to look through the mirror (Alice, Orphee [Cocteau]) of those meanings.

Wittgenstein says:

> A proposition is a picture of reality for if I understand a proposition, I know the situation that it represents. And I understand the proposition without having had its sense explained to me (1961, 39–40);

and

> If [the cited sentence] were set down in isolation I should say, I don't know what it is about. But all the same I should know how this sentence might perhaps be used; I could myself invent a context for it (1967, para. 525);

and

> We ask 'What does "I am frightened" really mean, what am I referring to when I say it?' And of course we find no answer or one that is inadequate. The question is: 'In what sort of context does it occur?' (1967, 188).

And Firth and many others would surely agree. All I am trying to establish here is that if many believe that meanings are determined from contexts, and if what I want to do is focus on my ignorance as to what constitutes context, then I can do it by looking at context through meaning, i.e. reversing the normal procedure.

Given some sort of contextless sentences and their meanings what is there – as a sort of lowest common denominator of my processes of guessing contexts – which can tell me something about the general process or object known as 'context'? But is this a sufficiently constrained thought experiment? Perhaps the range of contexts I could permisssibly guess for a given sentence would be too wide? Both 'permissibly' and 'too', surely, themselves beg not only questions but also contexts? Well, but given that we might find some elicitational and evaluative methods to circumambulate these problems, is the approach in general feasible? It seems as if this approach might *not* be reasonable, largely because it relies upon the assumption that the meanings of contextless sentences are, in very large measure, canonical; that is, that it is perfectly reasonable to talk about *the meaning* (NB. singular, single; NB. definite) of a contextless sentence. And there are reasons for imagining that this assumption is false.

First, the meanings of lexical items are not known with any precision, since they vary quite widely from individual to individual at a given moment of time, and quite widely within an individual from one time to another. Sampson (1973, 116) suggests that the rules of inference which yield the meanings of lexical items are different from those which give it the meanings of grammatical constructions (a) in being probabilistic, and (b) in being constant for a given individual only for a short span of time. He writes:

> If the meaning of a lexical item is as personal and temporary a thing as this, it is surely reasonable to say that it is outside the province of the linguist, without suggesting that it is necessarily available to other kinds of investigator, e.g., psychologists. (1973, 116)

Second, such differences between the lexical entries in different mentalities are not restricted to lexical items alone, but affect, in some ways more surprisingly, more worryingly, closed system items such as modal verbs and prepositions. Fillenbaum and Rapoport (1971) show by means of multi-dimensional scaling the extent to which the meanings of prepositions differ amongst individuals. And given the ways in which each of us creates the meanings of the items in our personal, cerebral (?), lexicon, perhaps we should not be surprised at such differences.

Third, rationalist and propositional ideologies require the manufacture and propagation of, and universal collusion in, a fiction of lexical constancy. Nevertheless, even in some mathematical research, which is imagined by outsiders to represent the acme of precision and accountability, we find such surprising remarks as:

> [if] you . . . ward off concept-stretching counter examples with monster-barring definitions . . . you will slide onto an infinite

> slope . . . you will be forced to incorporate [in your theorem] more and more 'rigorous' definitions couched in terms whose vagueness has not been exposed yet! But *you never get out of vagueness* (Lakatos, 1976, 100)

and

> *Rationality after all depends on inelastic, exact concepts! But there are no such concepts*. If you want mathematics to be meaningful, you must resign certainty. If you want certainty, get rid of meaning. You cannot have both. (Lakatos, 1976, 102)

Compare also Harrah on the desired relation (it might be a necessary one!) between rationality and deterministic meaning-making:

> It might be thought that since we want to study the behaviour of a rational *R*[eceiver], we should specify a rational *L*[anguage], a rational *k*[nowledge], and so on. Unfortunately the meaning of 'rational' is in dispute . . . so we shall not presume to be dealing with an *R* who is rational in any absolute or universal sense. As the first step . . . we decide to consider the rationality of 'scientific man' . . . But it can be argued that further narrowing is needed . . . we cannot define 'science' or 'scientific' in a way which is sufficiently precise. . . . Here we shall assume . . . that the explication may never be complete, that we have some rough notions about what [it] is or ought to be, that we may use these rough notions to guide our analysis. (Harrah, 1963, 9)

Fourth, in support of the preceding three points, the little which is known or surmised about the processes of remembering and recall indicates that each individual act of recall fairly radically alters the nature of the recalled item. Each time a scene is recalled, each time a word is used, the *contents* of the address, whose label *may* remain constant, will change in terms of the circumstances of that recall, of that use. If the Self is serviced and maintained largely on the basis of memories, and if memories by being exercised are constantly altered, then so much for the constancy of Self! Presumably this problem is a necessary and sufficient basis for yet another internal pathology of epistemology.

Lastly, and tautologically, we know, as individual creators both of our own meanings and those of others, that in practice contextless sentences *cannot exist*.

Are context and meaning different?

It is clear then, that we cannot guess the contexts of contextless sentences from the meanings of those sentences – at least we cannot do it in a fashion both sufficiently precise and controlled – in order to determine more deeply than hitherto the nature of context itself. The *nature* of this failure prompts a different sort of question, which takes us back to the possibility that our ideas about the determinability of meaning constitute a Batesonian pathology. The question is:

How do we know that context and meaning are different?

Or, equivalently, what evidence is there that context and meaning are not the same? I do not think that this question has been asked before, but Parker-Rhodes (1978) develops a theory and notation for the representation of utterable thoughts in which his use of context indicates that he might answer the above questions with 'we don't' and 'very little', respectively.

I will try to focus on the above questions by quoting Parker-Rhodes (PR) extensively, and commenting where relevant. Because I shall need to refer to the quotations under different headings, I shall number the quotations and thereafter refer to them by number.

Context and meaning are indissociable

The ostensions of the following sentences are peculiar, to put it mildly:

(i) *Here is a context which contextualizes no meaningful event*;
(ii) *Here is a meaningful event which has no context.*

I suppose that these ostensions abort simply because they attempt to indicate impossibilities. Lacking 'an essential quality of all known objects' (O'Brien, 1967, 135), they can only be members of Flann O'Brien's eternity '"[which] has no size at all," the Sergeant explained, "because there is no difference anywhere in it and we have no conception of the extent of its unchanging co-equality"' (1967, 133).

> (PR 1) no utterance can, in general, be understood in the absence of its context. (1978, 8)

Compare Firth (1957, 220), 'all texts . . . have . . . "the implication of utterance" and [the implication] of "contexts of situation".'

(PR 2) the amount of effective transfer of ideas which is possible in the absence of a context is very restricted. (1978, 25)

(PR 3) the concept of semantic deviance . . . has trapped many enquirers who have not been trained to ask on every occasion 'What is the context?'. A [semantically deviant] sentence (if not really ungrammatical) is simply one for which appropriate contexts are rarely encountered. (1978, 4)

(PR 4) the indispensability of the *context* to the understanding of an *utterance*. (1978, 33)

(PR 5) a context is not identical with a sequence of utterances, but with the corresponding sequence of what the utterances mean. (1978, 38)

If contexts and meanings are indissociable, they must either be different parts, or properties, of the same thing, or they must be different names for a single thing. In either event we should expect them to partake in, or respond to, the same sorts of forces or behaviours.

Contexts are utterable

Clearly this is a behaviour which contexts share with meanings, in so far as all contexts *are* utterable. About this there may be room for doubt even in PR's own mind – cf. (a) 'a context is an obscure entity arrived at by complex mental process' (1978, 9 [and PR 15 below]); and (b) if one were to ask a listener to re-express, or utter, the complex rhema (which is the context) using the same methods as s/he would for a simple rhema, one would find that s/he cannot do it in that way – or at least chooses not to do it in that way (1978, 48). In addition there may be doubt about the expressibility of any ineffable component of context. See PR 10, and further below.

(PR 6) anything which forms part of the context *can* be uttered; but whether or not it is so is not relevant to its status as part of the context. (1978, 34)

(PR 7) part of the context . . . [is] things which are not uttered at all [e.g. only humans talk]. (1978, 36)

(PR 8) nothing would be changed if [these context sentences] *were* uttered by an imaginary commentator . . . I don't mean them in any way to be *complete* as a statement of the context;

> they are selected only as being the points necessary to understand A's first remark [see PR 24 below]. (1978, 37)
>
> (PR 9) context has the rather vague sense of 'things not uttered which affect the meaning of things uttered'. (1978, 34) [for 'things not uttered' *sc*. 'things which *happen* not to be uttered']
>
> (PR 10) If on the other hand, there were anything strictly ineffable forming part of a context, then as such it would at some point affect the meaning ascribed to some utterance; this altered meaning could be discussed, and the discussion would involve expression, in some form, of the supposedly ineffable matter. We are therefore entitled to propose that any context at all can be *represented by* a sequence of utterances. (1978, 36) See also (PR 5).

The distinction PR gives us, then, is between something which happens to be unuttered (context) and something which happens to be uttered (meaning) – the distinction rests only upon *interest*. Or, in a completely cynical environment, chance, but I will not consider that further here. What we are interested in when we speak is what is *unuttered*, i.e. the context. But the distinction ('interest') does not inhere in the dimension of meaning + context, since, for two participants on different occasions, what is uttered on the one occasion (some several meanings) may be the basis of interest on the other (unuttered contexts).

Why then, one might ask, don't particular contexts for given pairs of participants become 'exhausted'? First because the Self is not constant; second because they serve as the means of establishing reciprocal interiorization (the creation of the 'we') (Laing 1967, 65ff.); third because repeated enquiry touches the immanent (Da Free John, 1980a; Wittgenstein, 1961) – see further below.

Contexts and meanings are (different names for, or views of) the same thing

This claim supports that in (A) above. It imposes something very like Bohr's Principle of Complementarity upon the context + meaning nexus.

> (PR 11) the 'context' of an utterance ideally includes everything both verbal and situational which may have a bearing on the interpretation of utterances emanating from it. A context is then an entity of the same kind as the *meaning* of an utterance. (1978, 35)

(PR 12) Utterances answer questions *about contexts* . . . If we are to regard comprehension as involving some kind of delocutionary inference, this must be an inference *from* utterances, understood as being *about* the context in which they occur. (1978, 34)

(PR 13) [in the absence of its context a sentence] *defines* a context rather than arises out of one. In that case it is proper to ask questions about it which treat it *as* a context. . . . But it is improper to ask the sort of questions which [treat it as a sentence having] a context independently defined. (1978, 34).

(PR 14) What, in fact, does an utterance 'represent'? . . . a 'thought'. I . . . use the term *rhema** for that which an utterance represents, for a given participant in a given context. . . . The word 'thought' can indeed be used of mental images insufficiently clear or conscious to be formulated as rhemata; but such 'arrhematic' thoughts will . . . not concern us further. (1978, 38) [* Gk. 'a thing spoken of']

See also (PR 5, 6, 9, above).

Context sometimes seems knowledge-like, or information-ish

But what *sort* of knowledge is this? Is it simply informational? Or does it also include feelings, anxieties, the unreadable hieroglyphs of the sub- and semi-conscious?

(PR 15) The normal purpose of conversation is to arrive at an agreed contextual understanding, or to celebrate its prior existence; it is frustrating when this purpose is not achieved, and we clearly need a word for saying so. It is natural, since a context is an obscure entity arrived at by complex mental process whereas words are immediately present to the senses, for contextual discrepancy to be attributed, formally, to the words rather than to the context; so we say 'I don't believe that', or even more pointedly 'I don't believe you'. But in fact these phrases do not impugn the sincerity of the speaker, so much as the accuracy of his information. (1978, 9)

(PR 16) if you admire a friend's walking-stick, and he tells you that it's made of beech, it matters not at all if your more expert eye detects that it is in fact hornbeam; you have the choice of either accepting a contextual model in which this distinction is not made, or of inviting its [the context's] amendment by such a remark as 'I'd say it's hornbeam'. What is ordinarily called

> disbelief occurs when two participants in a conversation *persist* in adopting divergent contexts. (1978, 8–9) [But is the first choice a *lie*?]

> (PR 17) ['The present King of France is bald'] belongs to a context which well-informed listeners will be indisposed to adopt. (1978, 11) [Context here seems to be equivalent to Harrah's *k* (1963, passim).]

> (PR 18) contextual data can affect how [lexical items] will be understood. (1978, 33)

> (PR 19) [in respect of contexts for an utterance] we aren't supposed to know anything at all. (1978, 37).

> (PR 20) there is no such thing as a 'null' context, this . . . implies that the sentence exists in a 'universal' context containing all knowledge (a notion which I demolish on set-theoretic grounds). (1978, 34)

Isn't there private knowledge – incommunicable components of Self and its selves – which must be involved in my construction of a context?

Different participants entertain different contexts

Simply by definition: different individuals have different knowledges, histories, expectations, interests . . . (cf. PR 15). There seems no *a priori* reason why a participant should not entertain *more than one* context at any given point in an exchange. (See further below.)

> (PR 21) What, then, can we say about deliberate lying? A liar is a person who chooses between two thoughts competing for expression on grounds of expediency rather than of truth. . . . Whenever someone known to have this habit speaks, this information forms, for a listener forewarned, a part of his contextual map. This means that the liar's remarks are still believed, but they will be believed to be expedient for himself rather than to be true of *his* contextual map. Under these circumstances it will be difficult, perhaps impossible, to achieve the normal congruence between the two contexts. (1978, 9)

> (PR 22) a listener's understanding of an utterance is never blocked by a supposed state of unbelief. The latter applies only to the listener's reconstruction of the speaker's grasp of (or presentation of) the context. Natural language thus does not

> operate a system of truth values like that of formal logic. There are no *false* statements . . . at most there are statements which are rejected, in the sense that the listener refuses to modify his contextual map in the direction invited. (1978, 9–10).
>
> (PR 23) each utterance, as it is comprehended by the listener – and each potential utterance which occurs to him as a result of the 'thought' phase of the cycle – is thus a contribution to the context, which it in general alters (for one or the other participant) in some point. The contextual map for each is thus built up in sequence . . . [which] is not wholly arbitrary but represents evidence of the relative prominence that the various contextual data have for the participants. (1978, 35–6)

This emphasizes the dynamic and constructional nature of context. Notice also the possibility offered by this formulation of a given participant entertaining more than one contextual structure *simultaneously* – since *more* than one 'potential utterance' may occur to him.

> (PR 24) the build-up of context from Alfred's point of view [intonation according to Halliday's method; context = not-A, not-B] . . .
>
> //1 There are/people/playing *ten*nis
> //1 They're/not/*here*
> //1 *Alf*red would/like to/play
> //1 Alfred/sees/*Beat*rice
> A: //2 Want a/game of/*ten*nis/Beatrice?
> B: //5 I'm/dead/*tired*//4 I'd/rather/*not*
> //4 People who're/*tired*//1 don't/*like*/playing/tennis
> A: //1 Come and/watch the/*others*/then
> B: //4 Oh I'd/*like* to/sit in the/sun a bit
> //1 It's/quite/*cold* today. (1978, 36)

Here there seems to me to be a difficulty about definiteness (and cf. (H) below). '*The* build-up' seems to imply, even if its incomplete (PR 8), that Alfred's opening remark could only have *one* context (for Alfred). But this surely cannot be true. Not only may Alfred have a motive other than wanting to play tennis. He may also entertain two or more compatible or incompatible motives. Worse, he may have *no motive at all* for making the remark he makes. And uttering *this* context would not be easy. Wittgenstein says (1967, 188) 'And do I always talk with very definite purpose? – And is what I say meaningless because I don't?' See also PR 8, 15, and 16 above.

Participants attempt to create convergent contexts by conversing

> (PR 25) [drawing] an inference from my utterance which I did not intend you to draw [can immediately occasion the] entertaining [of] divergent models of the context (1978, 32).

Presumably any particular participant cannot always guarantee to know at any given point in the exchange whether or not an 'unintended inference' has or has not been drawn. S/he can only know under precisely those circumstances in which The Other in some degree or another gives voice to the unintended inference or its consequence(s).

If, under the second of these conditions, the speaker *knows* that the 'unintended inference' has been made, it is surely not so much that the contexts *diverge* as that they make a mutual detour.

> (PR 26) [of the speaker and the listener] the listener has the harder job of deciding what one would have to have been thinking, in order to motivate the utterance he hears in the context he finds himself in. (1978, xiii)

But the argument here is centred on an incongruence which is barely visible. The context which motivates the utterance is the S[peaker]'s context; the context which the L[istener] finds herself in when trying to decide what S would have to have been thinking is the L's context. S's context and L's context are not the same. L cannot know S's context. Therefore L must make the decision about what S's utterance was motivated by *on the basis of a context which is not the 'correct' context for doing that determinately*. The build-up of context in PR 24 'from Alfred's point of view' is therefore far too deterministic and confuses the issue of PR 8. *We* may 'understand' Alfred's first remark in terms of the context-utterances given in PR 24, but Beatrice could never understand Alfred's first remark that way. Beatrice can only understand Alfred's remarks in terms of *Beatrice's* contexts, and conversely. If these *different* contexts are unuttered, how can the details of the differences become known? The answer is that they can't. Only in a very sketchy, dimly visible way can Beatrice know the manner in which Alfred's contexts are different from her own. *And then only if she is interested in knowing* – since it requires some considerable effort (cf. Pellowe 1984, 42ff.)

> (PR 27) [thinking about the listener's 'problem' leads one to ask about its end-product, and that is] the thought arising in the listener's mind as a result of his activity, which is (he

> hopes) the same thought from which the speaker's utterance arose (xiv).

But what *evidence* is there that the L *does* hope in this manner? When I consult my own fleeting awareness not only of the products, but also of the process of my understanding, I'm not often, if ever, aware of the sensation of hoping. And why is it appropriate that I do not entertain hopes of this sort? Because my understanding of A's remark can only ever be an incomplete approximation to the thought from which that remark arose. *And I know this.* I know that my understanding does not arise passively in me triggered by A's remark. It results from an active creative commitment on my part (see PR 26) – in terms of *my* contexts, *my* interests, *my* being. And I know that in these respects A and myself are different.

> (PR 28) There is no reason to doubt that the [expression phase] is typically a determinate process of algorithmic character . . . [but] it seems, from the lack of real progress, doubtful whether comprehension is an algorithmic process at all. It may rather be a questing search ('what would I have to have been thinking in order to say that?'), an open-ended enterprise bearing to expression something like the relation which, in the calculus, integration bears to differentiation. Failure to face up to this contrast may well have retarded our understanding of grammar in many ways. (1978, 17–18)

But if the questing search really operates on the basis of the question cited, what would we do if the hearer's answer to herself was 'I don't under*stand* what I would have to have been thinking to say that' (i.e. 'I don't believe I am *capable* of thinking what I would have to have been thinking in order to say that')? I guess from the logic of PR's position that he would interpret this as meaning that the Listener was thereby barred from comprehending the utterance. But this does not seem to me to accord with what frequently happens in conversational exchanges: even if one's answer to the question is as I have given it one ascribes a no-doubt vague, no-doubt multivalent meaning to the utterance. PR certainly cannot make appeal to some inexpressible component of L's context as a source of L's understanding in such cases, since PR has already claimed that all purportedly ineffable material in some context must, in fact, be expressible (cf. PR 10).

In addition, there seems a logical difficulty here. If expression is a determinate process, and comprehension an indeterminate one, how can their products be 'the same'? See also PR 15, 16, 21, and 22 above.

The paradox which causes the confusion I feel in the face of PR's position (cf. Introduction above) has one of its sources here, in the notion that participants, by conversing, can make their contexts converge. The other source is that contexts are utterable, that is, they are never ineffable (cf. PR 10).

First, on the one hand contextual discrepancy is attributed to the words, rather than to some context, because context is an obscure entity (PR 15); on the other hand any context whatsoever can be represented by a sequence of utterances (PR 10).

Second, on the one hand a participant can be frustrated by contextual discrepancy – implying his powerlessness in the face of that discrepancy (PR 15); on the other a participant can accept or amend The Other's contextual map (PR 16), or refuse to alter his own (PR 21).

Third, if their (initial) contexts are different for the participants (PR 21, 22, 23, 24), and if B's understanding of A's remark can only be a partial approximation of A's thought through *B*'s context(s), how can A's and B's contexts *converge*? I mean what possible measure of contextual convergence could one imagine? What could the underlying characteristics of such a measure be? Mightn't it be more perspicuous – more easily measurable – to claim that participants are interested in creating, not contextual convergence, but a mutual contextual richness?

Contexts sometimes seem to be separable from persons, meanings, incidents, or languages

But on *all* occasions when this seems to be a possible and reasonable state of affairs we must actually be dealing with some *second order context* that is, one which has been derived or abstracted from a first-order context. First-order contexts are those which are developed by real participants in real exchanges in real time. These are the types of contexts I have been gesticulating towards so far.

> (PR 29) I have omitted from the above example all potential context items which are not particular to the given incident. (1978, 37)

But how am I to distinguish what is particular amongst all that is potential in someone's context for a meaning – *including my own*? This stark uncertainty is surely the grounds for my entertaining more than one context at some moment in an exchange. And isn't the givenness of the incident only brought about by those exact particularities?

> (PR 30) The understanding of a contextual situation, though commonly assisted by linguistic means, is a goal definable independently of any particular language, and can be attained, by appropriately informed and sufficiently intelligent observers, irrespective of the languages they use. . . . To grasp a context is to grasp every rhema inferrable from the context, that is, from those [rhemata] conveyed by the rehearsal of the context. (1978, 49)

We may grasp a *situation*, but surely not a dynamic *context*, in the absence of knowledge of some language. The latter claim is in direct contradiction of PR 23. See also PR 6, 7, 21, and 24 above.

The case of the liar (PR 21 (cf. Pellowe 1984)) refutes, on a second, doubled ground, the supposition that participants in an exchange might share the context – what I called the Sharedness Problem above. We have already seen how S's context and L's context cannot be the same in first-order context terms.

I have mentioned the possibility of a participant having two compatible (or incompatible) contextual models simultaneously, though for ease of discussion I have usually assumed only one model for each participant. In the case of the liar it *must* be assumed that two incompatible models of context are simultaneously in operation (*at least* when s/he is lying). First the liar needs a context for the contributions to the exchange in which the lying is being done; secondly the liar needs a context for the exchange as it *would have been* if the lying hadn't been being done. Liars will tell you that their competence depends on a complicated form of 'book-keeping'. As I understand it, this must mean remembering the mapping between these two contexts over some period of time. A considerable skill in the service of a doubtful end.

Definiteness in respect of 'context' is always misleading

All definite references to context (the context, this context, etc.) will tend to mislead the reader, since as I have been trying to show, context is inherently ill-defined, (a) because it is dynamic, (b) because there are at least as many different first-order contexts concurrent in any exchange as there are participants.

> (PR 31) A sentence is not deviant in itself: the deviance is in the context which it calls forth. But a sentence which no

> context ever calls for is never uttered (at least, never in good faith: people can always make up examples); and what is never uttered is not an utterance and is not within the purview of a realist semantics. (1978, 4)

Here for instance, the implication is that some sentence can call forth only one particular context. A view which I am sure PR does not actually hold.

> (PR 32) Every utterance . . . is . . . *believed* within the limits of the context in which it is uttered. (1978, 7)

Some context for the uttering cannot be the same as some context for the believing.

> (PR 33) Disregard of the context as a real and independent element in any speech act has had many unfortunate consequences. (1978, 24)

Though I don't disagree with the thrust of PR's remark, the implication again, is that a given speech act only has one context. See also PR 3, 4, 7, 8, 10, 11, 12, 23, and 24 above.

Self-awareness of listener

> (PR 34) the speaker is normally quite unconscious of the original anatomy of his ideas, for they enter consciousness only in the course of their transformation into speech; it is the listener who has the opportunity, if only fleetingly, to observe the products of his comprehension. (1978, xiv)

And possibly also we may observe the process of our comprehension, at least in terms of the evocation and through-weaving of the cloud-like dynamics of our auto(?)-biography. And more certainly when we suspect that something is perverting, subverting or endoubting our grasp of meaning making.

Note also Firth's excellent question (1957, 191): 'What is the energy of listening? Of comprehension?'

What is context?/who is context?

Wittgenstein's starting point in the Tractatus is: 'The world is all that is the case' (1961, 7). It is, perhaps, not clear whether the totality [– of 'facts'?] to which he points does, or does not, include that which happens not yet to be known to us (i.e. whose 'case' are we looking at?). Nor is it singularly certain what the means and manner of judging facticity should be. Are errors, conceits, contradictions, deceits, 'false' beliefs, fancies, imaginings all components of the 'all that is the case'?

But what happens if I 'individualize' Wittgenstein's definition? – My world is all that is the case for me now. Insert the 'now' to handle the likelihood of the inconstancy of 'me'; the constantly changing force and detail of re-membered memories. Doesn't this formulation make contact with the texture I ascribe to my environment of selves, of meanings, of connections? And doesn't *this* gloss call up the idea of context? Then perhaps 'context is all that is felt to be the case by the construer in the now of construal. The term construer (C) is neutral as between Speaker (S) and hearer (H)'.

This seems to equate context and attention as directed inwards *and* outwards.

Context is inactive, (or *mu*, neither 'yes' or 'no', it makes no sense to ask about it), when *nothing* is being interpreted, that is, when interpreting is not occurring. Clearly the state when interpreting is not occurring is both of low frequency, and of short duration, in the lives of most, egoically-centred, human individuals. In sleep, at least one of the dreaming selves has some sense of what is the case, and is interpreting in its own, doubtless ripplesome, not wholly recoverable fashion.

But let me begin again.

What *is* context? Certainly it does a great deal of unpaid work in the humanities and social sciences. It is one of the most pervasive components, perhaps in the end the only component, in our background knowledge. Yet background knowledge is where we assume we have full knowledge, when all we actually have is complete ignorance (Lakatos, 1976, 45). And we have already seen that we don't know what anything *is* (Da Free John, 1980a, 35).

Novalis wrote: 'All that is visible clings to the invisible, the audible to the inaudible, the tangible to the intangible, perhaps the thinkable to the unthinkable'. This would have a parallel in the meanable clinging to the unmeanable ('and we know whatever that means' [Hemingway: *Across the river and into the trees* – of 'I love you']); the knowable clinging to the unknowable, and the utterable clinging to the unutterable (rather than to the unuttered). In other words, away with all these useless dualities! (Firth, 1957, 227–8): 'These dichotomies [mind and body, language and thought, word and idea, signficant et signified, expression and content] are a quite unnecessary nuisance, and in my opinion should be dropped. . . . The dualistic principle wrecks the empirical analysis of the language material.' And this last – the utterable clinging to the unutterable – was surely exactly at the centre of much of Wittgenstein's effort, *whilst* adjuring us to 'pass over the silence' that which cannot be spoken of, to gesticulate (with some longing) towards the unutterable.

If my intentions as a hearer (Pellowe, 1984) are in good faith, and if the speaker utters with a maximum of personal vulnerability – i.e. what Firth (1957) believed to be the most significant use of speech (the expressive rather than the informational) – then all of the me and all of the other is context for the other's remark to me. All dreams, memories, hopes, fears, knowledge, feelings, myths, times and places which have their nexus in me, as me – all of this is me and then in the same(?) manner, all of that Other is a context for this utterance. But what I am aware of *as* me varies from moment to moment in so many respects. Therefore the context which I am for myself varies proportionally, similarly, presumably moment-by-moment.

Two 'I's' are a context at some moment. You are your context for you. And I am my context for me. You are your meaning for you. And I am my meaning for me. Compare:

> One's modes of being are one's modes of meaning and; one means what one is (or, alternatively and equivalently, one is what one means) by behaving in such and such a way in one's context. (Lyons, 1977, 608)

Then we should always ask not 'What is context?' (or 'What is the context?') but *Who* is context? And this form of question focuses things in a different way, makes it possible to see how the duality might be dissolved.

But if my context is *me*, it cannot merge or converge with your context, which is you. Perhaps, though, I can mimic your self, and hence your context? And likewise you me? Momentarily, perhaps, we become our context for us (Laing, 1967). Our meaning becomes us for us. But then we fall away from some kind of oneness into egoity again. And maybe our endless blah blah blah blah blah is both an attempt to reach that oneness again – the ego's endless circling attempts to minimize itself without in the least intending to reduce its size and power – and a recognition that things were not always this way.

And under what conditions do we feel that things were not always this way? When do we sense that there is another, earlier, higher(?), use for utterance than the endless cavorting alienated Presenting of Ego to Everyday Life? Put another way, what is the source of our feeling that having our Selves as our context is not comfortable (the proscription of egotism), nor necessary (couldn't context, in spite of all we have said, be represented in and by our humanness?), nor sufficient (for all its stranglehold on our precious little lives, we are not satisfied by the Rule of the Ego)?

Two conditions seem to me to indicate that there was/is a form of context + meaning prior and higher to the egoic form I have written about so far.

The first of these is the peculiar feeling of one's *being spoken*. The second is that referred to by the phrase *like-mindedness*. It is possible that they are closely related. First, in general, I have not accomplished, do not and cannot accomplish, my own existence – I am being lived. I am not breathing my breath, pounding my heart – I am being happened (e.g. Da Free John, 1980a). And when I am being spoken, it is not at all the same feeling of wearying, unchangeable difference as I feel when I parade the supermarket of my ego-self, or watch with more, perhaps, than a hint of narcissistic voyeurism others parade theirs for me. Being spoken is, by contrast, an effortless connection with all *be-ing*. Wittgenstein (1967, 188–9, emphases added) points, maybe, to something of the sort:

> Describing my state of mind (of fear, say) is something I do in a particular context . . . . Is it, then, so surprising that I use the same expression in different games? *And sometimes as it were between games? And do I always talk with any definite purpose? And is what I say meaningless because I don't*? . . . But here is the problem: a cry, which cannot be called a description, which is more primitive than any description, *for all that serves as a description of the inner life*.

Second, like-mindedness seems to partake of a different form of context from the usual ones of egoic encounters. Exchanges of which we would want to use the term seem to be ones in which the like-mindedness is *itself*, in some strange way, the context. It is notable in such encounters, whether between co-workers, friends or lovers, that the formal structure of the exchange is defective in terms of surfacely present features, that some sort of 'densification' process takes over without any apparent agreement or signalling that this should be the case. Much more of the 'message' is carried by prosodic and paralinguistic, facial and gestural means. The participants themselves often become aware of this densification and when they do, it sometimes increases. It is as if like-mindedness creates a kind of rarifaction of the communicative atmosphere in which smaller and smaller signalling units can (perhaps because of the clarity and cleanness of the communicative air?) carry bigger and bigger contents.

'*If a lion could talk, we could not understand him*' (Wittgenstein 1967, 223). Two things in connection with this. (1) A good illustration of the depth and power of egoic thinking is the amount of time one might waste thinking about what Wittgenstein could have meant (intended or signified (again you see?)) by such a remark. (2) Even if I had a grammar and a dictionary of Lionese, I could not understand the presumptions (cf. Raine, above) of a lion, his context for him and my context for me would always fail to find comprehensible congruity. I could, in a phrase, never be like-minded with a lion.

I would like to say that there is a type of context which is similar in form and function to like-mindedness. That it is rare, in terms of the sheer volume of talking which gets done. And – this may turn out to be a difficulty – it is *also* a first-order type of context.

> We are all participants in a vast Realm of Nonsense, and we are struggling to make 'sense' of it by attaching ourselves to selected or experientially preferred phenomena. We are confronted by an infinite Chaos of Experience, and we each try to enforce an order and a limit on infinity via the self-limiting mechanisms of our own body-mind and independent consciousness. We each try to make a 'Universe' out of 'Chaos' by continually imagining an inner being, or mind, or soul that is 'I' and that is a fixed and independent center of experience. . . . But the truth of the matter is that we are terrified by our vulnerable mortality, and the infinite Chaos of the World-Process is not a Condition into which we tend to be joyfully and ecstatically surrendered. (Da Free John, 1980b, 165)

But *being* does not have anything to do with the verbal mind. Being is not un*real* because it is not verbal – it is simply a more fundamental, more profound dimension than that on which the verbal works.

> We think meaning encompasses everything, because we are in the mind of meanings. Actually however, meaning interferes with hardly anything. We really do not exist in a world of meaning. The world of meaning is reduced to the practicalities of ordinary life. . . . To enter into the universe totally, to enter into the sphere of existence itself, you must go beyond the world of meaning. You could still use words, but they do not quite have the force of meaning any longer, they are more like pointers, vague gestures, dancers. . . . We do not exist in . . .

> the world of meanings [but neither do we] exist in the world of non-meaning in the sense . . . of negativity, of vacuity (Da Free John, 1983, 30–2).

and Berger and Mohr (1982, 89):

> In life, meaning is not instantaneous. Meaning is discovered in what connects, and cannot exist without development. Without a story, without an unfolding, there is no meaning. . . . When we give meaning to an event, that meaning is a response not only to the known but also to the unknown: meaning and mystery are inseparable, and neither can exist without the passing of time.
>
> The visible has been and still remains the principal human source of information about the world. . . . It is thanks to the visible that one recognizes space as the precondition for physical existence. The visible brings the world to us. But at the same time it reminds us ceaselessly that it is a world in which we risk to be lost. The visible with its space also takes the world away from us. Nothing is more two-faced. (Berger, 1984, 50)

Can you unfold context? Why shouldn't it be as two-faced as the visible? Perhaps it *is* the two-facedness of the visible. What is *your* context for all of the preceding? How do I know if we are like-minded?

Notes

1. Thanks to Bob White and Graham McGregor for the invitation; and to Graham for his endless patience with my smithereening deadlines. Thanks to Shu Zhen for her humour and support in spite of my bearishness; and to Bob Lumsden for himselves, their critical senses, and their Accompaniment on the Way.
2. This, and three previous efforts (see references and *York Papers in Linguistics* 8 (1980) 97ff.), are part of an attempt to feel my way towards something like a quantum theoretic linguistics – how else can one interpret or incorporate the anti-dualistic remarks of Firth (1957, 227–8) and isn't it worth wondering why Firth's suggestions have been avoided? I thank Haj Ross and Bob Le Page for their own work towards such a goal.

References

Bateson, G. (1972) *Steps to an Ecology of Mind*, San Francisco, Chandler.

Bateson, G. (1985) *Mind and Nature: A Necessary Unity*, London, Fontana (Flamingo).
Berger, J. (1984) *And our Faces, My Heart, Brief as Photos*, London, Writers and Readers.
Berger, J. and Mohr, J. (1982) *Another Way of Telling*, London, Writers and Readers.
Capra, F. (1982) 'Buddhist Physics' in S. Kumar (ed.) *The Schumacher Lectures*, London, Abacus, 121ff.
Da Free John (1980a) *The Four Fundamental Questions*, Clearlake, California, Dawn Horse.
Da Free John (1980b) *Scientific Proof of the Existence of God Will Soon Be Announced by the White House*, Clearlake, California, Dawn Horse.
Da Free John (1983) *God is Not a Gentleman and I Am that One*, Clearlake, California, Dawn Horse.
Fillenbaum, S. and Rapoport, A. (1971) *Structures in the Subjective Lexicon*, New York, Academic Press.
Firth, J.R. (1957) *Papers in Linguistics 1934–1951*, London, Oxford University Press.
Harrah, D. (1963) *Communication: A Logical Model*, Cambridge, Massachusetts, MIT Press.
Hurford, J.R. and Heasley, B. (1983) *Semantics: A Course Book*, Cambridge, Cambridge University Press.
Hymes, D. (1972) 'On Communicative Competence' in J. Pride and J. Holmes (eds) *Sociolinguistics: Selected Readings*, Harmondsworth, Penguin, 269ff.
Katz, J.J. and Fodor, J.A. (1963) 'The Structure of a Semantic Theory', *Language* 39, 170ff.
Laing, R.D. (1967) *The Politics of Experience* and *The Bird of Paradise*, Harmondsworth, Penguin.
Lakatos, I. (1976) *Proofs and Refutations: The Logic of Mathematical Discovery*, London, Cambridge University Press.
Lyons, J. (1977) *Semantics* 2, London, Cambridge University Press.
Moore, G.E. (1939) 'Proof of the External World', *Proceedings of the British Academy*, XXV, reprinted in G.E. Moore (1959) (ed.) *Philosophical Papers*, London, Allen and Unwin.
O'Brien, F. (1967) *The Third Policeman*, London, McGibbon and Kee.
Parker-Rhodes, A.F. (1978) *Inferential Semantics*, Hassocks, Sussex, Harvester.
Pellowe, J. (1984) 'For Our Selves We are Silent' in C. Nicholson and R. Chatterji (eds) *Tropic Crucible*, Singapore, Singapore University Press, 37ff.
Pellowe, J. (1986) 'Hearers' Intentions' in G. McGregor and R.S. White (eds) *The Art of Listening*, London, Croom Helm, 5ff.
Raine, K. (1985) *Defending Ancient Springs*, Cambridge, Golgonooza.
Sacks, O. (1985) *The Man Who Mistook His Wife for a Hat*, London, Picador.
Sacks, O. (1986) *A Leg to Stand On*, London, Picador.

Sampson, G. (1973) 'The Concept "Semantic Representation"', *Semiotica* 7 (2), 97ff.
Wittgenstein, L. (1961) *Tractatus Logico-Philosophicus*, London, Routledge and Kegan Paul.
Wittgenstein, L. (1967) *Philosophical Investigations*, Oxford, Blackwell.
Wittgenstein, L. (1969) *On Certainty*, Oxford, Blackwell.

Part two

Listener response and communication

Chapter five

Eavesdropper response and the analysis of everyday communicative events[1]

Graham McGregor

Introduction

This chapter is based on research which investigates a particular case of listener response, namely that involved in the *post hoc* interpretation of everyday speech events by third parties whom I shall refer to as *eavesdroppers*. The research in question is principally concerned with the systematic study of ordinary members' knowledge and practices about what is communicated and what communicates between speakers and hearers in the course of creating such events. By adopting a listener-oriented approach to analysis, we hope to demonstrate the methodological and theoretical gain of taking into account 'ear-work'; albeit in the special sense with which we are concerned here.

The motivation for such an approach is not as readily obvious as might first appear. Readers might like to compare the nature of other contributions to this volume as an indication of both the need for, and implications of, analysis based on recipiency and response. As far as interpersonal communication is concerned, a conventional view of the interactional process provides for a sender (speaker) *and* a receiver (hearer). Yet it is the production skills of the former that analytic models tend to be centred upon, whether descriptively or theoretically derived. It was this speaker-oriented bias in language study in general that prompted the collection of papers presented in McGregor (1986a). My co-author on this occasion, and in McGregor (1986b), drew to my attention a similar bias in the treatment of literary text by the continued exclusion, in discussion, of the creative capacities of its *readers*. This chapter is subsequently offered as part of a wider and expanding programme of research that seeks to contribute towards redress of such bias by focusing on skills of *interpretation* rather than production, particularly as these may be employed in the analysis of everyday communicative events. The perspective adopted here is not without its problems, as we shall see, but it does offer the analyst a novel and extremely rich site for research.

Studies of everyday verbal exchange

Investigation of naturally occuring talk continues to engage scholars from a variety of disciplinary backgrounds. However, whilst its study is becoming increasingly recognized as worthy of attention in its own right (cf. the extensive literature produced in the last decade in particular[2]), the would-be analyst continues to face what Grimshaw (1982, 15) describes as 'fundamental methodological (and practical and ethical) and theoretical problems'. A major difficulty for analytic method is that the communicative effects and/or results of what has gone on are, in participant terms, 'always an EMERGENT phenonemon, explicitly specifiable only in retrospect (and then by way of simplifying procedures that may well distort their experience)' (Dore and McDermott, 1982, 386). Thus as Labov and Fanshel (1977, 350) point out, 'Working with real conversations of real speakers poses a profound and perhaps insoluble problem for the external observer, and we may refer to this as the "problem of correct interpretation".' The consequences of this problem are of course that analysts 'can never hope to have *all* the knowledge the participants shared themselves', as Labov and Fanshel (1977, 35) recognize.

To take a case in point, Grimshaw (1982), for example, reports a singular lack of success in fully understanding the episode of verbal interaction he presents for analysis both in his roles as *objective analyst* and *retrospective participant*. Notwithstanding his difficulties in this regard, Grimshaw suggests a number of percipient avenues for research, the first of which is central to the argument I seek to develop here. It is that there is a need to extend our analyses, and hence understanding of verbal exchange, by means of 'more adequate cognitive and cultural models of participants' knowledge and practices' (1982, 38). But *how* can we begin to provide such models, and *what* can they contribute to our understanding of the speech communication process?

Interpretive sociolinguistics

The research I have developed to address these questions makes use of analytic and descriptive techniques derived from a variety of disciplines that have studied communicative activity in naturally occurring talk, and particularly those pioneered by John Gumperz (1982a; 1982b), wherein participant and non-participant observation of speech events is used to facilitate a closer understanding of how linguistic and social knowledge interact in discourse interpretation. Gumperz's work is significantly different from other linguistic and sociolinguistic traditions which seek to investigate language use in naturally occurring social contexts because it 'focuses on the strategies that govern the actor's use of lexical, grammatical, sociolinguistic and other knowledge in the production and interpretation of messages in context' (1982a, 35). This 'interpretive sociolinguistic approach' as he calls it, aims to document and test the claim that interpretive analysis of talk in key naturally occurring situations 'can yield significant insights into the communicative processes that underlie categorization, intergroup stereotyping, evaluation of verbal performance and access to public resources in modern societies' (1982b, vii).

The substance of this claim is investigated through a series of case studies exploring situations of intergroup communication and the role of particular communicative phenomena therein. In order to find out what is going on in such situations from the participants' point of view, Gumperz develops a general theory of 'conversational inferencing', that is, 'the situated or context bound process . . . by means of which participants in an exchange assess each others' intentions, and on which they base their responses' (1982a, 153).

A typical method which is used to find out what kind of inferences are made is to play a recording of a particular exchange, or at least some episode from it, to a panel of listeners, including some of the individuals who were involved as participants. Individuals are then asked 'to explain what they thought the speaker intended to convey in speaking as he did and to evaluate the effectiveness of his verbal strategies'. This method enables Gumperz to develop hypotheses about the kind of social assumptions that judges must have made in order to interpret and evaluate the exchange in a particular way. However, the method does not attempt to describe and account for these assumptions in any systematic way. Neither does it consider the extent to which they are held by different individuals, such that one might explain, for example, any variations that may occur within and between different judgers and the judgements they make.

We suggest, therefore, the need to extend and develop Gumperz's work by means of a programme of research that confronts two major issues: (i) The extent to which members of the same speech community share the interpretive capacity Gumperz describes; (ii) What this capacity involves in terms of individual perceptions of how what has gone on in some instance of talk becomes communicatively significant for its participants.

Eavesdropper respondents

In order to broach these questions, I have sought to devise an analytic tool flexible enough to elicit the tacit assumptions of ordinary members about what communicates and what is communicated in respect of different kinds of talk, and rigorous enough to allow subsequent comparisons between the informant judges used for this purpose, namely, participant and non-participant eavesdropper respondents.

Presumably focused participants in verbal exchange may be supposed to know what is going on communicatively, and this knowledge, in turn, influences and is displayed in what goes on. We might therefore expect individuals from the same speech community to possess the ability to describe such exchanges, if only from their own point of view and of course in retrospect. This ability was first recognized in any explicit sense in a brilliant series of lectures given by the late Harvey Sacks (1967–72) whose ideas about talk are characterized by their emphasis on practical reasoning and social cognition. Sacks's work presuppposes the use of interpretive procedures that are learned by individuals as a general phenomenon, the mechanisms of which are displayed in even the smallest and most fleeting fragments of verbal exchange. To the extent that these mechanisms are shared, that is related to the values, norms and concerns of others, they become what Sacks terms *observables*. Thus individuals 'can deal with and categorize and make statements about communicative events previously unseen'; they can act as *inferencing-making machines* (Sacks, 1985).

Exactly how one might begin to elicit and identify such inferential work as some instance of talk was actually in progress is, of course, highly problematic since I take it that direct questioning of the participants would simply result in a breakdown of the communicative process (cf. McGregor, 1986a). However, individual capacity 'to deal with and categorize and make statements about communicative events' can be investigated from another perspective, that is, from outside what Goffman referred to as the *participation framework*. The analytic approach which I am suggesting is consequently distinct from theoretically-oriented models of the kind recently put forward by Sperber and Wilson

(1986), for example, and analytic modes developed by conversation and discourse analysts (Levinson, 1983, Chapter 6 provides a useful review of these two traditions). It is distinct because its data consists of eavesdroppers' interpretive, oral responses to particular discourse fragments, and its method is 'experimental'. The term 'experimental' is used here to describe 'any method which entails the direct manipulation of an informant's responses'; as opposed to the methods of 'introspection' and 'inductive analysis' suggested by Milroy (1987, 1–5). I should point out that no criticism of other approaches is implied by the perspective adopted here, the present work is rather intended to be complementary. I make this point because like Stubbs (1983, 175), I aver that 'no single level of analysis will ever be able to say all there is about a conversation', and moreover because the prospective analyst of talk needs all the encouragement he/she can get!

Let us now consider the method used for investigating the capacity of ordinary members to describe and evaluate some instance of verbal exchange by undertaking interpretive work in the third-person.[3] We will consider thereafter the methodological and theoretical implications of this work for discourse studies in general.

Studies of eavesdropping

In order to determine the extent and/or willingness of third parties to give interpretive responses to some instance of verbal interaction, I provided various different individuals with the opportunity to listen to and comment on previously recorded speech activities. The studies in question were an attempt to investigate the interpretive capacity of participant and non-participant eavesdropper judges without attempting to pre-empt or pre-judge what they might listen for.

Three pilot projects using different judges (singly and in pairs) were undertaken with the aim of eliciting as wide a range of judgements as possible.[4] The use of pairings was an attempt to minimize the effect of audience design (Bell, 1984), and hence analyst influence, by encouraging spontaneity of interaction between judges. In these studies, the instructions eavesdroppers were given were made as general as possible in order to try to avoid directing their listening behaviour. Thus judges were simply invited to listen to and comment on various different extracts of talk on the basis that one could not predict the significance of particular kinds of information, for particular individuals, in advance. All comments which judges gave were noted and/or tape-recorded and form the basic corpus of data for the analysis which follows. I will consider the comments of non-participant judges only.

In all thirty non-participant judges, fifteen men and fifteen woman of varying ages from the university community at Newcastle, participated in the research. They included undergraduate and postgraduate students, as well as academic and ancillary staff. None of the judges had any linguistic training. Each judge listened to segments of talk ranging from forty seconds duration to five minutes, selected from tape-recordings I had made. The selection of segments was problematic because I did not want to provide either too much, or too little material for individuals to listen to. Thus on the one hand, I wanted to avoid overwhelming them with material, and on the other, I wanted to be certain there would be enough material to prompt some comment rather than none at all. My worries on this score proved unnecessary since the method was to elicit a very substantial corpus of comments. All the recordings were of dialogues to help facilitate speaker recognition for purposes of eavesdropper and analyst reference.

Inspection of the corpus revealed that whilst eavesdroppers provided extremely variable responses to the conversational extracts, both in kind and quantity, a great many of them consisted of strikingly similar kinds of declarative statement. Excluding comments about what they could actually hear, and comments addressed to me directly, two major types of statement were identified. These typically involved a predicator and argument describing some state of affairs about either perceived surface characteristics of the exchanges, ('There was lots of overlapping speech'; 'She spoke quite slowly', etc.) or providing information about who the participants were and what they were involved in doing ('Two friends were having a chat'; 'That was an argument', etc. – see further below).

Some 1,277 descriptive statements of these types were identified and provide the basic data for the discussion which follows. I have labelled these statement types *observations* and *inferences* respectively, on the model of Hayakawa's (1952, Chapter 3) categorization of the language of reports, where he suggests that the report of what we have seen, heard or felt constitutes the basic symbolic act for purposes of the interchange of information. On further inspection, *observations* were found to refer to four distinguishable characteristics of the exchanges.

(1) *Observations* about lexis (e.g. 'They use words like bona fide and relationship'; 'Words such as junk and rip-offs are used'). There were 14 descriptive statements of this type referring to the participants' use of particular words and phrases.

(2) *Observations* about subject matter. Some 32 descriptive statements were of this type and these referred to what the participants talked about (e.g. 'They talk about a range of topics, black holes, how to teach, how to get money'; 'They talk about student-teacher relations').

(3) *Observations* about sequential organization. These included descriptions of within-turn verbal phenomena (e.g. 'There is lots of hesitancy, uhm, uh and so on'; 'There are plenty I means, uhms and you knows') as well as descriptions of dialogic phenomena (e.g 'There is some overspeaking'; 'It's interspersed with them talking over each other'; 'There are gaps when they didn't know what to say'). Some 93 examples were of this kind.

(4) *Observations* about prosody. In this category, eavesdroppers offered descriptive statements about a variety of prosodic and paralinguistic phenomena (e.g. 'He was a bit low and mumbly at times'; 'She spoke very quickly'; 'Her voice went up when she said "however" '; 'The word "mud" was stressed'). 146 statements of this type were identified.

The frequency and distribution of *observations* in the three studies as a whole is given in Table 5.1.

The nature of these *observations* are indicative of the ability of particular eavesdroppers to act as naive discourse analysts. Indeed, the descriptions they offered about such textual phenomena could be inspected for pattern in much the same way as ethnomethodological studies try to establish how participants act within their own social worlds. In this sense *observations* could

Table 5.1 Observations

	LEX.	*SUB.*	*SEQ.*	*PRO.*	*TOTAL*
Study 1	7	12	23	8	50
Study 2	1	7	37	71	116
Study 3	6	13	33	67	119
TOTAL	14	32	93	146	285

LEX. = lexis; SUB. = subject matter; SEQ. = sequential organization; PRO. = prosody.

always be verified by checking them against a transcribed record of the exchanges. 285 or 22.3 per cent of the total number of statements were of this kind. Now what about *inferences*?

As far as possible, *observations* exclude *inferences* since *inferences* involve evaluative or judgemental work that cannot be verified in the same way, that is, they consist of descriptive statements imposed on the data in order to make sense of the type and substance of talk. 992 descriptive statements, or 77.6 per cent of the total number were of this kind. That gives us a ratio of about three *inferences* to every one *observation*. Although we are concerned with decontextualized interpretation here, this is an interesting finding which appears to lend support to Sperber and Wilson's (1987) arguments for preferring an inferential as opposed to code model of communication.

Table 5.2 gives the frequency and distribution of *inferences* in each of the three studies.

Two major categories of *inference* were identified from the descriptive statements eavesdroppers provided. These were:

(1) *Inferences* about setting, in which the exchanges were located in both space and time (e.g. 'It took place in an office'; 'It was in the kitchen or home of one of the participants'; 'Two blokes are chatting in a boiler room' ; 'It's a casual encounter'; 'It's in their coffee break').

Only 38 statements of this kind were offered. The relative paucity of comments about setting may be usefully compared to the number (954) describing the participants and the nature of their interactional behaviour. The difference is remarkable, but might be explained by Bell's (1984) suggestion that topic and setting are subservient to the addressee variable in communicative terms. Eavesdropper judgements would certainly appear to provide strong supporting evidence that this is indeed the case as I think comments about the participants themselves and what

Table 5.2 Inferences

	SET.	*PAR.*	*TOTAL*
Study 1	21	197	218
Study 2	9	396	405
Study 3	8	361	369
TOTAL	38	954	992

SET. = setting; PAR. = participants.

they were perceived to be doing show. It is to these comments we now turn.

(2) *Inferences* about the participants and what they were perceived to be doing are represented in descriptive statements that provide essentially two kinds of information:

(a) Information about the social identity of the participants, including age, sex, social and educational background, place of origin, speech style, and affective states and attitudes; in other words what Abercrombie calls indexical information. These statements include both specified social stereotypes and named person prototypes (e.g. 'The first guy was a Geordie'; 'One was older than the other'; 'The woman who said shockingly was definitely posh'; 'She's got a very fruity voice, sort of actressy'; 'Sounds as if he's in a bad mood'). 312 statements were of this kind. Since these judgements were elicited without prompting, they may help to form the basis of more controlled experimental work which stems from *participants*' perceptions of what is considered to be communicatively salient; as opposed to those simply assumed by analytic design. One advantage of this approach is that third-party eavesdropper judges do not of course affect speaker style, since their listening skills are applied in *post hoc* interpretive work.

(b) Information about the type of speech activity involved. The notion of 'speech activity' is taken from Gumperz (1982a, 166) who defines it as 'a set of social relations enacted about a set of schemata in relation to some communicative goal'. Gumperz recognizes that speech activities are not precisely listable since the action they constitute is indicative of ongoing, co-ordinated and interactive effort. Thus, whilst 'Speech activities can be characterized through descriptive phrases such as "discussing politics", "chatting about the weather", "telling a story to someone", and "lecturing about linguistics"' (1982a, 166), such phrases are only a guideline for how communicative events may be interpreted. What is important about these phrases is not what they can contribute towards delimiting particular kinds of event, though they may well help towards this end, but rather the means they provide for specifying the perceived constraints on verbal action and on how this action might be interpreted by others. In other words, they provide a means whereby necessary forms of social and communicative knowledge (imagined, stereotypical or real), can be brought to the surface and articulated in a form that becomes researchable.

Thus, the 642 statements in this category demonstrate the capacity of different individuals not only to distinguish between different kinds of talk on the one hand as in Gumperz's examples (cf. 'It's easy chatty conversation'; 'It's a discussion between colleagues'; 'It's like two old blokes I heard in a bar'; 'That was an interview'); but also to monitor and recover the perceived nature of negotiated and negotiable relationships, both interpersonal (e.g. 'They didn't know each other very well'; 'One man is entertaining another to coffee. He plays the role of host and asks all the questions'; 'They're obviously friends but clearly not related'), and discoursal (e.g. 'He wants to do something but isn't sure about it. He was sounding out'; 'One of the speakers was probing for advice').

An important facet of eavesdroppers' interpretive work, in an inferential sense, appears to have been based on appraisal of both the communicative *key* (the tone, manner or spirit in which an act or event is performed – after Hymes, 1972) and *effect* (for them) of particular utterances or sequence of utterances. The comments offered for such instances were rather different in kind from the *inferences* we have considered thus far, since they were essentially the results of interpretive glossing of specified data segments (cf. ' "Really" is ambiguous. It's not convincing. It had shades in it'; ' "Yes" marks understanding rather than agreement'; 'When he said "that sounds good", he didn't mean it sounded good, he meant it sounded bloody awful').

Whether it is overtly stated by eavesdroppers or not, there seems to be a necessary relationship between such glosses and *observations* about prosody in particular. The nature of this link and its implications for interpretive work on discourse fragments are explored in some detail in McGregor (1986a). As far as other kinds of inferential statement are concerned, the obvious question is from whence they might derive? *Inferences* could have been and sometimes were based on what had been observed as we have suggested. Occasionally, the two would be directly linked by eavesdroppers in statements such as, 'One of the speakers sounded eager but hesitant. It came from the way he said things, maybe his tone'; 'They were obviously educated, they used words such as bona fide and relationship'. However, whether or not this link was made in any overt sense, we presume that eavesdropper *inferences* could only have been deduced or based on guesses from necessary forms of social and linguistic knowledge, whether this knowledge was based on real or imagined, interactional experience.

In order to begin to determine more precisely what this

knowledge might be, we can work backwards, as it were, from each type of inferential statement. This procedure obviously entails a higher level of inferencing based on the kinds of professional knowledge that analysts necessarily bring to bear in handling their data (cf. the ethnographic approach of Agar, 1980). It may be argued that what is being suggested here is merely a methodological bind; *inferences* about *inferences* about *inferences*. The danger of infinite regress is real enough but misses the point, since what we can gain by working in this way is a means of providing evidence as we work from data to theory in the analysis of communicative events. Presumably, the more interpretive evidence we can collect, the stronger our analytic claims can become. But what is the source of such evidence?

In offering comments about setting, eavesdroppers presumably provided answers to the questions of where, when and why the exchanges took place. These answers could only be based on knowledge about the temporal and spatial parameters of speech events. To identify and describe the individuals concerned in these events, eavesdroppers would have to ask who the participants were and what they were like. This would require knowledge not only of individual person prototypes but also social group and relational stereotypes as we have suggested. To then answer the question of what these participants were doing in communicative terms, knowledge of communicative norms and processes would be pre-requisite.

Given the descriptive framework we have outlined, and that we can begin to formally model something of ordinary members' knowledge and practices about the nature of interpersonal communication, it remains to briefly consider something of the methodological and theoretical implications the present approach might have for analysis of everyday verbal exchange in general.

Some implications of eavesdropper inferencing

On the basis of the work undertaken to date, it has been possible to compare the frequency and distribution of inferencing practice among and between different eavesdroppers. The differences between male and female judges, for example, is particularly illuminating in this respect, especially in the apportioning of sex marked stereotypes (cf. McGregor, 1985). Lay as opposed to professional inferencing provides another important parameter for helping to explain differences within and across different judgers and the judgements they made, as is the distinction between participant and non-participant inferential work (see,

McGregor, 1983; 1986a). Indeed, we ought to be able to generate and test various hypotheses about possible co-occurence relationships between eavesdropper inferences and various other informant variables: age, ethnicity and social network ties are three that spring readily to mind.

Moreover, by proceeding in this way with different kinds of talk and different eavesdroppers, we hope to have demonstrated that it is possible to elicit and identify interactional phenemona and processes *that are not normally verbalized by participants in talk*. The nature of these processes, as perceived by ordinary participants, have been little explored despite the fact, as Gumperz (1982a, 37) points out, 'that there is every reason to suppose that [they] play an important role in everyday interaction'.

We suggest, accordingly, the need for further research. Quite simply, interpretive sociolinguistic work of the kind that we have outlined can and ought to be investigated in its own right. It *can* be investigated, as my own and Gumperz's work have shown. It *ought* to be investigated because we take it that if a linguistic phenomenon is spoken about by native language users, it merits our professional concern. Quite apart from the kinds of interesting information that it might yield, investigation of third-person inferencing may also serve to provide investigators with an important source of evidence as they move from data to theory. The link between the two, however indirect, is not always acknowledged in discourse research and this surely has implications for our role as professional *responders*, whether it be as analysts and/or creators of interpretive theories.

Notes

1. This chapter is an extended version of a paper delivered to Sociolinguistics Symposium 7, University of York, April 1988, and I am grateful to those participating members who heard it for offering useful comments.
2. This literature is now so rich and well known that detailed reference here was thought to be unnecessary.
3. The need to distinguish between different kinds of listener to talk, and what such distinctions might involve is presented in McGregor (1986b, 59–60).
4. These studies are variously reported in McGregor (1983, 1984, 1985; 1986a; 1986b).

References

Agar, M. (1980) 'Stories, Background Knowledge and Themes: Problems in the Life History of Narrative', *American Ethnologist* 7, 223–39.

Bell, A. (1984) 'Language Style as Audience Design', *Language in Society* 13, 145–204.

Dore, J. and McDermott, R.P. (1982) 'Linguistic Indeterminacy and Social Context in Utterance Interpretation', *Language* 58, 347–98.

Grimshaw, A.D. (1982) 'Comprehensive discourse analysis: an instance of professional peer interaction', *Language in Society* 11, 15–47.

Gumperz, J.J. (1982a) *Discourse Strategies*, Cambridge, Cambridge University Press.

Gumperz, J.J. (1982b) *Language and Social Identity*, Cambridge, Cambridge University Press.

Hayakawa, S.I. (1952) *Language in Thought and Action*, London, Allen and Unwin.

Hymes, D. (1972) 'Models of the Interaction of Language and Social Life' in J.J. Gumperz and D. Hymes (eds), *Directions in Sociolinguistics*, New York, Holt, Rinehart and Winston, 35–71.

Labov, W. and Fanshel, D. (1977) *Therapeutic Discourse*, New York: Academic Press.

Levinson, S.C. (1983) *Pragmatics*, Cambridge, Cambridge University Press.

McGregor, G. (1983) 'Listeners' Comments on Conversation', *Language and Communication* 3, 271–304.

McGregor, G. (1984) 'Conversation and Communication', *Language and Communication* 4, 71–83.

McGregor, G. (1985) 'Lissnty Mi Toknty Yi: A Look at Linguistic Variation from the Listener's Point of View' in H.J. Warkentyne (ed.) *Papers from the Fifth International Conference on Methods in Dialectology*, British Columbia, Canada: University of Victoria, 258–99.

McGregor, G. (1986a) 'The Hearer as "Listener Judge": An Interpretive Sociolinguistic Approach to Utterance Interpretation' in McGregor, G. (ed.) *Language for Hearers*, Oxford, Pergamon, 153–84.

McGregor, G. (1986b) 'Listening Outside the Participation Framework', in McGregor, G. and White, R.S. (eds) *The Art of Listening*, London, Croom Helm, 55–72.

Milroy, L. (1987) *Observing and Analysing Natural Language*, Oxford, Blackwell.

Sacks, H. (1985) 'The Inference-Making Machine: Notes on Observability' in T. Van Dijk (ed.) *Handbook of Discourse Analysis* 3, London, Academic Press, 13–23.

Sperber, D. and Wilson, D. (1986) *Relevance*, Oxford, Blackwell.

Stubb, M. (1983) *Discourse Analysis*, Oxford: Blackwell.

Chapter six

Accommodating troubles-talk: the management of elderly self-disclosure[1]

Nikolas Coupland, Karen Henwood, Justine Coupland, and Howard Giles

Perspectives on recipiency

Our starting point is the belief, shared by contributors to this volume, that the role of the listener is under-represented in descriptive and explanatory linguistic research. The move towards a more interactionally-grounded sociolinguistics (cf. for example, Gumperz, 1982; Brown and Levinson, 1987) does promise a reversal of an unfortunate trend. The general position we wish to argue in this chapter, however, is that even when recipiency issues are foregrounded, there are still crucial issues concerning the *dimensions of recipiency* that an interactional sociolinguistics needs to address. That is, we see it as quite possible – and indeed commonplace – for the listener's role to be considered within theoretical constraints which leave the dynamics of interactional sequences seriously under-explained. We shall discuss the empirical data presented in the chapter in terms of communication accommodation theory (cf. Giles, 1984; N. Coupland, J. Coupland, Giles and Henwood, 1988; Giles, Coupland and Coupland, forthcoming). Therefore, by way of introduction to our own approach to issues of recipiency, we begin with a very brief review of alternative possible formulations.

There are numerous approaches which can claim to be listener-sensitive simply by involving *multi-party descriptions*. Paradigmatic studies within conversation analysis have insisted that our understanding of talk must reflect the sequential complexities and patterns that comprise everyday spoken exchanges. It is clear that the mechanics of conversation are themselves intrinsically recipient-sensitive. Conversational behaviours (classically of turn-taking, but in multiple dimensions) are, for example, precision-timed to the interlocutor's behaviours and highly-organized interpersonally (see Atkinson and Heritage, 1984 for a recent collection of work in this broad tradition). Another tradition has come to see multiple possibilities of *listener-adapted performance*, the operation of immediate, real-time interpersonal effects on communicative behaviour and less direct effects. Bell (1984), for example, documents the complex ways in which speech (Bell considers predominantly dialect data) can be 'designed' to take account of audience characteristics. Data show that addressees, auditors, overhearers and eavesdroppers can be distinguished partly by the constraints they variously impose on speakers' performances. Clearly, non-co-present audience-members/groups can also systematically influence stylistic choices, as for example when a radio DJ simulates co-presence (Montgomery, 1988) or signals degrees of community affiliation in dialect (Coupland, 1988).

The stimulus for a great deal of work on adaptive speech processes is Giles and co-workers' model of accommodation processes. In its early forms, speech accommodation theory (SAT) set out precisely to explain speakers' motives and behaviours in relation to addressee speech characteristics, and to identify patterns such as 'speech convergence' and 'speech divergence' operating between participants (for a recent review of the theory's development cf. Giles, Mulac, Bradac and Johnson, 1987). But whereas early work in SAT was principally concerned with relatively straightforward adaptive processes, often at the level of dialect-variation, much recent consideration has been given to the array of socio-psychological variables underpinning the selection of diverse communication strategies in dyadic exchanges, and subsequent evaluations and attributions. This recent emphasis on *strategic sociolinguistic interplay* is a far more powerful invocation of recipiency concerns than the two approaches listed above. It has required the theory to be recast as a 'communicative accommodation theory' (CAT). The agenda set by the expanded accommodation framework is to model and explain degrees and types of communicative 'attuning' in discourse, and contextualize these with considerations of social norms, beliefs and expectations, self- and other-categorizations, and interactional goals, as they influence both encoding and decoding choices. Figure 6.1 (from N. Coupland *et al.*, 1988) summarizes the principal current scope of communication accommodation theory.

CAT offers lines of interpretation that are not obviously open to less integrated recipiency-interested approaches. In particular, we find there to be a historical tendency for sociolinguistic research to involve 'listeners' in (what we would call) a *cooperativity* paradigm. The dominant assumptions are that

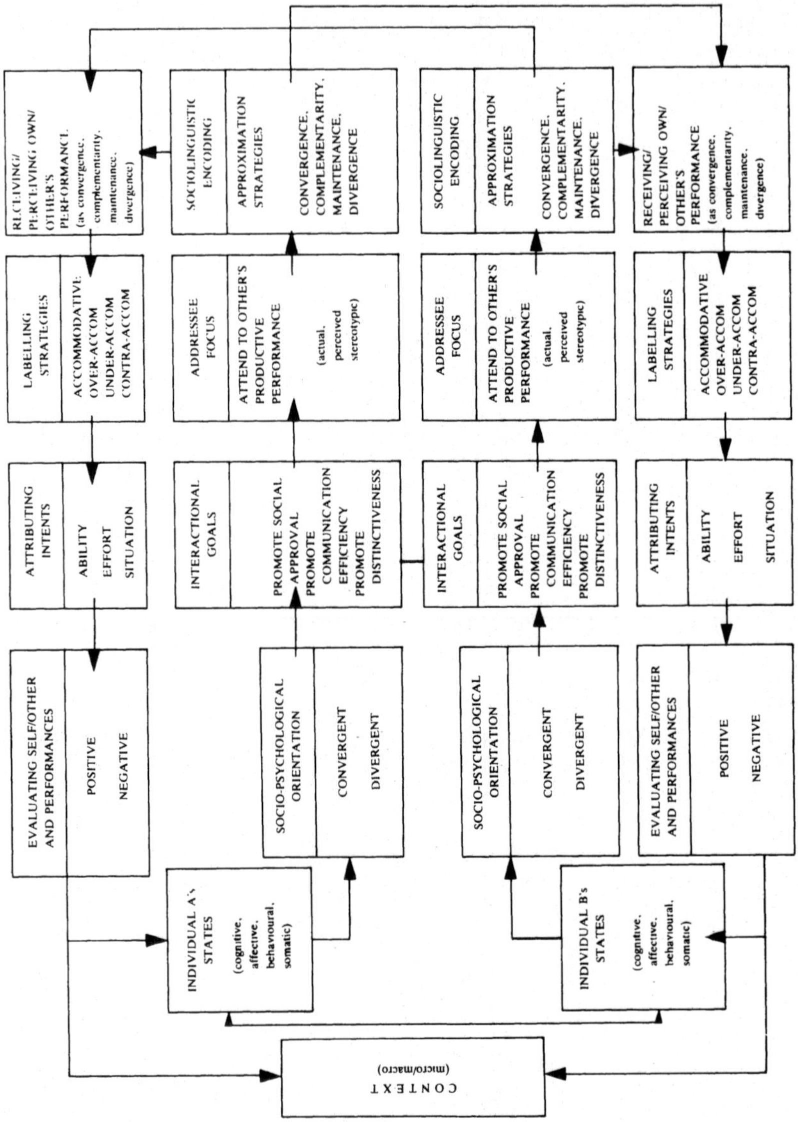

Figure 6.1 A generalized model of SAT processes

speakers and listeners routinely demonstrate shared assumptions, rely on shared code-knowledge, and participate in the shared production of social interaction. These assumptions are obviously correct to the extent that sharing is fundamental to any interpretable exchange of meanings. On the other hand, we must distinguish those categories of shared knowledge that are (a) intrinsic to a community's linguistic resources (e.g. a language or repertoire of languages, a dialect or repertoire of dialects); (b) intrinsic to community-members' understanding of basic principles governing social interaction (e.g. turn-taking conventions, or Gricean co-operative maxims), and (c) social norms for how resources and norms should be implemented in various settings (e.g. politeness conventions). While it has been claimed that there may be a general set to converge linguistically to one's interlocutor (Giles and Powesland, 1975), thus placing some dimensions of accommodation within category (c) above, the accommodation model generally offers possibilities well beyond the three categories. The model allows us to chart a full range of strategic alternatives in talk, including 'counter-attuning' (the motivated reduction of co-operative behaviour) and recipients perceiving communication directed at them to be 'over-accommodative' or 'under-accommodative' (cf., again, N. Coupland *et al.*, 1988).

Therefore, we would argue that recipiency-inclined research also needs to develop *a conflict paradigm*, exploring those contexts when the immediate, predictable co-operativity of talk can encode and of course actively construct interpersonal or intergroup dissonance of some sort (cf. Coupland, Giles and Wiemann, forthcoming). Figure 6.1 points to the possibility of individual participants' contributions being better or worse 'attuned' even at the procedural level. Also, semblances of textually attuned interaction can clearly disguise socio-psychological processes which themselves constitute conflict – of interactional goals, assumptions or ideologies. 'Well-attuned' procedural talk can itself represent some failure in relation to interactional goals. Construals of 'desirable interchange' can be mis-matched across participants, and perceptions/evaluations of ongoing talk can of course themselves differ.

Self-disclosure in talk between the generations

From such a conflict perspective, this chapter will examine patterns of recipiency to elderly speakers' intimate disclosive talk, or 'painful' self-disclosure (PSD). Two previous papers have examined this phenomenon, from first a descriptive and second a distributional point of view (cf. J. Coupland, N. Coupland, Giles and Wiemann, 1988; N. Coupland, J. Coupland, Giles, Henwood and Wiemann, submitted). In a large corpus of video-recorded interactions, we have found elderly female conversationalists frequently disclosing highly intimate information to new female acquaintances, both young and elderly. In the current chapter, however, we consider the extent to which elderly PSD is a product of recipient behaviours, and the far broader question of how such intergenerational sequences in turn contribute to the maintenance of intergenerational attitudes and communicative orientations. PSD is a mode of elderly talk which does indeed seem to fulfil important goals and needs for some elderly people. Also, PSD sequences seem to be co-operatively managed and to show high levels of procedural attuning in our data, particularly when the recipients are young (in fact in their 30s) rather than elderly peers. At the same time, however, we want to show that PSD constitutes a social practice (indeed, we argue, a sociolinguistic routine) out of which themes of intergroup conflict tend to arise. We shall show PSD as fertile ground for the evocation of negative stereotypes of the elderly and their communicative styles (for example, as grumbling, grim, rambling and egocentric speakers).

But in particular, we want to use the accommodation model to trace the highly complex and sometimes inconsistent functioning of elderly stereotypes in young recipients' responses to elderly PSD. These stereotypes, we argue, are invoked as part of a process by which the potential problematicality of elderly PSD is rationalized and denied by the young listeners. Overt evaluations of elderly PSD by young people do not uniformly recognize PSD to be problematical, despite the arguably inevitable threat to recipients' 'negative faces' (in the sense of Brown and Levinson, 1987). During PSD sequences and in subsequent evaluative activity, therefore, elderly and young people, we argue, engage in role-consistent, complementary behaviours which nonetheless endorse a fundamental conflict in inter-group relations. Overall, we try to demonstrate how, across the full range of their behaviours, attributions and evaluations in relation to elderly self-disclosure, the younger participants collude in producing and sustaining PSD, and thereby in the reproduction of intergroup stereotypes, and the maintenance of intergroup distance.

The data contexts

We build our argument around analyses of two different data-sets. The first is a corpus of 40 videotaped interactions[2] where pairs of volunteer subjects, women aged 70–87 and 30–40 years, were asked to 'get to know one another'. Participants were given no further instructions and were left alone, knowing they were being video-recorded, for eight minutes. (Each pair was also recorded for two minutes after their 'get acquainted' session, unaware that cameras were still running, though these two sub-contexts are not distinguished in this report.) The elderly women, most with (grossly characterized) upper-working-class backgrounds, were members of two Day Centres in Cardiff, Wales; most lived alone and were widowed. The young women were mostly lower-middle-class and married, and were recruited through an advertisement in a local newspaper. Twenty of the dyads were intergenerational (young-old); ten were peer-young and ten peer-elderly. According to the study-design, therefore, each subject participated in two interactions, one within- and one across-generation.

From this data-set, we shall give a brief overview of the distribution of what we define to be 'painful' self-disclosure sequences, then summarize and exemplify the roles played by recipients of PSD, in eliciting and responding to elderly PSD sequences. As reported in detail in the J. Coupland *et al.* (1988) study, we identified all PSD sequences in the data according to a pre-determined schema of topic-categories: reported bereavement, severe ill-health, immobility, loneliness, disengagement, and an assortment of family, financial and social troubles. All sequences were transcribed (using notation developed from that of Jefferson, as summarized in Atkinson and Heritage, 1984). Of course, we can make no claims as to the intrinsic or actual 'painfulness' of the states and events being disclosed, and use the term PSD as a convenient gloss. The analyses relate to a taxonomy of four phases in the management of PSD discourse (reproduced as Figures 6.2a-d in the Appendix). The taxonomy exhaustively lists alternative strategies which disclosers and recipients variably use in the pre-contexts to disclosures being made, the encoding of disclosures themselves, recipient next-moves, and first moves towards closing on-going PSDs. (A detailed distributional account of disclosers' roles in PSD sequences is to be found in N. Coupland *et al.*, submitted).

The second data-set was gathered as an attempt to expose some of the attributional and evaluative processes that underlie recipiency behaviours, and upon which our discourse analyses of the interactive data can provide only a speculative commentary. An evaluative follow-up study was designed in which young women, on the whole similar in age to the younger group in the interactive study, listened to 16 diverse audio-extracts (each of approximately half a minute) chosen from intergenerational encounters in the video-taped study. Details of the design and procedures used in the interactive study were made clear to the groups of listeners before they heard the extracts. Nine of these were from PSD sequences, chosen to represent variously contextualized and developed 'painful' disclosures on topics of ill-health, bereavement and loneliness. The remaining seven were randomly chosen from non-'painful' sequences of elderly disclosure, including some clearly positive reports (talking proudly about children and grandchildren or current social activities) and some expressions of dissatisfaction or of current difficult (but still not 'painful' in our defined sense) circumstances. The listeners were asked to imagine themselves in the roles of the younger women they heard on tape, and to describe how they felt, what influenced them most, and what was most problematical for them as (supposedly) the younger persons involved. A set of prepared questions was used to elicit relatively free discussion[3] on these issues among small groups of women about the extracts they had heard, and on the theme of elderly PSD in general. Discussions in eleven groups (involving a total of forty-three women) were audio-recorded and parts transcribed.

We think we are fully cognizant of the limitations of this research procedure. The (probable) experiential gaps between the young individuals in the two studies, the immediate versus the reflective contexts, the dyad versus the group contexts, and the predictable face-considerations in the young evaluators' public presentations of their apparent reactions to the PSD stimuli all conspire to hide 'genuine' evaluations from our inspection. On the other hand, we doubt that any de-contextualized and enduringly 'genuine' patterns of response can ever be available to us as researchers (if at all). Our aims were correspondingly humble and, we think, realistic. We argued that young women's discourse on the theme of elderly PSD was amenable to analyses not different in kind to those employed in the original (interactive) study. While confidence in the overtly simple judgements expressed in the group-discussions would be unwarranted, a further interpretive analysis would give a sense of the kinds of attributions of elderly self-disclosure available to young people in either accepting or denying its problematical nature. We would be interested in how beliefs about older people are represented in a specific context of talk, and more tendentiously even consolidated and constructed discoursally (cf. Wiemann *et al.*, 1987). The procedure could therefore be seen as benefitting from two of its apparent limitations. The group context might predispose specifically inter-group formulations, with a clear picture emerging of how generational stereotypes can mediate responses to intergenerational talk. Also, the real-time, reflective, evaluative process that we would be tapping into might itself be crucial to the formation and perpetuation of inter-group attitudes.

Patterns in the management of elderly PSD

The interactive study revealed clear generational differences in amounts of 'painful' self-disclosure. In summary, PSD in the defined sense occurs in thirty-two of the forty encounters, and accounts for highly variable proportions (between 1 per cent and 57 per cent) of speaking-time (mean = 13.7 per cent). In these gross distributional terms, PSD is a major component of encounters involving at least one elderly participant, where it occupies far more time (approximately 16 per cent) than in peer-young encounters (approximately 6 per cent). Half the peer-young encounters, but only 10 per cent of the encounters involving at least one elderly participant, have no PSD. Furthermore, in the cross-generation encounters, almost the whole of PSD is talk about the elderly's (and not the young's) 'painful' experiences. Elderly speakers in the data engage in PSD to roughly equal extents across peer and intergenerational contexts. These findings seem to support the general observation that the elderly speakers in our data are behaving significantly more 'disclosively' than the younger women, though we would want to specify this claim through much more detailed attention to the contextualization of elderly PSD.

Some relevant findings emerge from the analysis of pre-contexts to 'painful' self-disclosures in the data. It is apparent that elderly disclosers here do play a major role in determining their own disclosing. This may seem almost tautological, though our taxonomy of alternative attested pre-contextual types (see Figure 6.2a in the Appendix) shows that PSDs can be also triggered by recipients' eliciting behaviours. Again, they can be in a sense self-generating, triggered by previous textual happenings with no apparent will on the part of participants to either elicit PSD or to disclose. In fact, more than half the PSDs in the data

(53 per cent) are determined interactionally by disclosers themselves rather than being directly/indirectly elicited (26 per cent) or being textually generated (20 per cent). The elderly (who, we have seen, are almost always the sources of PSD here) are responsible for determining slightly more than half the total of PSDs, whether conversing with younger (53 per cent) or older (59 per cent) speakers. The observation that the elderly are behaving 'disclosively' is therefore supported in the more particular sense of seeming to design their talk, at least in half of the attested cases, as PSD.

On the other hand, we see it as highly significant that the young participants also elicit PSD from their elderly interlocutors to a considerable extent – 34 per cent of instances, contrasting with elderly speakers eliciting only 12 per cent of instances from their peers. We take this to be evidence of the young sharing responsibility for the engendering of elderly PSD. The two processes (elderly disclosure and young elicitation) are of course not in competition, except possibly in respect of particular sequences. The young's eliciting role will require particular disclosive acts, but will more generally legitimize elderly disclosive behaviour; conversely, elderly disclosure will establish interactional norms which legitimize eliciting behaviour.

Certainly there is a complementarity across the patterns of pre-contextualization we find in the data. We are reticent, however, to see the young's role here as purely accommodative to the elderly's wishes or to norms established in particular interactions. A qualitative focus is revealing. The data contain instances of young women's eliciting behaviours which presuppose interrogatory rights they would certainly not have in peer-young conversations (and which may not, of course, be endorsed by particular elderly conversationalists either). On one occasion, a young speaker (Y10) asks *is your husband still alive?* (in a context where there is no on-going PSD talk). Y06 asks E06 *do you sleep alright when you get to bed?* when previous talk has been on the general theme of reading habits. These are surely intrusive questions in first-encounter conversations, even though we have no access to recipients' (the disclosers-to-be) own evaluations of them. Such questions, and the category of direct elicitations as a whole, impose obligations upon elderly interlocutors either to disclose or to prevaricate. The category of indirect elicitations (see again Figure 6.2a) subsumes questioning strategies which give rise to PSDs less predictably, though they certainly enable such disclosures. When Y11 asks her elderly interlocutor *where are your family living now? are they all fairly close to you or are you quite spread out?* she taps an area which may well be reported as a 'painful' experience (and was, in this instance). Even indirect elicitation acts can therefore be seen as potential threats to the equilibrium of discourse, and threats that are often tolerated by young elicitors.

The eliciting role of the young is confirmed in our analyses of the final phase of PSD sequences – moves towards closing (cf. Figure 6.2d in the Appendix). By far the most common strategy of all alternative move-types listed here is for the young recipients in the intergenerational context to elicit on related but non-painful discloser-topics. And the elderly amongst themselves never do this. (The elderly's most frequent strategy in responding to other elderly's PSDs is to match a painful self-disclosure with another from their own experience.) When a particular elderly disclosive sequence has run its course, typically facilitated as we shall show by diverse young response-moves, it falls approximately equally (in frequential terms) on the discloser and the recipient to move the discourse on to a new topic. Young participants most commonly choose to re-orient talk away from PSD by drawing further self-disclosure from their partners.

It is in the area of responses to PSDs that we get the clearest evidence of the young's and the elderly's generalized roles in relation to PSD. It is apparent in the interactive data that elderly recipients of elderly PSD are often accommodating or attuning to their interlocutors in their next-moves (see Figure 6.2c in the Appendix) along a dimension of group-identity. The young, on the other hand, are attuning more in respect of the particular (inter-individual) topic being disclosed upon. Often, the basis of *elderly* responses to PSD is in-group solidarity, appealing to the shared experience of ageing. While pointing to shared experience as a solidarity act, and thereby we might expect accommodative, we in fact find that it can also *inhibit* the development of particular PSD sequences. For example in extract 1 (from Interaction 07),

Extract 1 (from I07)

line

1 E03 but (sighing) it's (.) it's just erm (.) I don't get
out [
2 E04 just can't do
3 the things we used to do=

4 E03 =I I (.) couldn't do it love no
[
5 E04 I can't *walk* like I
used to
[
6 E03 well
7 no and I got a stick now this thing
[
8 E04 well I haven't got a stick=
9 E03 =no=
10 E04 =but I can't go up=
11 E03 =no=
12 E04 =I walked from our Derby and Joan club yesterday to
go
[ ][ ]
13 E03 yes yes
14 E04 home=
15 E03 =yes
[
16 E04 and I had to stop *three* or *four* times on the way
[
17 E03 that's right
yes
18 you're you're short of breath
[ ]
19 E04 it's like a (.) with my breathing=
[ ]
20 E03 I do
21 E03 =yes
[
22 E04 and also=
23 E03 =yes=
24 E04 =my legs don't seem too (.) dainty
[
25 E03 no of course they don't we're
26 all the same

E04's particular disclosure of immobility *I can't walk like I used to* (line 5) is overlapped by E03's *well no and I got a stick now* . . . (lines 6–7). Reporting the shared experience of mobility problems does not offset the fact that E03's self-reference truncates her partner's on-going self-disclosure. The resulting effect (we suggest) is not altogether positively accommodative because it also inhibits the development of the particular disclosure in progress. Moreover, the fact of generalizing these experiences explicitly to the group (*no of course they don't we're all the same*, lines 25–26) is simultaneously depersonalizing. Perhaps E04 has not been allowed or enabled to develop her particular disclosure of immobility and breathing difficulties as fully as she might have wished. As an in-group member, E03 can short-circuit the disclosure by contextualizing and rationalizing it (cf. J. Coupland *et al.*, 1988) with a move towards closing the disclosure.

In extract 2 (from I20), this in-group convergence option for elderly peer recipiency builds on what is in fact a very locally shared experience.

<u>Extract 2</u> (from I20)

line

1 E09 (puts on glasses) oh that's better I don't like the
2 light (.) I never had anything wrong with my eyes before
3 E10 well well
4 E09 yeah till about six months ago and then it came (.) er
5 E09 conjunctivitis? it's like er a lot of irritation
[ ]
6 E10 (sympathetically) ah ah dear god
7 E09 yeah never mind (.) it'll go I expect (laughing) one day
[
8 E10 I get
9 a lot of noise in my ear=
10 E09 =oh that's with our age as well
[
11 E10 have you got (.) have you got that?
[
12 E09 I get that yes
13 E10 you *get* it?
14 E09 (emphatically) *yes* see you can't they can't do a thing
15 with that=
16 E10 =that that's right (.) that's what the doctor s
[
17 E09 yeah it's just like a lot of er (.) buzzing
18 and (.) blocked you know ears are blocked

E09 too is a sufferer from tinnitus, the focus of the PSD she receives. Still, E09 chooses to frame the expression of solidarity in group terms: she responds with *oh that's with our age as well* (line 10).

There is clearly a strong potential sense of shared pain in the joint experience of being elderly and all that this can suggest in terms of experiencing bereavement, degenerating own health and so on. But it is perhaps surprising that sharing such experiences, and in many cases the will to disclose them, does not on the whole lead the elderly to engage in recipiency behaviours (including next moves to PSDs) which promote the telling of particular sequences. PSD discourse in general may well not be inhibited by elderly responses, though the benefits to elderly disclosers in terms of positive face (see N. Coupland *et al.*, submitted) cannot accrue. The phenomenon of combative matching of PSDs that we identified above in fact suggests that the telling function can override recipiency concerns altogether for elderly conversationalists at times. There are grounds for believing that much elderly PSD is designed for non-elderly audiences, and can only fully achieve its face-promoting function in the intergroup context.

The *young* as recipients show a clear tendency to attune their responses to elderly PSD in respect of the particularities of the on-going disclosure. They signal interest and engagement, and thereby often sustain PSD both in particular and in general terms. Although several options are open to them as makers of next-moves to PSD, the young rarely have recourse to the expression of shared experience, and of course never to the essential generational in-group experience. Signalling surprise at an elderly PSD, for example, which itself demonstrates engagement with the particular topic being revealed, is a frequent young recipients' next-move. If we assume that elderly disclosers of painful experience are disclosing at least partly because of the need for interactive engagement (and the benefits to identity this in turn brings), recipient surprise is a valuable endorsement of the news-worthiness of the telling. If the telling is somehow cathartic, surprise is presumably therapeutic.

Extract 3 (from I06)

line

E03 (sighing) and um anyway they had a house then in
Bristol (.) Bristol (.) had their own house there (.)

3 but things didn't seem to go (1.0) very well you know
4 (1.0) and er (.) one day he came home (.) and he said
5 um (.) she's gone (2.0) with two little kids ((and))
[ ]
6 Y03 (quietly) oh dear
and how *old* were *they*?
7 E03 well the one was in his arms she he was about um
twelve months old
[
8 Y03 she left
9 the children? she left the ch
[ ]
10 E03 yes
11 E03 twelve month old
12 Y03 mm
13 E03 and the little the little girl was (.) four and a half
[
14 Y03 good
15 heavens above and *where* did she go?
16 E03 she went back home to her mother=
17 Y03 =(tutting) oh dear *left* the children

In extract 3, Y03's high-rise intonation contour on the last two syllables of *she left the children?* (lines 8–9), as well as her *good heavens above!* (lines 14–15) are part of an extensive repertoire of sustaining and attuning recipient-moves the young employ. Sympathy is encoded, either verbally (*oh dear* at line 17 of the extract, and in other extracts: *ah there's sad yeah* [I33]; *oh that's a shame* [I10]; etc., or prosodically and facially/posturally at appropriate points. Sometimes the affective signal is 'focused' on particular items of content isolated through selected reformulation of what the discloser has said: in extract 3, *(tutting) oh dear left the children* (line 17); or through explicit evaluative glosses: in I22, *oh that couldn't have been easy*. Initiations maintaining the topic of an ongoing PSD are also common in young next-moves. In extract 3, *and how old were they?* (line 6); and *and where did she go?* (line 15) explicitly require the teller to elaborate the content of her PSD. Some of very many further instances are *is he still there* [in a mental institution]? (I06); *how long ago were you widowed?* (I21); and the following sequence (extract 4) from I13:

Extract 4 (from I16)

line

1 E07 . . . now er (.) I'm dreading (.) tomorrow and (.) Sunday
2 Y08 oh you're it's just Monday to Friday that you go (.)
oh
[
3 E07 so it's (.) everything's getting
4 me ((down)) and I'm going into hospital on Monday
5 Y08 oh are you?
6 E07 and I'm a little bit erm
7 Y08 bit worried (.) how long are you going to be in hospital?

Overall, the various contributions we have shown the young participants making intergenerationally justify labelling them as facilitators (Holmes, 1984), particularly of elderly PSD. Their quite frequent role in eliciting PSD runs contrary to what Berger and Bradac (1982, 82) suppose is normative for interrogative behaviour among new acquaintances. These authors conclude that 'it appears that interrogative strategies which are impersonal, i.e. non-intimate and de-individuated, are more acceptable initially than are highly personal strategies'. Moreover, our data deny Berger and Bradac's subsequent claim that 'highly personal internally focused strategies are likely to inhibit self-revelation' (1982, 82). This is not the case when our elderly speakers are questioned on aspects of their personal states and experience. In their major function supporting on-going PSDs, the young in our data generally fulfil the role Coates (1986, 115) and others have considered prototypically female in inter-sex encounters, providing above all solidarity and support to interlocutors. In the sex-roles literature, this conversational orientation has been considered a powerless role, though we are reticent to classify the young as globally powerless in relation to the elderly here. While in terms of amounts of talk and personal focus the elderly do very clearly dominate, the young are equally clearly dominant in the domain of discourse-management, through their eliciting behaviour. The relational character of our intergenerational data is very much that of interviews (in the 'chat-show' mould, not selectional interviews), with the young enabling and sustaining extended spoken performances by the elderly.

Problematicality

At this point, we need to address the question of why the young adopt such a facilitative orientation to elderly PSD, when there seems to be an intrinsically 'painful' element, at least in potential, to the telling but also the '*receiving*' of negatively valenced, intimate self-disclosures among new acquaintances. There are grounds for predicting that recipiency to elderly PSD is 'problematical' to the young, in one or more of several dimensions. In Brown and Levinson's (1987) terms, painful self-disclosure predictably threatens a recipient's negative face: her rights to unviolated personal space. Simultaneously, the discloser exposes her own positive face (her desire to be approved of/thought well of) by indulging in counter-normative self-disclosive behaviour (Berger and Bradac, 1982).

At the most basic level, the emotional loading of many of the disclosures we have considered 'painful' inevitably intrudes on recipients' negative face-rights, particularly given that our data are first-encounters between strangers. Beyond this, young recipients of elderly PSD are forced into selecting among response-options, all of which bear potential face-threats in their own right. If a recipient discourages on-going 'painful' disclosure (perhaps by selecting a pre-closing move, or shifting topic onto non-painful self- or other topics), there is an immediate threat to her positive face. The discloser may find her strategy under-accommodative (cf. J. Coupland *et al.*, 1988), socially or even morally deficient: the discloser thinks the recipient is not resourceful or courageous enough to be recipient of PSD, and incidentally not as brave in this respect as the discloser herself is being in threatening her own face through disclosure. If a recipient chooses the options which encourage disclosure (for example through eliciting further information or through supportive back-channelling in the manner we have seen the young most typically employ), she accepts the prospective threat to her own negative face: she may have her emotional space invaded once again. And of course there will be a recurring positive face-threat in the need to encode further responses.

The above represents, at least from a theoretical perspective, a potentially intractable accommodative dilemma. It would not be surprising if the competing considerations of face resulted in no desirable or even tolerable response suggesting itself to some recipients on occasions. The lack of relevant shared experience we have pointed to above compounds this problem, removing the potential for group-solidarity marking that is a perennially available referrent for the elderly. It is therefore most surprising how rarely the flow of discourse reflects these problems we anticipate.

<u>Extract 5</u> (from I18)

line

1 E08 =because when I was a widow you see after eleven years
2 I had three little children you see to bring up I worked
[ ]
3 Y09 mm
4 E08 very hard I done everything *cook* er parlourmaid
5 *every*thing I done
6 Y09 mhm
7 E08 well I had to get a living you see=
8 Y09 =oh yes yes (1.0) mm (2.0) oh well (3.0) um (.) I was
9 going to say I'm I've started working again I've got a
10 little daughter and I've just started back to work

A sequence such as that in extract 5 does suggest that the young recipient (Y09) experiences problems in maintaining the flow of talk. However, the young population in our data seems highly socially skilled in this respect, and such instances are rare. We have little textual evidence of problematicality, therefore, although certain recipient-responses to disclosures do seem to suffer an intrinsic inadequacy that we suspect is perceived by recipients themselves. In I40, Y20 offers a 'contextualization' move *so this is really good for you isn't it then to be able to go somewhere like this*. Her elderly interlocutor (E20) has said she has been widowed for twenty-one years. The contextualization, even if it is in itself appropriate, makes unwarranted assumptions about the elderly interlocutor's particular circumstances and needs. Appreciating this (if she does) will be uncomfortable for the young recipient, who is nevertheless trying to reinterpret disclosed information in a positive light: to 'look on the bright side' (cf. Jefferson, 1984). Jefferson (1984, 363) also notes the propensity of recipients (who are young in our terms) in her data to propound extravagantly optimistic responses.

At this point in the argument, then, we have no coherent explanation for the young's tolerance of, even their propensity to generate, interactional sequences which carry threats to both participants. It is in the domain of the attributional and evaluative components of accommodation processes that we will find the most satisfactory explanations. So, we turn now to the second data-set, the evaluative study, as a basis for further analysis.

The evaluative study

The preceding discussion has raised the possibility that PSD recipiency may be problematical in several overlapping dimensions. Most generally, we have argued that PSD in the context of our interactive study will impose some *affective* load upon recipients, who may experience discomfort or embarrassment, frustration or perhaps even boredom. The discourse analyses showed little evidence of *procedural* or sequential difficulty, which we would take to be represented by recipients showing difficulty in finding any plausible next move to PSD. Again, we hypothesized that the accommodative dilemma of responding to PSD might constitute a strategic difficulty: a next move may be found, though it would fail to satisfy recipients' own appraisal of what would constitute a desirable or at least adequate strategy at that point in the discourse. In our explorations of the evaluative group-discussion data, we were initially interested in whether participants would overtly recognize any categories of problem to be associated with PSD recipiency, and if so, which.

In fact, such recognition of specific problems directly associated with receiving PSD is uncommon. There are certainly references to procedural difficulties, but only very rarely of the sort anticipated. VB in DG6[4] and DB in DG10 do comment on the limited range of options open to recipients of PSD, by observing that there is often no option but to give sympathy or to change the subject (which is itself acknowledged to be difficult to achieve). More often, experienced procedural problems are said to take the form of expressed dissatisfaction with the recipient roles of the elderly speakers in the extracts, that they were interrupting and inattentive listeners (see, for example, extracts 6 and 7).

Several other discussants raise the problem of powerlessness, being unable to control the developments of topics or themes in intergenerational conversation. PE and GR (in DG4) suggest that sudden changes of topic (as when an elderly speaker in the stimulus recordings chains a PSD on the subject of an abdominal rupture to one on her failing eyesight) are difficult to respond to. HC in DG7 comments that *it is hard to get a conversation to where you want it to go with older people*.

Extract 6 (from DG6)

line

1 R what was it about the snippets of conversation that
2 you found the most problematic?
3 VB um (.) the fact that the the older person interrupted
4 you all the time (.) whatever you
[ ]
5 R mhm
6 VB you said (.) she wasn't really listening (.) she had
7 her own mind her own thoughts and she was just
8 preparing the next thing she was going to tell you
9 didn't really listen to the question

Extract 7 (from DG7)

line

1 HC oh when they didn't stop and listen to you and they
2 just sort of carried on with what they were saying all
3 the time when you were trying to say something and
4 they would just . . . continue and sort of butt in before
you'd finished your question completely
[ ]
5 DR yeah
[
6 R yeah
7 HC taking it on to a different tack um that's difficult

There is of course an affective dimension to each of the procedurally focused complaints above, but specific affective consequences are mentioned very rarely. RT in DG10 responds to a disclosure on loneliness as follows: *she just came across as if she wanted to moan to somebody and that was really embarrassing*. RT and KM in the same discussion ascribe this to a conscious intent on the part of some elderly people: *they are trying to make you feel sorry for them in some way*. But most recognition of the affective impact of PSD is generalized into a discourse of sadness and sympathy for elderly people, living and having lived difficult lives. Extract 8, for example, sees LJ expressing a global response to the condition of being elderly.

Extract 8 (from DG10)

line

1 R right (.) what . . . did you find influenced you most?
2 LJ . . . um (1.0) you know if they're having problems with
3 health and this sort of thing then it affects you I
4 think very definitely it does to me anyway (.) um (.)
5 if they're feeling lonely and depressed then that oh
that hurts me very strongly
[ ]
6 R mm
7 R is there was there a particular snippet there that
8 you . . . can remember in that respect?
9 LJ um (2.0) I think . . . the emphysema one I think really
10 went home (.) that one um (1.0) and oh the very lonely
11 people (.) I think there were a couple of those who
12 were very very lonely (1.0) I felt sorry for those
13 because you then think of people who are in that
14 situation um and there must be thousands of people like
that all over (.) the world

It is important to note that the invocation of the social group (*thousands of people like that all over the world*, line 14) necessarily attenuates any experience of problems in relation to PSD in particular, and of course in relation to the particular instances of PSD in the stimulus material. And the most consistent pattern we find in the group-discussions is the recognition of problematical elderly life circumstances working to *deny* problems of PSD recipiency (the issue the researcher was attempting to explore quite systematically in the evaluative study). This process of contextualization is apparent in extract 9.

Extract 9 (from DG6)

line

1 R was it just the . . . bereavement that you found might have
2 been difficult to respond to or was there anything
else?
3 PE well no just the general situation of old age . . . I mean
4 it just seems to me that old age is very often a sad
5 situation and I don't think there is an awful lot can
be done about it

```
                 [
6  MS                I didn't find
7       it difficult
          [
8  ML       no
9  PE  I mean I didn't find it difficult either but I think
10     that's the situation it's it's you just accept that I
11     mean when you're talking to old people
       [
12 MS  they like to talk about their husband who passed away
13     seven years ago
                [
14 PE  yes I agree
       [
15 ML   yes
16 MS  they like to have a chat about it
17 ML  yes it's lovely it's yes yes and if you listen
                                                [    ]
18 MS                                             yes
19 ML  I mean you don't have to say anything
                                        [    ]
20 MS                                      no
21 ML  just let them unburden
```

In answer to R's question, PE observes that *old age is often a fairly sad situation* (lines 4–5) and that little can be done about it. MS interjects to deny she finds PSD *difficult* (lines 6–7) and PE seems to feel the need to match MS's denial and redress her earlier statement to some extent. ML even maintains that it is *lovely* (line 17) – to listen to old people talking about lost loved ones – which appears to transform the suggestion of problematical recipiency into satisfaction at some sort of altruistic, perhaps therapeutic, involvement. The discussion at this point works in various ways to deny what we have seen as the essence of PSD talk. It is now glossed as the elderly having *a chat about it*, and *liking* to engage in such talk (line 16): an image of talk which is both enjoyable and superficial is constructed in the discussion discourse. Problematicality is subverted to the extent that ML claims *I mean you don't have to say anything* (line 19): recipients are implied to be free from any significant involvement.

For some discussants, the very generality of what they perceive as undesirable elderly behaviours in talk is used to downgrade the degree of problematicality they cause. In Extract 10, for EB and RW, it is the fact of those [modes of talk] being *routine* (lines

7–8) that leads to their view that PSD in not problematic for them as listeners.

<u>Extract 10</u> (from DG5)

line

1 R is there anyone here who feels that (.) um me asking
2 the question what was problematic doesn't doesn't
3 really resonate with how they felt does anyone feel (.)
4 that they didn't find (.) the ext responding to the
5 snippets snippets of conversation problematic? (1.5)
6 EB on the whole no=
7 RW =on the whole no because one's come across those before
[ ] [ ]
8 EB routine
9 NL yes
[
10 EB one's
11 come across those before . . .
12 RW well I've got a granny of eighty-five who's continually
13 saying she's lonely she's not lonely at all because
there's a visitor
there[ ]
14 R yes
15 RW just about every hour of the day into the house
[
16 R mhm
17 RW but she says she's lonely and nobody comes to visit her
[
18 R mhm
19 RW and in some respects you have to take it with a little
20 bit of a pinch of salt=
21 R =mhm
22 RW um (.) what people say
23 MC yes they play for sympathy they're very much like some
24 some elderly people are very much like young children
25 they want to be the centre of attention for as long as
possible

This is a perplexing claim, until it is made clear by both RW and MC that they accept that elderly PSD is routinely unfounded. Their ageist suggestion is that *you have to take it with . . . a pinch of salt* (lines 19–20), and that some elderly *play for sympathy* (line 23). MC finally invokes the classic inverted-U stereotype of the old as children (cf. N. Coupland and J. Coupland, forthcoming).

A discourse of elderly stereotyping[5] is in fact structurally integrated into other patterns of argumentation in the group-discussions. Stereotyping here operates at different levels of inclusiveness, with both categorical and less inclusive characterizations, and the invoking of stereotypical themes may convey quite different sentiments depending on the way these themes are expressed (cf. the idea that stereotypes may be held in different ways, Henwood, 1986). We find labels such as *cantankerous* (GD in DG3), *depressing* and *moaning* (HP in DG3), *boring* (ML in DG3), *selfish* (KM in DG10), and *rambling* or *rattling on* in conversation (EK in DG5; KM in DG10). But such stereotypical ascriptions are often counter-balanced by less pejorative themes, such as the discourse of sadness and sympathy for old people we referred to above. Discussants will often focus on exceptions to stereotype-conformity, thereby apparently legitimizing their negative ascriptions to the out-group. In GD 4, NL says *it can be a b rather boring to be with an old person for any length of time and a bit frustrating and you feel a bit resentful of the time you have to spend . . . it's the sort of duty thing*. She then immediately restricts the currency of her observations with *it's an exceptional person that makes you feel like that*, and the more positive global view is bolstered by another participant's (HP's) contribution that *some of the conversations* [in the stimulus material] *were quite buoyant . . . it was an elated sort of conversation*. Pejoration seems to be in turn enabled by this up-swing; HP adds *but some were very downcasting very sort of moaning type conversations*.

The ebb and flow of stereotyping and counter-stereotyping in the discussion-data seems to reflect a normative constraint, in public discourse in a liberal democracy, that naked categorical assertions about social groups are undesirable. We are prepared to construe a good deal of the more positive ascriptions within the stereotyping talk as a veneer of tolerance and liberal sentiment over some generally endorsed beliefs about the elderly as undesirable interactional partners and problematical conversationalists. Of course, as we noted earlier, their 'actual' beliefs are not open to analysis. What seems most significant in the group-discussion data is the readiness with which young discussants appeal to group-formulations – positive, negative, or both – in the context of questioning about particular sequences of PSD. The pervasive denial of specific problems associated with PSD recipiency is achieved only through adopting the broader perspective. Such problems (as *we* construed them) are either dissolved into highly general, recognized inadequacies of intergenerational talk, or are reduced to an irrelevance by comparison with considerations of the elderly's problematical lives. Either way, the availability of group-salient, stereotypical formulations of old people intervenes crucially in what we originally conceived as an exercise of evaluation and response.

Discussion

Intergenerational PSD sequences appear to be an interactional routine[6] which is very substantially enabled and supported by recipients, and leads to (superficially) complementary sociolinguistic/non-verbal behaviours, but which can nevertheless sustain and promote dissonance at the intergroup level, through endorsing social stereotypes. In approaching the sequence as a routine, we are claiming it is not only sociolinguistically regulated (cf. Coulmas, 1981) but in an important sense self-regulating. If young and old contributions to PSD discourse are 'prefabricated' or communicative sets, they achieve this position through sociopsychological processes in the environment of intergenerational talk itself. They are not mere formulae (as most of the instances in the Coulmas collection are), but are apparently preferred generational strategies for the management of intergroup relations in respect of PSD. The very complementarity or high level of attuning of talk in procedural terms (that we commented on in the earlier discussion of PSD discourse) consolidates stereotype-consistent behaviours (probably by both parties in intergenerational talk), which come or continue to be seen as 'the way things predictably are'.[7]

The recipiency role of the young is therefore ultimately highly ambiguous. As we have shown, recipients do a substantial amount of work to bring about interactional patterns that ultimately distance them from their interlocutors. They guarantee 'attuned talk' only in the immediate sense of generally keeping the conversation flowing. 'Attuning' rather needs to be seen to operate at different 'levels', where contradictory tendencies can be apparent. The behavioural (well-attuned 'sociolinguistic encoding') level fronts complex socio-psychological (attributional and evaluative) processes. Perceived 'problems', that seem (to us) to be an inevitable consequence of intimate self-disclosing to strangers, may be subjected to even 'deeper' attributional scrutiny by participants. Attributional considerations can impose a more global evaluation, often more positive, and lead to the denial of 'problems' that would seem to be intrinsic to PSD recipiency.

We have witnessed some aspects of these processes of attributing and evaluating past communicative experiences as real-time events, occupying discourses subsequent to those that were the initial focus of attention in this chapter. The group-discussions, where the young overtly 'rationalize' elderly PSD in talk with their peers, may be representative of commonplace in-group discourses through which evaluations of inter-group experiences are reached. Through this process of transformation, we see problems in one sense denied, but in another sense perpetuated and consolidated. The ground is seemingly also laid for new initiatives by recipients (in the same or a later encounter) which guarantee the continuation of intergroup non-alignment and ideological conflict. The young come to evaluate elderly PSD positively only through (and at the cost of) perceiving the elderly as a disenfranchised out-group needing special consideration. Recipiency to elderly PSD by the young is only to be regarded positively to the extent that intergenerational conversation is pseudo-consultation. The young seem to accept, sometimes enthusiastically, their opportunity to make some sort of therapeutic intervention in the lives of the elderly. However appropriate this might be in particular cases, it nevertheless inevitably constrains the roles elders can fulfil in intergenerational talk. The more general consequence is the imposition of a rigidly inter-group frame on talk between younger and older adults, which must perpetuate the social alienation elders so often consider their greatest handicap.

The accommodation model we introduced at the beginning of the chapter captures quite well the complexity of these processes in respect of intergenerational PSD. Referring to this model (see Figure 6.1), let us assume that 'sociolinguistic encoding' represents elderly PSD and young supportive recipiency behaviours to PSD. The young may then perceive their own and interlocutors' behaviours as (respectively) 'over-accommodative' and 'under-accommodative'. The elderly are seen as under-accommodating in that they make insufficient allowance for the burden (affective and interactional) that PSD imposes upon recipients. The young see themselves as over-accommodating: having to transcend the 'normal' bounds of the recipiency role. In the past, we have tended to assume that these evaluative labels signal some sort of miscommunication and probable interactional dissatisfaction with 'problems' in interaction. However, the discussion data show the young (in talk) attributing elderly PSD largely to 'situation' (an option specified in the model), in terms of elderly life-circumstances, beliefs about talk, needs for talk, plus their own responsibilities *vis-à-vis* 'therapeutic' intervention.

In the process of making these attributions, the young's potentially negative evaluations of elderly PSD (the model's next box) are often recast as, transformed into, more positive evaluations, through mediating considerations of elderly stereotypes. Subsequently (again in the model's terms), these evaluations enter the 'context' component as a form of learned or reproduced 'knowledge' about the old and about intergenerational talk, which again predisposes recipients (as 'Individuals B' in the model) to adopt presumably convergent psychological orientations to the elderly next-time-around. The classic 'positive accommodative' interactional goals of promoting social approval (maintaining and responding supportively to PSD) and communication efficiency (selecting discourse strategies, such as elicitation and expressing sympathy) are adopted and will advance talk according to a conventional intergenerational schema. Ultimately, then, we have a cyclical process explaining the transmission of intergroup attitudes, including predispositions for modes of talk, through experiences of talk. If our interdisciplinary model has captured some of the complexities of multi-party PSD management, it may prove to be of some more general utility in understanding intergroup communication, and particularly the difficulties and satisfactions of talk between the generations.

Notes

1. The research on which this report is based has been supported by the Economic and Social Research Council (ESRC, United Kingdom), reference number G002220022.
2. Interactions in this corpus are referenced with an 'I' prefix to a two-digit number – I01 – I40. Participants in these interactions are identified with either 'E' (elderly) or 'Y' (young) prefixes to two-figure digits – E01 – E20; Y01 – Y20.
3. As a further means of triangulating in on these same issues, quantitative measures were also taken from the same population of evaluators. Space precludes reporting of this phase of the investigation here. But it may be important to note that participants in the group-discussions had already completed a questionnaire task on the subject of elderly PSD before engaging in the discussion phase. They were presented with ten rating-scales on which they subjectively assessed various dimensions of their affective responses (a number of which tapped experienced problematicality) to the elderly speakers' disclosures across the 16 extracts. They also rated

how conscious they were of PSD occurring, the extent to which they felt this to be 'typical' of old people, and gave written answers to explain why elderly people might disclose personal information like this. Finally, they answered a general question about their frequencies of contact with older people.

4. Participants in the group discussions are referenced by (fictitious) initials. R refers to the researcher leading the discussion-groups. Individual group-discussions are identified with the prefix DG.
5. Stereotypes of old age have been widely researched, cf. Braithwaite, 1986; Branco and Williamson, 1982; Brubaker and Powers, 1976; McTavish, 1971; Rosencrantz and McNevin, 1969; Sigall and Page, 1971. The discourse analytic perspective we are adopting here does not mesh well with these predominantly experimental and questionnaire-based studies. They have, for example, tended to use a restricted set of descriptive labels which do not relate easily to ascriptions of the elderly made by particular groups in contexts. A task for future research is to explore possibilities and means of reconciling work in the laboratory tradition with ethnographically framed investigations of the employment of social stereotypes in interaction.
6. We hypothesize there is a set of such routines, including ideological matching sequences (cf. N. Coupland *et al.*, 1988) and age-disclosure sequences – Coupland and Coupland, forthcoming).
7. There is, in fact, some recognition of the scripting of intergenerational sequences in the group-discussion data. In DG8, JC says (of the stimulus PSD extracts): *a lot of these are very classic types of conversations that you have with elderly people . . . if you talk to elderly people you talk similar scripts.*

Appendix

Pre-context alternatives represent three broad means by which subsequent disclosures are triggered in our data: recipient-determined (direct or indirect elicitations of PSD by recipients); textually determined (where considerations of conversational coherence predispose or require PSD); and discloser-determined (where the pre-context to PSD is established by the discloser herself). These three groups represent (respectively) strong-to-weak obligations to disclose, as they might be experienced by disclosers; similarly, the three categories seem to us to correspond with there being few-to-many discoursal options available to them.

Disclosive modes are distinguished in terms of 'staging' – the thematic prominence afforded to the 'core' of a disclosure – and sub-types of 'elaboration' – the extent of development or complexity of functional units in the telling of a disclosure.

Recipient next-moves are the diverse minimal and full moves which variously encourage or discourage further PSD, and are tentatively and subjectively ranked in Figure 6.2c according to this principle.

Moves towards closing are the first contributions, in each of the PSD sequences, made either by discloser or by recipient towards closing the topic of on-going PSD (whether or not they achieve closure in the flow of discourse).

Figure 6.2 A taxonomy of strategies in four phases of disclosive sequences

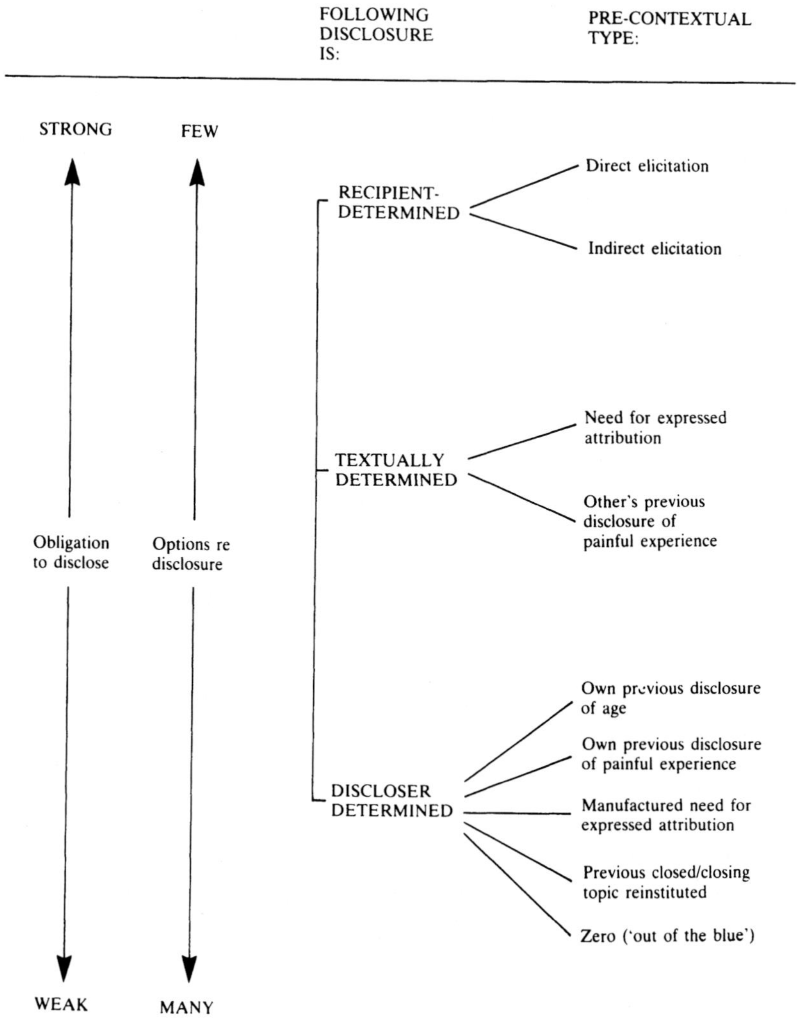

Figure 6.2a Precontexts

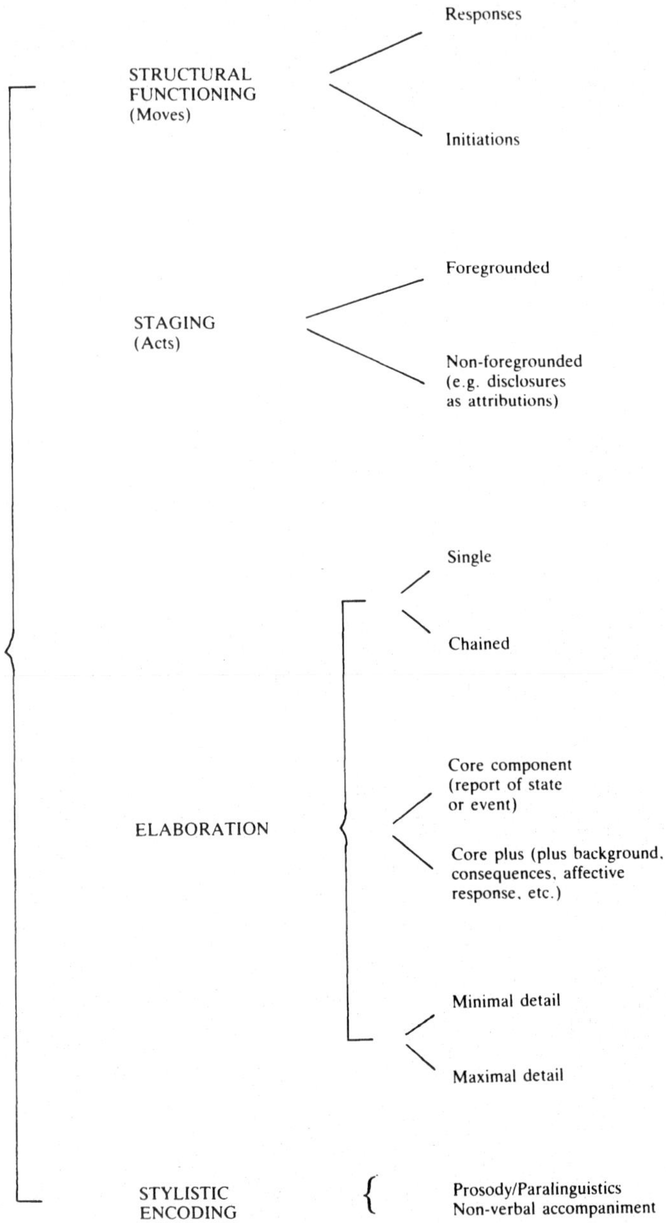

Figure 6.2b Modes of disclosure

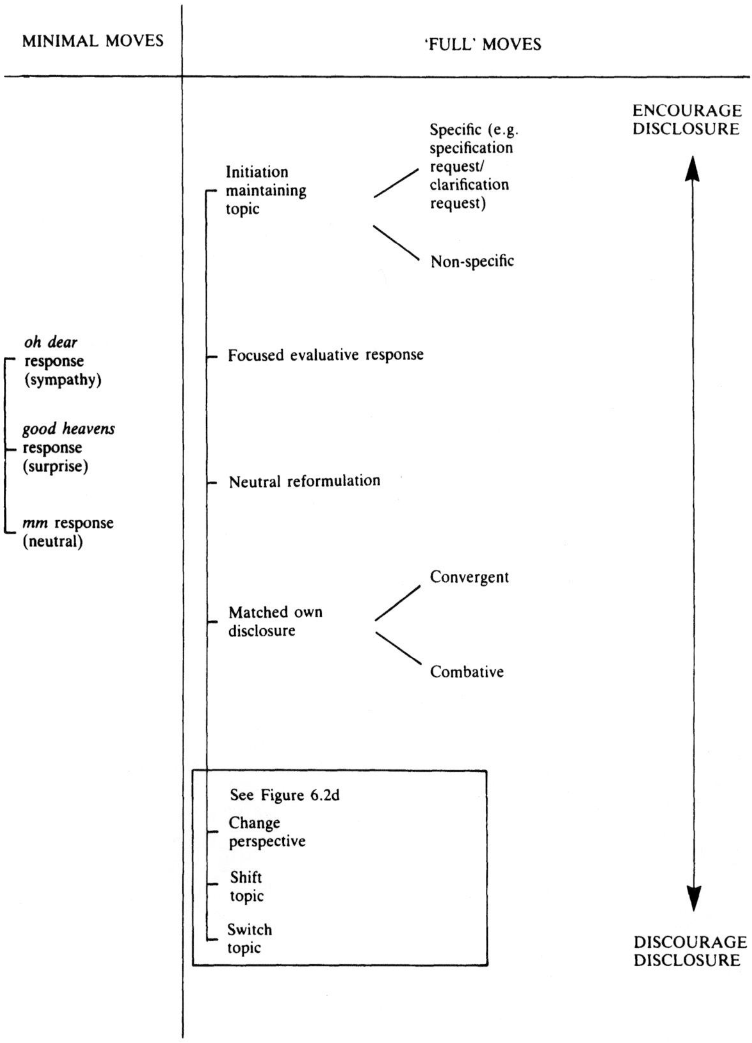

Figure 6.2c Recipient next-moves

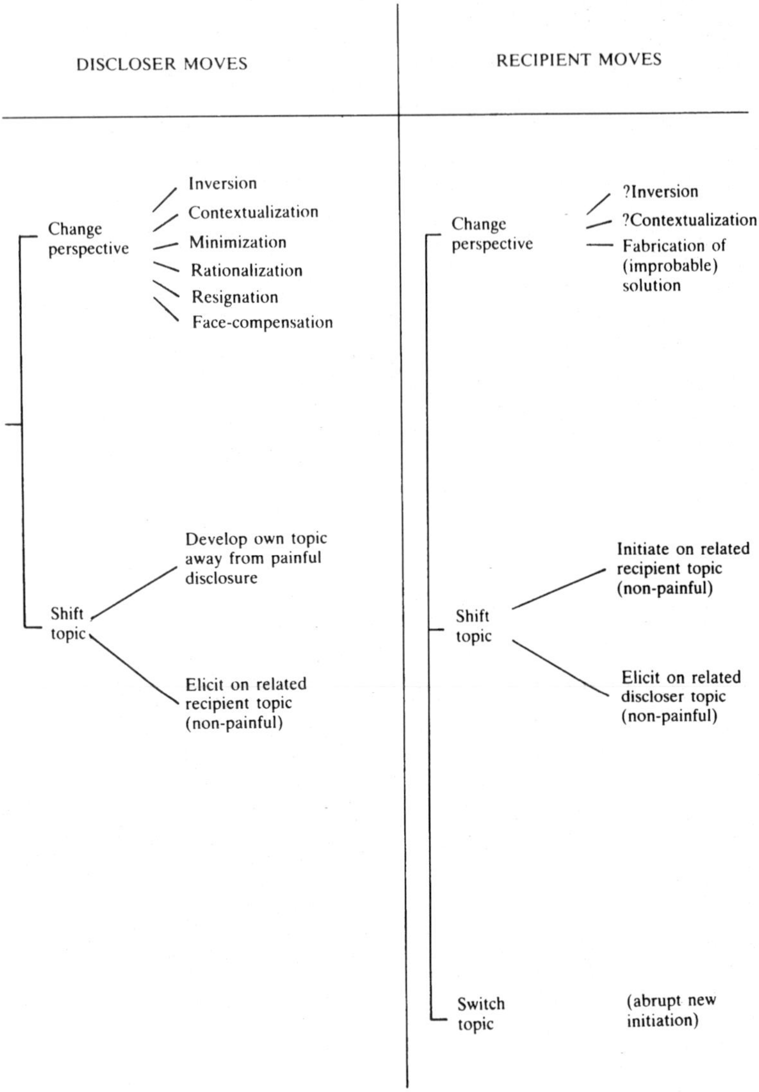

Figure 6.2d Moves towards closing

References

Atkinson, J.M. and Heritage, J. (eds) (1984) *Structures of Social Action: Studies in Conversation Analysis*, Cambridge, Cambridge University Press.

Bell, A. (1984) 'Language Style as Audience Design', *Language in Society* 13(2), 145–204.

Berger, C.R. and Bradac, J.S. (1982) *Sequence and Pattern in Communicative Behaviour*, London, Edward Arnold.

Braithwaite, V.A. (1986) 'Old Age Stereotypes: Reconciling Contradictions', *Journal of Gerontology* 41(3), 353–60.

Branco, K.J. and Williamson, J.B. (1982) 'Stereotyping and the Life-Cycle: Views of Ageing and the Aged' in A.G. Miller (ed.), *In the Eye of the Beholder: Contemporary Issues in Stereotyping*, New York, Praeger, 364–410.

Brown, P. and Levinson, S. (1987) *Politeness: Some Universals in Language Usage*, Cambridge, Cambridge University Press.

Brubaker, T.H. and Powers, E.A. (1976) 'The Stereotype of "Old": A Review and Alternative Approach', *Journal of Gerontology* 31(4), 441–7.

Coates, J. (1986) *Women, Men and Language*, London, Longman.

Coulmas, F. (1981) *Conversational Routine: Explorations in Standardized Communication Situations and Prepatterned Speech*, The Hague, Mouton.

Coupland, J., Coupland, N., Giles, H. and Wiemann, J. (1988) 'My Life in Your Hands: Processes of Self-disclosure in Intergenerational Talk' in N. Coupland (ed.), *Styles of Discourse*, London, Croom Helm, 201–53.

Coupland, N. (1988) (ed.) *Styles of Discourse*, London, Croom Helm.

Coupland, N. and Coupland, J. (forthcoming) 'Language and Later Life' in H. Giles and P. Robinson (eds), *Handbook of Language and Social Psychology*, London, Wiley.

Coupland, N., Coupland, J. *et al.* (forthcoming) *Age-Identity and the Management of Age-Disclosure in Intergenerational Talk.*

Coupland, N., Coupland, J., Giles, H. and Henwood, K. (1988) 'Accommodating the Elderly: Invoking and Extending a Theory', *Language in Society* 17.

Coupland, N., Coupland, J., Giles, H., Henwood, K. and Wiemann, J. (submitted) 'Elderly Self-Disclosure: Interactional and Intergroup Issues'.

Coupland, N., Giles, H. and Wiemann, J. (forthcoming) *Handbook of Miscommunication and Problematic Talk*, Clevedon, Multilingual Matters.

Giles, H. (1984) (ed.) *The Dynamics Of Speech Accommodation*, *International Journal of the Sociology of Language* 46, Amsterdam, Mouton.

Giles, H., Coupland, N. and Coupland, J. (eds) (forthcoming) *Contexts of Accommodation: Developments In Applied Sociolinguistics*, Cambridge, Cambridge University Press.

Giles, H., Mulac., A, Bradac, J.J. and Johnson, P. (1987) 'Speech Accommodation Theory: The First Decade and Beyond' in M.L. McLaughlin (ed.) *Communication Yearbook 10*, Beverly Hills, California, Sage, 13–48.

Giles, H. and Powesland, P.F. (1975) *Speech Style and Social Evaluation*, London, Academic Press.

Gumperz, J.J. (1982) *Discourse Strategies*, Cambridge, Cambridge University Press.

Henwood, K.L. (1986) 'The Social Psychology of Stereotypes: A Critical Assessment', unpublished PhD Thesis, Bristol.

Holmes, J. (1984) 'Hedging Your Bets and Sitting on the Fence: Some Evidence for Hedges as Support Structures', *Te Reo* 27, 47–62.

Jefferson, G. (1984) 'On the Organisation of Laughter in Talk about Troubles' in Atkinson and Heritage (eds), op. cit. 346–69.

Jefferson, G. (1984) 'On the Organisation of Laughter in Talk about Troubles' in Atkinson and Heritage (eds), *Structures of Social Action: Studies in Conversation Analysis*, Cambridge, Cambridge University Press, 346–69.

McTavish, D.G. (1971) 'Perceptions of Old People: A Review of Research Methodologies and Findings', *The Gerontologist* 11, 90–101.

Montgomery, M. (1988) 'D-J Talk' in N. Coupland (ed.) *Styles of Discourse*, London, Croom Helm, 85–104.

Rozencrantz, H.A. and McNevin, T.E. (1969) 'A Factor Analytic Analysis of Attitudes Toward the Aged', *The Gerontologist* 9, 55–9.

Sigall, H. and Page R. (1971) 'Current Stereotypes: A Little Fading, a Little Faking', *Journal of Personality and Social Psychology* 18(2), 247–55.

Wiemann, J., Coupland, N., Giles, H., Rowlands, P., Henwood, K. and Coupland, J. (1987) 'Beliefs about Talk: Intergenerational Perspectives', paper presented at the Speech Communication Association Convention, Boston, Masssachusetts, November.

Chapter seven

The interpreter as listener: an observation of response in the oral mode of translating

Ian Mason

Introduction

In the written mode of translating, the translator's response to a source-language text (ST) is subject to all kinds of modifications before it appears in the form of a target-language text (TT); re-reading of ST, matching of ST message with 'world knowledge', re-formulation of TT in accordance with the translator's writing skills and awareness of target language text norms, judgements of the effect of particular TT forms on TT readership, etc. For all of these reasons it is difficult to perceive the translator's immediate response during the reading process. It is posited here that in the oral mode of translating generally known as simultaneous interpreting, where the translator's response is immediate, what we hear if we tune into the translator's output is much closer to being a reflection of the listening process. A comparison of several interpreters' output from the same ST may provide evidence of differences in the 'text world' of the interpreters as listeners.

The mechanics of simultaneous translation[1]

A brief description of the mechanics of the exercise will suffice for our purposes here; fuller descriptions of what simultaneous translation involves are available in, e.g., Gerver (1976), Goldman-Eisler (1980), Lederer (1981). The typical situation is that of the conference theatre equipped with sound-proof booths for translators. Speakers' ('Orators') output is relayed to the booths where the translator ('Interpreter') listens through headphones and concurrently utters a translation which is then relayed back to the auditorium where conference participants ('Audience') can listen to it by tuning into the translator's channel on a specially provided receiver. As many languages can be catered for as there are booths and translators, so that the audience may comprise participants listening directly to the floor in language A, others listening to a TT in language B, others in language C, others alternating between several output sources, and so on. But the responses of the audience as listeners, although an intrinsically interesting subject of study (e.g. the matching of Orator's paralinguistic features with delayed TT output), is not at issue here. Our precise concern in this contribution is, as outlined above, the response of the translator as listener.

Relevant features of simultaneous translation

A number of factors impose constraints upon the particular type of listening activity involved in simultaneous translation. They can be listed as follows:

Divided attention

Speaking at the same time as O(rator), I(nterpreter) has to run several processing activities concurrently. In addition to processing current input (ST signal), s/he has to translate the immediately previous input, encode output and monitor current production (TT signal). Time available for evaluative/reflective listening is thus curtailed.

Ear-Voice Span

The necessary time lag between reception of ST and production of TT is generally known as the Ear-Voice Span (EVS – see Gerver, etc.) and is said to vary between two seconds and ten seconds approximately, depending on individual style, on syntactic complexity of input and on language combination. Variations in EVS can, of course, be taken as a rough measure of the size of the stretch of discourse currently being processed. In general terms, the shorter the EVS, the closer will the translation adhere to the form of ST. The correspondence is however not absolute. But whereas EVS is at least measurable, the length of text being processed at any given time during written translation is not observable in the same way.

Participants in the speech event

In the particular kind of speech event under consideration, there are no interlocutors as such and there is no face-to-face interaction. In effect, the relevant features of the situation are that

> 'I' is able to see 'O' but 'O' does not (in general) see 'I';
> 'I' is able to see 'A' but 'A' does not (in general) see 'I'.

It will be seen that, defined as such, certain features of simultaneous translating are akin to those of communication by telephone. But there are important differences; crucially, 'I' cannot communicate with 'O' nor 'A' with 'I' so that there is no opportunity for conversational repair mechanisms in the sense of requests for clarification or repetition, etc. (cf. Levinson, 1983, 339). First-time comprehension of ST input is therefore at a premium.

Further, speeches for simultaneous translation tend to be of a particular kind. In many cases (although not in committee work), the mode of ST will be written-to-be-read aloud and the propositional content will be non-trivial with sustained and planned development of a single topic. Delivery will of course be affected by whether ST is spontaneous speech or written text and may even be influenced by the fact that the text is to be simultaneously translated. But it will not be affected by the pressures of face-to-face interaction. Indeed, the interpreter as listener is in a totally different situation from that of the participant in conversation who negotiates meaning with an interlocutor. The situation is more akin to that of listening to a briefing without any opportunity for interrupting, asking questions, etc.

Motivated listening

An entailment of the above is that the simultaneous translator cannot be a *selective listener*, as can the participant in casual conversational exchange. A response will be required to the entirety of ST and not merely to interesting aspects of it. However, this requirement for evenness of monitoring has to be understood in the light of what we know about the physiology of listening; as McGregor and White put it:

> Recent research into the physiology of listening establishes that we do not simply 'hear' all the sounds generated by others

> because of the complexity of the auditory system which is always selecting, sifting, making sense of and interpreting a wide variety of accoustic signals. (1986, 1)

In this sense, the simultaneous translator will use cues for comprehension and anticipate forthcoming input in the same way as other listeners do (and the translator's output will sometimes provide evidence of such anticipation – see Seleskovitch, 1976, 104). The creative role of the interpreter-as-listener will be constrained but not impaired.

Continuous response

A further concomitant of the situation is that, given the requirement of divided attention and immediacy of response, the simultaneous translator concentrates on processing only current input. In other words, there is likely to be less matching of current input with prior text-presented knowledge[2] than is the case in other forms of discourse processing such as listening to monologue or, particularly, reading. Whereas co-textual cues do form an important part of the translator's interpretation of text, preference is probably granted to the immediate pre-text over earlier text segments. In this respect, it would be interesting to make a study of simultaneous translators' recall of input immediately after performance. de Beaugrande and Dressler (1981, 195) report the results of an experiment in which participants were required to 'listen to or read a text and then to recall the content', so that the 'systematic pattern of additions, omissions, and changes manifested in their reports' could be studied as evidence of the listening/reading process: inferencing, building a 'text-world model', matching current input against 'stored world-knowledge', etc. The scope for empirical studies of this natúre in the domain of simultaneous translation is apparent (for one such study, see Gerver, 1972).

Background knowledge

Precisely because of the requirement of immediate output and the reduced scope for mature reflection on the relevance to current processing of previous text segments, the need to be able to activate relevant patterns of stored knowledge is crucial to the simultaneous translator. Acquisition of such relevant contextual knowledge is thus an important part of translator training and an essential part of the conference interpreter's preparation for work. In particular, it constitutes a central factor in the creation of listener meaning, knowledge activated for the purpose of constructing a text-world model to serve as the basis for TT output.

Characterization of the listener

It will be appreciated from what precedes that the simultaneous translator constitutes a special category of listener. The data to be presented in the pilot study that follows is characteristic of the mode of discourse in which the conference interpreter normally operates: that of formal monologue within a one-to-many addresser/addressee framework. As such, the data is quite unlike the informal conversational data of most empirical studies of speaker/listener strategies. As Milroy notes,

> Interlocutors in unplanned discourse have a range of strategies for monitoring comprehension, for clarifying and for repairing mistakes and misunderstandings as they follow the facial, gestural and interjectional cues which accompany interactions. Constant repetition and repair are important components of communication in context. (1986, 18–19)

In these circumstances, responsive listening involves not only the construction of a text-world through conversational inferencing but also the active negotiation of meaning between interlocutors. In our own case, on the other hand, the interpreter/listener's audible response is not one of interaction but rather of *sympathetic impersonation*. In other words, 'I' will seek to relay to 'A' a faithful version of 'O's text-world, mediated through 'I's own listening process. Moreover, in terms of the categories of listener proposed in McGregor (1986, 59), following Goffman, the simultaneous translator is in some sense a *ratified participant* not specifically addressed by the speaker; but in another sense, s/he is an *overhearer*, physically isolated from the speech situation, and able to engage, within the limits suggested above, in a certain amount of evaluative listening.

The data

In the remainder of this article, we wish tentatively to suggest a way in which empirical study may be used to test the initial hypothesis, namely, that the output of the simultaneous translator may provide evidence of the listening process and that comparison of several different outputs from the same ST will evince the construction of different text-world models by different listeners. For the data on which this pilot study is based I am greatly indebted to my colleague Janet Altman. It consists of the recorded and transcribed output of five trainee interpreters from each of five French ST speeches and was originally collected in order to serve as the basis for a study in error analysis to be published in due course. The value of this data lies in the opportunity it provides for comparison of several different outputs from the same ST and in the fact that, being trainees, the subjects are more prone to error than professionals would be; as Milroy (1986) posits, the study of breakdown may throw light on what is actually going on when communication is successful.[3] But this pilot study is not concerned with interpreters' *errors* as such; rather, given the objective of 'sympathetic impersonation' suggested above, we are looking for evidence of *interpretation* of ST in the sense of inferencing, etc.

Naturally, the empirical evidence is subject to certain kinds of interference. First, the translation process itself involves linguistic reformulation, which may in itself lead to a less-than-perfect representation of *what the listener takes speaker meaning to be*; in other words, output may not wholly reflect the listener's mental image of ST meaning. Second, the process of self-monitoring and auto-correction of output by 'I' means that the latter can, as it were, cover his/her traces as a listener; the listener's initial mental representation of speaker meaning is subject to modification for the purposes of, e.g., improvement in the quality of TT expression or revision of initial interpretation of speaker meaning. But the latter is part of the process of responsive listening. Moreover, unlike written translation output, simultaneous output will often show up this revision process since, in revising, the simultaneous translator cannot erase or 'cross out' what has already been said. Evidence of responsive listening is thus to be found in hesitations, false starts, corrections, etc. Third, it is of course the case that differences in listeners' text-world model are not the same as differences in their model of the real world, a construct which pre-exists the utterance of ST. But, as suggested above, the process of matching current input against the real-world model should, in the case of a competent translator, condition the construction of a text-world; and it is evidence of this that we are seeking. For the simultaneous translator, the 'line of least resistance' is the calque, an adherence to the lexical and syntactic form of ST, with minimal concessions to TT norms or to representation of speaker meaning. In the output of trainees, the calque tends to occur whenever processing tasks are too burdensome. Regarded as preferable to breakdown, it enables processing to continue in the hope of 'clearing the channel' for what is to come next. The calque however masks evidence of the listening process – or indeed, provides evidence that creative listening is not taking place, is being crowded out by other processing activities. But at points where ST is *inexplicit* or otherwise elliptical, the translator is often obliged to be *explicit* in order to ensure continuity of sense in TT; in other words, s/he is forced into text-world construction. Such instances proved to be the most fruitful source of evidence of the listening process in the data studied.

Analysis

The transcribed data were scanned for evidence of creative listening processes. The examples which follow are illustrative of the various categories perceived. (A fragment of ST is given first in each case, followed by the corresponding output of several trainees, labelled for convenience a, b, c, etc.)

(1) il existe des régions entières de la Communauté dont les routes, par exemple, sont financées par les credits du FEDER

a. entire regions within the Community whose roads have been financed by allocations from the ERDF

b. entire regions within the Community where roads, for example, are built enti. . . and maintained entirely by Community funds

In (1), the segment *routes . . . financées* is inexplicit in that it is not clear exactly what is being financed. Whereas (1a) passes on the non-explicitness, in (1b) we find evidence of the listening process at work; a model is constructed (presumably by activating the world-knowledge frame [EEC regional funding]), in which the money is provided for *building* roads. This model is then found to be untenable (entirely? all roads?), again by appeal to knowledge of the way the world works, and consequently modified to include *maintenance*. Thus the translator as 'sympathetic impersonator' works beyond the inexplicitness of the encoded message (ST) towards a representation of speaker meaning. In this example as in others, it is not of course the historical facts (of Community funding, etc.) which are at stake but rather the listener's interpretation of what was intended.

(2) Je rappellerai que, de 1980 à 1984, la proportion des chômeurs de longue durée est passée, selon les pays membres, de 17 à 46 pour cent en 1980, et de 27 à 59 pour cent en 1984. Je dois, pour être honnête, dire qu'un seul pays échappe à des chiffres aussi impressionnants; c'est le Danemark qui ne compte que 6 per cent de chômeurs de longue durée

a. . . . this country only had 6 per cent of long-term unemployed people

b. . . . which only has 6 per cent long-term unemployed people

c. . . . which with only 6 per cent o. . . long-term unemployed is the only country . . .

d. . . . which has only 6 per cent of, um, the population as long-term unemployed

e. where only 6 per cent of the employed . . . unemployed are long-term unemployed

A notorious problem for simultaneous translators is the expression of percentage figures whose terms are not clearly stated. In French, the problem can be compounded by the linguistic similarity, but crucial semantic distinction, between, e.g. *6 pour cent de chômeurs/6 pour cent des chômeurs*. In such circumstances, inferencing is bound to occur – except where, as mentioned earlier, the burden of other processing tasks temporarily overwhelms responsive listening. (2a) and (2c) above show evidence of this; while (2a) is merely a calque – producing in this case an unsatisfactory TT rendering – (2c) narrowly avoids it but, in common with (2b), presents the information as non-problematic, thus passing on to the receiver of TT the onus of interpreting what are the terms of the percentage figure. This is of course not to say that inferencing has not taken place: there is no mechanism which determines that mental processes are necessarily encoded in text. But (2d) and (2e) are interesting in that they do show evidence of listening processes at work. In (2d), the audible hesitation ('um') is evidence of the listener's need to include the terms of the percentage in his text-world model. Hearer meaning is then directly attested in 'the population'. Evidence for this solution is not forthcoming from co-text as transcribed in (2): there is no suggestion that percentages of population are being considered. It is more likely that stored knowledge of the world is at play here. The relevant knowledge frame might be (unemployment in EEC countries), known to include such figures as 10 per cent or 12 per cent, say, of the population. Within this frame, a figure of 6 per cent for long-term unemployed might not seem unreasonable. Matching of text-presented knowledge against world-knowledge takes place and the result is deemed satisfactory for immediate processing purposes. (2e) also entertains this interpretation – or something similar to it – with '6 per cent of the employed'; but here, matching against either text-model (previous percentages of, e.g., 59 per cent could not possibly have been in terms of the employed) or world-model (6 per cent of the employed is perhaps not exceptionally low) causes a re-interpretation. The result ('6 per cent of the unemployed are long-term unemployed') is found to be consistent with the listener's text-world and real-world models and processing proceeds.

It will be appreciated that these accounts of appeal to world knowledge and to text-world models are, of necessity, speculative: we have no direct access to listeners' mental processes. That such construction of meaning takes place however can hardly be in doubt. Examples (3) and (4) provide further evidence.

(3) . . . ces pays, de taille plus petite, ont eu une tradition d'expatriement de leurs chercheurs, de leurs savants . . .

a. expatriation . . .
b. exporting . . .
c. brain drain . . .
d. a sort of migration . . .

(4) . . . il y a eu une discussion sur le chômage. . . . La Commission a été chargée de faire une étude sur les phénomènes d'économie submergée et de travail au noir . . .

a. the black market
b. black market labour
c. black workers

In each case, solution c. appears to be the result of activation of stored world-knowledge. The fact that (3c) is entirely appropriate while (4c) is denotationally inaccurate need not bother us here; in both cases, the problematic ST item has been instinctively linked to a familiar world-knowledge frame. In (4c), it would appear to be a case of association, within the [unemployment] frame, of the problem itself with those notoriously affected by it.

As for evidence of matching against previous text-presented knowledge, J. Altman's study shows how previous exposure to the frame [*Committee on Energy, Research and Technology*] ensured that all interpreters in the group, on hearing at a later stage *la commission de l'énergie et des technologies nouvelles*, re-introduced the item 'research' – a case of listeners hearing or interpreting what they automatically expect to hear.

Example (5) presents further evidence of the *non-explicit* > *explicit* category but also shows how listeners search for key words to aid interpretation.

(5) L'autre difficulté tient au retard quantitatif

a. The other difficulty is more quantitative in nature
b. The other difficulty is . . . concerns quantitative matters
c. The other difficulty regards quantities . . . quantitative contributions
d. The other difficulty regards . . . the lower level of spending, the quantitative . . . amount with which these countries are now lagging behind
e. The second difficulty is the amount . . . of ground that we have to make up in terms of R and D spending

(5) represents a complete sentence on its own, so that in order to make sense of *retard quantitatif*, the listener is compelled to relate it to the immediately preceding co-text to which it is cohesively related:

Nous sommes confrontés à une insuffisance quant à la participation, la contribution à l'effort de recherche scientifique dans ces deux pays, et c'est véritablement un handicap pour apprécier l'apport de chacun de ces deux pays

The processing difficulties involved in this scanning of previous text input are reflected in the hesitation displayed by each of (5b–e) at this particular juncture. Now, it is interesting to note that (5d) and (5e), relating incoming data to the overall topic of the text-model they have constructed, both feel the need to make the link explicit in their output. But the text worlds are not identical for each of the two listeners: the shift in perspective ('we' vs. 'these countries') reveals a difference of hearer meaning not so much at this particular juncture of ST as at the level of the text-world model as a whole, involving perception of ST producer's attitude towards his topic. Once again, it is the point at which ST is non-explicit or involves a level of abstraction that brings the simultaneous translator to reveal evidence of the listening process. Moreover, there is evidence that the complexity of the processing tasks involved here in the time available leads listeners to give priority to certain incoming information over other items. Faced with the pair *retard quantitatif*, it seems significant that all five interpreters perceived/reported the item *quantitatif* while only two (5d and 5e) reflect *retard* in their output. In the absence of systematic evidence, one can only speculate on the reasons for the selection of the qualifier over the head word; a possible explanation would have to do with what is perceived as 'new' as opposed to 'given' information. (Previous text had referred to a deficit on the part of the countries concerned without actually using the item *retard*). But the scope for further empirical research is again apparent; the regularity of such procedures should be amenable to testing.

In addition to key concepts and lexical networks, the listener's text world will also include indications of the pragmatic focus which emerges as ST unfolds. Awareness of the dominant contextual focus (cf. Werlich, 1976, 39) can be an invaluable aid to the interpretation of incoming text, as Example (6) illustrates:

(6) C'est une bonne orientation. Il faut la mener à bien.

a. This is an important point and we must carry it through

b. This is a good, um, orientation . . . and will be successful

c. This is a . . . good programme and we must . . . put it to good use

d. This is a *good* and positive direction in which to move, we must make *sure* that we make definite progress

[NB – in (6d), italic denotes emphasis.[4]]

On the criterion of a current-input-only translation, it is apparent that (6b) is in error. But the sensitive listener relies here not only on the current text item *il faut* for a deontic interpretation but also on the emergent dominant illocutionary force of ST as a whole. The prevalence of such items as *il nous faut, doit, nous devons donc, prenons donc conscience*, etc. establish beyond doubt the hortative nature of speaker meaning. (6a and 6c) have no doubt picked up this intentionality but it is (6d) who, by positive emphasis in his TT output, provides direct evidence of the responsive listening process.

Finally, the creative role of the listener can occasionally be perceived when the ST speaker employs metaphor (or when an opportunity for metaphor in TT arises). It must be remembered that the simultaneous translator's response has to be immediate,

EVS being no longer than a few seconds. In these circumstances, the translator often resorts to a calque, which may be more or less appropriate to context; but the substitution of an equivalent metaphor not infrequently provides a fleeting insight into the listener's text world. Examples (7), (8) and (9) illustrate the process.

(7) Nous sommes à un tournant

a. We are at a watershed

(8) Là encore les vrais progrès seront difficiles

a. In this area once again, we have a stony road ahead of us

(9) . . . des pays tels que l'Espagne et le Portugal, à moindre titre la Grèce, servent en quelque sorte de chevaux de Troie de la pénétration technologique . . .

a. . . . could serve as a springboard for other countries to penetrate . . . (the European market)

Again, the felicity of (7a–9a) is not at issue: rather, it is the immediate response of the translator seeking, as suggested earlier, to be a 'sympathetic impersonator', which shows the listener at work. In simultaneous translating, the listener is often induced to provide evidence of the listening process in ways which differ from the processes of conversational interaction.

Summary and conclusion

The data which served as the basis for this pilot study of the role of the simultaneous translator as listener have yielded evidence of some ways in which listeners, in their interpretation of speaker meaning, build their own text-world model; the process of inferencing involved in this relies on both co-textual cues and the activation of relevant patterns of stored world-knowledge. Evidence of these processes at work was perceptible when the translator (i) revised his/her initial response, often with signs of hesitation, or (ii) offered an explicit response to non-explicit ST input or (iii) used figurative or metaphorical expression in response to some ST concept or expression. In some cases, erroneous or otherwise inadequate translation was also traced to the listening process.

It does seem that there is enough evidence here to warrant a proper empirical study of the role of the interpreter as listener. As it stands, the pilot study is unsatisfactory in a number of ways.

The samples quoted from the data were given here for purposes of illustration and constitute much less than a complete listing of all instances observable in the data as a whole. Moreover, the database itself is far too small for any emerging trends to be treated as a systematic indication of the types and degree of inferencing involved in the listening process. Using the facilities of the interpreting laboratory with its multiple translator booths, it would be possible to gather data on a systematic basis, providing for comparison of many simultaneous TT outputs from the same ST. Even with such a corpus of material, however, the analyst would encounter serious problems which have not been resolved here. They have to do with the fact that the process of inferencing is not wholly separable from the translator's processing and monitoring of TT output; the translator is both listener and speaker, and it is the results of the latter process which provide the only available data for studying the listening process. And of course, inferencing is taking place all the time in language processing, whereas only occasionally is evidence of it available in TT output; much more of the listening process is hidden from the analyst. In the study of any particular sample, the exact role of listening will be difficult to determine. Nevertheless, the comparison of output by several translators from the same ST stimulus does provide evidence of differences of interpretation; experiments might be set up to test response to specific categories of ST input (varying degrees of incoherence or inconsistency, varying levels of abstractness) or to match actual output against translators' post facto recall of the meaning of ST. In ways such as these, it is hoped that the study of simultaneous translation may be able to contribute in some way to our understanding of the active role of the listener.

Notes

1. The term 'simultaneous trranslation' is preferred here to the usual term 'interpretation' for the sake of clarity. The latter term may of course refer to the overall translation process (as in, say, 'conference interpreting') or it may refer to that part of the whole process generally known as 'comprehension'. Following Green and Morgan (1981, 177), we prefer the term 'interpretation' to 'comprehension' since it better reflects the creative role of the listener and avoids the view of ST as a 'message to be decoded', as if there could be some kind of 100 per cent decoding of a perfectly encoded message.
2. Cf. de Beaugrande and Dressler (1981, 202–4). The terms 'text-presented knowledge', 'world knowledge', although convenient, are strictly speaking unsatisfactory in that knowledge implies facts; in the

model of language processing subscribed to here however, language users' experience of the world about them is seen as a social construct. 'World meaning' is something we create rather than something which pre-exists.

3. Lederer (1981, 88) adopts a similar view. The results of her empirical study of interpreters' output show how auditory cues are used for constructing a message – a process which she calls *la suppléance mentale*. But the process is most apparent when errors are committed: 'on détecte plus facilement la suppléance lorsqu'il survient des erreurs car on peut alors retracer le raisonnement qui, à partir de quelques indices, a engendré l'énoncé faux'.
4. Since intonation patterns and emphasis may provide important clues to the listener meaning of the translator, a properly constituted corpus for sociolinguistic study of the output of simultaneous translators would need to incorporate a satisfactory form of notation for such features, as well as for audible hesitation ('um') and timing of pauses.

References

de Beaugrande, R. and W. Dressler (1981) *Introduction to Text Linguistics*, London, Longman.

Brislin, R. (1976) (ed.) *Translation. Applications and Research*, New York, Gardner.

Gerver, D. (1972) *Simultaneous and Consecutive Interpretation and Human Information Processing*, London, Social Science Research Council Research Report, HR 566/1.

Gerver, D. (1976) 'Empirical Studies of Simultaneous Interpretation: A Review and a Model' in R. Brislin (ed.) *Translation, Applications and Research*, New York, Gardner, 165–207.

Goldman-Eisler, F. (1980) 'Psychological Mechanisms of Speech Production as Studied Through the Analysis of Simultaneous Translation' in B. Butterworth (ed.) *Language Production, 1: Speech and Talk*, New York, Academic Press, 143–54.

Green, G. and Morgan, J. (1981) 'Pragmatics, Grammar and Discourse' in Cole, P. (ed.) *Radical Pragmatics*, New York, Academic Press, 167–81.

Lederer, M. (1981) *La Traduction simultanée*, Paris, Minard.

Levinson, S. (1983) *Pragmatics*, Cambridge, Cambridge University Press.

McGregor, G. (1986) 'Listening Outside the Participation Framework' in G. McGregor and R.S. White (eds), *The Art of Listening*, London, Croom Helm, 55–72.

McGregor, G. and White, R.S. (1986) (eds) *The Art of Listening*, London, Croom Helm.

Milroy, L. (1986) 'Comprehension and Context: Successful Communication and Communicative Breakdown' in G. McGregor and R.S. White (eds), *The Art of Listening*, 17–42.

Seleskovitch, D. (1976) *Interpretation, A Psychological Approach to Translation* in R. Brislin (ed.), 92–116.
Werlich, E. (1976) *A Text Grammar of English*, Heidelberg, Quelle and Meyer.

Chapter eight

Responsive listening as part of religious rhetoric: the case of black pentecostal preaching

Christine Callender and Deborah Cameron

> We say to you, perfect yourselves in oratory, cultivate all the fields of knowledge, make your sermon mentally and rhetorically all it ought to be (C.H. Spurgeon).

Introduction

Ritual speech events, including religious ceremonies, have long been among the major concerns of anthropologists and ethnographers of speaking, especially those working in traditional societies and so-called 'exotic' cultures. Less attention has been paid to this whole area by sociolinguists and discourse analysts investigating language use in urban western contexts. In this paper, we bring the methodologies of speech ethnography and conversation analysis to bear on a phenomenon so far little-studied, at least in Britain: the language of Black Pentecostal preaching.[1] We will argue that both methodologies are appropriate, because the religious rhetoric of Black Pentecostals can be related on one hand to general patterns of Black verbal culture, and on the other, to the sort of conversational organization recently identified in secular forms of rhetoric, especially political oratory. We will further argue that from either point of view, the role of the listener emerges as crucial in structuring the overall performance of preaching.[2]

Data for this analysis were audio-recorded over a period of several weeks at two Pentecostal assemblies in London, C. Temple and K. Temple, which had previously been approached for permission to conduct research.[3] There are important differences between the two Temples. K. Temple, located in a prosperous area of London, is part of the 'moderate' Elim Pentecostal movement which avoids the more 'extreme' or unorthodox modes of worship. It meets in a very large, rather impersonal building and attracts a multiracial, upwardly mobile congregation. C. Temple, by contrast, is a smaller and more traditional assembly. It is situated in a working-class, inner city area, and its members are predominantly working class West Indian women.

Both Temples did in fact make regular recordings of their meetings as a form of 'tape ministry', so participants were accustomed to the presence of audio equipment and we had no difficulty obtaining consent to our using recordings for research purposes. All the meetings where recordings were made were also attended by Christine Callender (who as a member of the Afro-Caribbean community in South London had ties of kin and friendship with practising Pentecostals). Callender noted contextual information to go alongside the recorded data, and was able where necessary to follow up points in conversation with participants and with the Pastor at C. Temple. Recordings were transcribed using a notation adapted from Atkinson, 1984; the main symbols are shown below.

SYMBOL	EXPLANATION
CT	C Temple
KT	K Temple
C[ongregation]	All those present in the church excluding the Preacher.
M[ember]	A member of the church.
P[reacher]	------------
E[lder]	A senior member of the church.
T[estifier]	A person called upon to give testimony.
XXXXXXXXXXXXXXX	Loud applause.
xxxxxxxxxxxxxxx	Quiet applause.
XXXXxxxxxxxXXXX	Applause amplitude increases/decreases.
-x-x-x-x-x-x-x-	Isolated clap/spasmodic clapping.

|----(8.0)----|	Duration of applause from onset to nearest tenth of a second.
P: One step to [day [One step	Continuation of talk through and beyond overlapping talk.
pol ↑ itically and ↑ morally ↓ bankrupt	Upward/downward pitch movement in immediately following particle.
0.5 (.)	Numbers indicate pause lengths to nearest tenth of a second. Dot indicates a micro-pause.
I *say* to ↑ *YOU*	Capital letters indicate more loudly spoken particles. <u>Underlining</u> indicates extra emphasis.

Preaching as a form of interactive discourse

The language of sermons and testimony may seem, on the face of it, an unpromising topic for the linguist interested in the role of the listener. In British culture, preaching is commonly assumed to be a non-interactive performance in which one dominant speaker's discourse is passively attended to by a silent congregation who have few opportunities to display listening activity even through the limited 'affiliative responses' permitted by other types of public rhetoric (such as clapping, cheering, heckling, etc.). But this is a narrow and ethnocentric view. It is contradicted by the practice of at least one religious group in Britain, namely Pentecostal Christians, especially those who belong to the many flourishing Afro-Caribbean churches.

Preaching and testimony in Black Pentecostal meetings are marked not by a respectful, attentive silence but by frequent interventions from members of the congregation as well as from the congregation acting as a body. To the outside observer, a recording of Pentecostal worship gives the impression at times of almost chaotic, random speech – much of it simultaneous or 'contrapuntal' (Reisman, 1974). It is clear, however, that the intervention of the congregation into the discourse of the preacher or testifier is highly valued. The Pastor of C. Temple explained that the sermon is 'a good way of inspiring people to action', by which he meant not only action in the outside world, but more immediately, participation in the sermon itself. Thus the power and success of preaching is measured in part by the strength of response it evokes.

Illustrations will demonstrate this point, and give something of the 'flavour' of the Pentecostal sermon with its constant interventions. We will begin with an extract from the K. Temple transcripts. Here congregational response was less in evidence than at the more traditional C. Temple, but on one occasion recorded by us, a visiting preacher exhorted those present to stronger and more frequent intervention. In this extract, some responses are spontaneously produced by members, while others are deliberately elicited by direct questions ('did you hear that?') and requests for a particular response ('how many can say Amen to that?')

<u>Extract one</u>

P: Obstacles and difficulty does not kill a Christian it solidifies him
M: Amen

P: Amen
M: Amen

P: Jesus did not come to make life easy but he has come to make champions out of difficulties
C: Amen

P: how many can say Amen to that [and make champions oh-h-h-h did you
C: Amen [XXXXXXXXXXX

P: hear that [Jesus have come to make a champion
M: [yes I heard you Amen
M: that's right

In the C. Temple by contrast direct elicitations were rare. A rhythm of interactive overlapping and simultaneous speech was often established, as in the following extract which demonstrates the way members become increasingly involved in the discourse.

Extract two

P: The Bible says God is not willing that any man should perish and all should come to repentanc [e pu [t on the
M 1: [Yes
M 2: [Amen

P: [be [st robe put a ring on his hand shoes on his feet (.)
M 2: [preach it
M 3: [Hallelujah Hallelujah Hallelujah

P: bring forth the fatted calf and kill it [let us have
M 1: [ye [s
M 2: [Amen

P: music [cause he who was dead is alive
M: [yes

On examination, extracts like one and two turn out to be highly organized rather than random or chaotic. The questions we wanted to examine concerned precisely this organization. How do listeners to a sermon or testimony make appropriate interventions at appropriate points? What is the effect of such interventions on the progress of the speech event? And at a deeper level of analysis, what shared norms and beliefs underlie or explain the interactive nature of Pentecostal preaching?

The organization of pentecostal preaching: a comparison with political oratory

In the last few years, the conversation analyst Max Atkinson has developed an analysis of political speech-making which places more stress than previous work on the contribution of the audience (Atkinson, 1984). Atkinson proposes that the usual conversational mechanism of turn-taking (Sacks *et al.*, 1978) is not absent from public speech events, but is rather adapted to different conditions. Whereas in ordinary talk, members are constantly attending because of the likelihood that a point will come when they may take or be allocated a turn, in political speeches the incentive to keep listening lies in the opportunity members have to make 'affiliative responses' such as clapping and cheering at appropriate points. Atkinson further proposes that the competent orator will signal appropriate points for audience response by using particular rhetorical devices such as two-part contrasts, three-part lists, the projection of names and intonational cues (1984, 49–83). If orators did not provide such signals, and listeners had not learned to orient to them, it would be difficult to co-ordinate collective responses like applause successfully.

Can this sort of analysis be applied to Pentecostal preaching? There is no incongruity in suggesting similarities between religious and political rhetoric, especially in the context of Black community norms. Atkinson comments on the borrowing of religious conventions by Black political orators, notably Dr Martin Luther King, while Geneva Smitherman (1980, 165) notes that 'black verbal style exists on a sacred-secular continuum'. C.H. Spurgeon, a writer on homiletics much respected by Pentecostalists, makes an explicit analogy between the skills required by the politician and the preacher; he asks, 'shall the representatives of the nation attain an expertness of speech beyond the representatives of the court of heaven?' (1976, 143). Bearing all this in mind, we set out to look for the rhetorical devices identified by Atkinson in the data from the two Pentecostal assemblies.

Contrasts and lists in Pentecostal preaching

The major rhetorical devices identified by Atkinson as 'clap-traps' to which listeners respond with applause are two-part contrasts and three-part lists. These do indeed turn up in the sermons we analysed.

An example of a two-part contrast cited by Atkinson is the following, from the UK General Election campaign of 1983:

MRS THATCHER: which example will be most likely to make it
pause (0.7)

1 {the renunciation of the means of national of self defence (0.4) which the banners of Faslane and Greenham call for (0.7)

2 {or the swift and sure response of our young [men in the south Atlantic] just a year ago

AUDIENCE: [x-xxXXXXXXXXXXXXX]
---------------(8.0)---------------

(Atkinson, 1984, 75).

We found comparable contrasts in the Pentecostal data. For instance, extract one (above) contains two effective contrasts, each of which elicits a response of *Amen*:

P: 1 {Obstacles and difficulty does not kill a Christian

2 {it solidifies him

M: Amen

---

and

P: 1 {Jesus did not come to make life easy

2 {but he has come to make champions out of difficulties

C: Amen

(KT)

It seems that the contrast is an effective device in many different types of rhetorical performance.

Lists of three are very common in political speeches. Atkinson points out that three is the minimal number of elements which can properly constitute a list, and suggests that orators structure their points in threes for this reason. He gives examples like the following, again from the 1983 Tory campaign.

MR TEBBIT 1 ⟶ Labour will spend and spend
2 ⟶ and borrow and borrow
3 ⟶ and tax and tax

(Atkinson, 1984, 60)

We found the list of three occurred fairly regularly in the discourse of preachers. For example:

Extract three

P: 1 → Angel Michael did not go to the cross at Calvary
: 2 → Angel Michael did not go to Mount Calvary
: 3 → Angel Michael did not rise again

(KT)

Here the preacher actually makes the same point twice in order to end up with a list of three. Another example is this:

Extract four

T: Now the word repent means to have
1 ⟶ a change of heart
2 ⟶ a change of mind
3 ⟶ a change of direction

(CT)

But the pattern reported by Atkinson, whereby listeners wait for the completion of the three parts and then respond, was all but absent from our data. Neither of the above extracts elicited any response from the congregations to whom they were addressed. Sometimes, on the other hand, members would acknowledge each part of the list:

Extract five

1 → P: They can't see the goodness of God
M: Praise him

2 → P: And the joy in the presence of the Lord
M: Amen
praise him

3 → P: And the pleasures at his right hand
M: Amen

(CT)

In other words, it seems that listeners too participate in producing three part lists, rather than simply attending to them in the talk of preachers (cf. also the *Hallelujah* sequence produced by M 3 in extract two above).

Another common pattern was for members to respond at the point where the pattern of the list was broken:

Extract six

T: 1 ——→ I smoked
2 ——→ I swore
3 ——→ I committed fornication
You name it I done it
M: Yes

(CT)

Many of the lists in our data, whether or not they evoked a response, had more than three parts. For instance:

Extract seven

P: 1 ——→ God is looking for giant killers
2 ——→ God is looking for devil destroyers
3 ——→ God is looking for demon casters
4 ——→ God is looking for miracle workers
5 ——→ And God is still saying myself I bore on the tree what you couldn't have been able to bear yourself

(KT)

This extension of the three-part structure can be linked with a distinctive 'Black verbal style' which we discuss later on.

Atkinson's observations on political speechmaking had some utility in describing our data. But it was clear that our data were more complicated than Atkinson's in a number of ways. In political oratory there is a clear, two-level hierarchy, speaker: audience. The speaker speaks and cues collective responses, usually applause, from the audience as a whole. Occasionally an individual listener may initiate (e.g. by heckling) but this is regarded as a deviation from the norm. In Pentecostal preaching, by contrast, it is not always the whole congregation that responds: often it is an individual, and that individual may be responded to by another, and so on, producing the 'chaining' effect we see in the following extract:

Extract eight

P: Some people are prosperous and they say prosperity
  has killed more than adversity [so here he has money
M: [Y [es
M: [Yes
M: A [men
M: [praise the Lord

(CT)

Alternatively the listener's response may trigger a response from the original speaker, leading to a 'call and response' sequence inserted into the discourse, as we see in extract one above where a member's *Amen* is responded to by the preacher and produces a further response from the member.

Extract one

P: Obstacles and difficulty does not kill a Christian
  it solidifies him
M: Amen

P: Amen
M: Amen

The fairly orderly pattern of turn-taking described by Atkinson, where speakers' contributions are punctuated at predictable junctures by short periods of collective response breaks down in our data. Furthermore, the Pentecostal listeners have a much greater range of possible responses than the political audience's clapping and cheering. They use various expressions like *Amen*, *praise the Lord*, *Hallelujah*, *yes*, *that's right*, *preach it*, all conveying a specific meaning and message. How do listeners select and time the appropriate expression? It seems they must be using more varied and complex strategies than those described by Atkinson; and it also seems that they are less directly dependent on a small set of cues provided by the preacher. In other words, the relatively passive role Atkinson proposes for listeners (recognizing the right place to clap by using a restricted set of signals) has to be expanded in order to account for the organization displayed by sequences like those in extracts one and two above. To understand that organization fully we must place Pentecostal speech events in their religious and social context.

Pentecostal belief and its effects on discourse

The Pentecostalist movement is best described as a 'biblicistic-ecstatic' revival movement whose outstanding characteristic is the doctrine of spirit baptism manifested in 'glossolalia' (speaking in tongues). Its origins can be traced to the USA at the turn of the century, from where it spread all over the Christian world. In Britain its strongest base was in Wales until the 1950s.

The association of Pentecostalism with people of African descent has been well-documented. Bloch-Hoell (1964) shows that by 1936 American Pentecostalism was principally to be found in the southern states, where it flourished especially among Afro-American communities. (There is, incidentally, also a strong association of this sort of religion with the poorest groups and with women rather than men.)

The movement was also strong in the Caribbean, and its salience in the British Isles today is mainly a consequence of the large scale immigration which took place from the West Indies between 1951 and 1962. By the mid 1960s, Calley (1965) counted sixty-one assemblies with a combined membership of nearly 11,000. These commentators suggest that Afro-Caribbeans in Britain found it necessary and desirable to 'import their preachers and their sects ready-made' (Calley, 1965, 72) because they found the indigenous Christian churches both uninspiring in terms of religious practice and uncongenial in their hostile and racist attitudes to Black worshippers.

Calley points out various differences between the Pentecostal approach to religion and that of other Christian denominations. He sees Pentecostalism as embodying a 'ritual' as opposed to 'intellectual' approach, and claims that one function of glossolalia is to allow intellectually weaker members to make valued contributions to communal acts of worship. Communality is emphasized and continually reaffirmed in Pentecostal practice, so that a successful leader 'is one who can stimulate his congregation to respond as a group, who can make members lose their own individuality in an impassioned, sometimes hysterical identification with the church' (Calley, 1965, 74).

While it is possible to detect in Calley's remarks – his allusions to hysteria and intellectual weakness, for instance – a patronizing and even racist attitude, he is right to point out that Pentecostalism values the passionate and emotional as much as the intellectual, and that it emphasizes community over individuality. The passionate and communal atmosphere of Pentecostal worship is related to the central place it has in Black community life; it also has implications for the kind of language to be found in Pentecostal contexts. Two points in particular are pertinent here, and we shall take them in turn.

First, we may observe that the interactivity of speech events in Pentecostal meetings reflects the importance of collectivity and mutual solidarity; hence the concern of preachers and testifiers actively to involve members of the congregation in the discourse of preaching, and the concern of members themselves to encourage and evaluate that discourse. This mutual concern can be seen more clearly if we examine the range of responses available to members, in order to demonstrate what kinds of interaction are going on between speakers and listeners.

Geneva Smitherman (1977) distinguishes four types of response in her study of 'Talkin' and Testifyin''. The most common type is the *co-signing* response which indicates agreement with the speaker's point, and is realized by *yes*, *praise the Lord* and *Amen*, which are by far the most frequently-occurring responses in our data. A stronger but less common co-signing response is what Smitherman calls *On-T*, indicating that a point is 'right on time'. One realization of this is, in fact applause, which occurs from time to time in both Temples. For instance:

<u>Extract nine</u>

P: God say my glory I will give no man
-x-
my prayers I will give to no angel
-x-
I get my gl [ory
C: [xxxXXXXxxx

(KT)

Two further types of response discussed by Smitherman have a different function, though still one which emphasizes solidarity between preacher and congregation: they encourage the preacher to go on with the argument. Smitherman calls the first of these types the *encourager*, and it is often realized by *preach it* or *preach it preacher*. We see this, for instance, in extract two, a sequence in which members signal both agreement and encouragement to the speaker.

P: . . . all should come to repentanc[e (etc.)
M 1: [Yes
M 2: Amen, preach it

The second type is the *completer*, where a member completes or repeats the speaker's point:

Extract ten

P: Here we see he says repent and be baptized in the name of Jesus and everyone of you who is baptized
P: will receive
M: will receive

(CT)

To sum up, then, the interactive nature of Pentecostal preaching is co-operatively achieved by speakers and listeners who share an awareness of the importance of solidarity and communal feeling, in addition to a knowledge of the conventions by which these things are expressed.

A second point concerns the emphasis Pentecostals put on discourse being 'impassioned' as well as rational (we say 'as well as' and not 'rather than' because despite Calley's comments it is clear preachers and testifiers are expected to expound intellectually coherent arguments). Within Pentecostalism, great importance is given to the workings of the Spirit in inspiring speakers. The idea that one's speech is not a wholly conscious production but is somehow 'given' to the speaker, who becomes a spiritual vehicle, is obviously relevant to any understanding of the phenomenon of glossolalia; but it is also relevant to the analysis of preaching.

One of the characteristics of Pentecostal preaching which outside observers find most extraordinary is the tendency for preachers to break off from their ordered expositions to participate in lengthy and sometimes quite disorderly sequences which are not merely tolerated but positively valued. The following is a typical example, where an Elder introduces the testifier, and this exchange ensues:

Extract eleven

E: Oh glory to God a young man that love the Lord. Let us praise the Lord for him
M 1: Praise God praise God, glory praise the Lord [praise him
T: Hallelujah Lord Jesu [s

T: Hallelujah Lord Jesus
M 1: Praise [the Lord
M 2: [Amen

T: Thank you Lord Jesus Hallelujah
M: praise

T: Hallelujah [Lord Jesus Hallelujah
M 1: [Hallelujah [Hallelujah
M 2: [Praise him

T: Thank you Lord Jesus Hallelujah
Praise the Lord everybody
C: Praise the Lord

(CT)

Here an exchange between the testifier and a member is kept going for several turns. As it goes on others join in: the result is increasing amounts of simultaneous speech. At a certain point the testifier exhorts the entire congregation to praise the Lord. Only after this does the testimony proper begin.

In fact it is quite common to find long sequences like this one marking the opening and closing of speech events within the meeting (e.g. sermons and testimonies). When preachers announce the biblical texts on which they plan to expound there is often a series of *praise the Lords* or *Hallelujahs*.

Extract twelve

P:	One of the verses of the scriptures that turn my life round is what I'm preaching from tonight one Peter two twenty four Hallelujah
M:	Hallelujah
P:	Hallelujah
M:	Hallelujah

(KT)

The function of this kind of sequence is to raise the spiritual temperature, generating an 'ecstatic' mood in which the message itself can be received. A certain degree of disorder is welcome as a sign of spiritual inspiration (the Holy Ghost after all is not to be constrained by the polite rules of garden-party talk). Yet at a different level we can see that the discourse is not so disorderly: it has a regular, repetitive and ritualistic quality and is brought without difficulty to a climax (in extract eleven, the congregation's collective *praise the Lord*).

Our analysis so far leads us to assert that speakers and listeners at the two Temples we studied work together to orient their jointly-produced discourse to two important norms of Pentecostal practice: (1) that talk should reflect and reinforce the cohesiveness of the group, emphasizing the importance of communal bonds and mutual solidarity in its interactive form; and (2) that the centrality of spiritual inspiration should be recognized through the value accorded to spontaneous and impassioned exchanges which do not necessarily advance the argument of a sermon or testimony.

Pentecostal preaching and black verbal culture

If awareness of the norms of Pentecostal religion is important in understanding the interactive and participatory style of preaching in our data, the general characteristics of Black verbal culture can also throw light on specific stylistic features.

Black verbal style – the style of speaking of African peoples as it has evolved in Africa, America and the Caribbean – has been studied in many contexts other than the religious one, and it has often been remarked that Black rhetorical modes are different from white ones. Kochman (1981, 97) says that in public speech the Black style is 'high-keyed; animated; interpersonal and confrontational' whereas the white style, especially among middle-class educated speakers, is 'low-keyed; dispassionate, impersonal and non-challenging'. Particular attention can be drawn to the following features of Black speech events.

Turn-taking

In the Black idiom, according to Kochman, the general rule is 'interrupt when you can'; this is not perceived as an infringement of others' rights. A consequence is the high level of simultaneous speech in Black discourse, something also noted by Reisman (1974) in his study of an Antiguan village where he claims that speaker self-selection does not preclude the previous speaker carrying on. We have already pointed out that Pentecostal preaching includes many interruptions and episodes of simultaneous speech. Both the norm of 'spontaneity' referred to earlier and the more general norms of turn-taking in Black culture favour this outcome.

Repetition

Black verbal art (exemplified for instance by oral narrative performance, ritual insults and verbal duelling, etc.) often makes use of extensive repetition. As Smitherman observes (1977, 142) 'believing that meaningful sounds can move people, the Black speaker capitalizes on effective uses of repetition'.

Repetition is very characteristic of Pentecostal preaching, not only in 'call and response' sequences where key words and phrases like *Hallelujah* and *praise the Lord* or *Amen* pass repeatedly between preacher and congregation, or between one member and another, but also in the matter of the preacher's exposition:

Extract thirteen

P: We are the extension of God
We are the extension of God
We are the extension of God

(KT)

This extract is, of course, a three-part list as well as exemplifying repetition.

A rather similar phenomenon is what we might label 'elegant variation', a near-repetition or paraphrase like 'I bring you good news; I bring you glad tidings'. It is likely that this reflects a familiarity with the style of the Bible itself: given the importance of religion among Black communities in America and the West Indies, it is probable that the Bible has contributed a great deal to Black rhetoric in those areas.

The value placed on repetition in Black verbal culture may explain why we so often encounter lists of more than three parts in Pentecostal preaching. Lists are repetitive structures which allow the speaker to build up a point. Prosodic features of pitch and stress and rhythm can be used to signal the completion of a list and invite congregational response. And this leads to a consideration of the next topic.

Prosody/'Tonal semantics'

Although we wish to place on record the crucial importance of prosody in Pentecostal preaching, we must also make it clear that in a paper of this scope we can hardly scratch the surface of the complex phenomenon Smitherman (1977) calls 'tonal semantics'. It merits an extended treatment of its own. Nevertheless it is worth pointing out that many of the cues which signal important points, and to which listeners respond, are indeed prosodic. Among the most common are the following:

Rhythmic speech and clapping

Preachers sometimes clap rhythmically and time their utterances to the resulting beat.

An example is given in extract nine.

<u>Extract nine</u>

P. God say my glory I will give no man
-x-
my prayers I will give no angel
-x-
I get my gl [ory
C. [xxxXXXXxxx

(KT)

'Intonational contouring' and 'talk-singing'

These terms refer to a practice common to many Black orators of shifting repeatedly from high to low key, placing heavy stress on the high-key segments which are also pronounced loudly. The result is a rhythmic, sing-song effect which Pentecostals associate with 'getting into the spirit'.

Extract fourteen

P: ↑you make up your mind today and ↑GOD is going to
meet you halfway [(.) THANK you ↑JE↓sus THANK you
M1: [Praise [the Lord Amen
M2: [That's good [
M3: [Amen
[Praise God
M 4: ↑JE↓SUS (0.5) I wonder if ANY↑bo↑dy is going to COME
and ↑talk to ↓GOD today ↑ANY↓one of you ↑con↓vince?
Convince just the ↑FIRST step (.)

Conclusion

In our analysis of data from two Pentecostal groups we have explored the characteristic style used in preaching, relating this to Atkinson's analysis of political speeches, to ethnographic studies of Black verbal culture and to the 'local' norms of Pentecostal belief and practice. We have also shown the extent to which Pentecostalists are called upon to be literally 'responsive listeners'. The responses they jointly and severally provide are not 'optional extras' or 'icing on the cake'. They are a central means whereby the discourse is advanced and the values Pentecostals hold dear – group solidarity, spiritual inspiration, joy in the Lord – are affirmed and reaffirmed.

Notes

1. An exception to the prevailing neglect is Sutcliffe and Tomlin (1986), which is a useful but very general account of the Black churches in Britain. Patterns of language among Pentecostals (both Black and White) have been studied ethnographically by Homan (1978; 1981).
2. 'Preaching' here refers to any point in a meeting where one speaker addresses a discourse to the whole congregation – that is, not only the sermon but also 'testimony' by individual members. From a religious perspective these are separate events within the meeting, but from a linguistic or rhetorical point of view they appear similar.
3. All fieldwork and transcription was carried out by Christine Callender. We are grateful for the co-operation of the two Temples and especial thanks are due to Pastor Sappleton of C. Temple for his extensive assistance at all stages of research.

References

Atkinson, J.M. (1984) *Our Masters' Voices: The Language and Body Language of Politics*, London, Methuen.

Bloch-Hoell, N. (1964) *The Pentecostal Movement*, London, Allen and Unwin.

Calley, M.(1965) *God's People: West Indian Pentecostal Sects*, London, Oxford University Press.

Hill, C. (1963) *West Indian Migrants and the London Churches,* London, Oxford University Press.

Hill, C. (1969) 'Some Aspects of Race and Religion in Britain', University of London, mimeo.

Homan, R. (1978) 'Interpersonal Communication in Pentecostal Meetings', *Sociological Review* 26, 499–518.

Homan, R. (1981) 'Crises in the Definition of Reality', *Sociology* 15, 210–24.

Kochman, T. (1981) 'Classroom Modalities: Black and White Communicative Styles in the Classroom' in Mercer, N. (ed.), *Language in School and Community*, London, Edward Arnold.

Reisman, K. (1974) 'Contrapuntal Conversations in an Antiguan Village' in Bauman, R. and Sherzer, J. (eds), *Explorations in the Ethnography of Speaking*, Cambridge, Cambridge University Press.

Sacks, H., Schegloff, E. and Jefferson, G. (1978) 'A Simplest Systematics for the Organisation of Turn-Taking for Conversation' in Scheinkein, J. (ed.), *Studies in the Organisation of Conversational Interaction*, New York, Academic Press.

Smitherman, G. (1977) *Talking and Testifying*, Boston, Houghton Mifflin.

Smitherman, G. (1980) 'White English in Blackface, or Who do I Be?' in Michaels, L. and Ricks, C. (eds), *The State of the Language*, London.

Spurgeon, C.H. (1976) *Lectures to my Students*, London, Marshall, Morgan and Scott.

Sutcliffe, D. and Tomlin, C. (1986) 'The Black Churches' in Sutcliffe, D. and Wong, A. (eds), *The Language of the Black Experience*, Oxford, Blackwell.

Part three

Responsive readers

Chapter nine

Where interpretation stops[1]

Robert Sharpe

Before I discuss reader response theory and its continental cousin, reception theory, in any detail, I will try to 'place' them with respect to another major movement in literary theory of the past few decades. Like other contemporary movements in literary aesthetics such as deconstruction, reader response theory is a reaction against the text-centred theories of the sort which were the orthodoxy in their different ways in both Britain and the United States. Both Leavisite criticism and the New Criticism took the text as the object of critical interest and, to a large extent, divorced the text both from its time and from the response of its readership. In this introductory section, I shall compare text-centred, deconstructive and reader response theories and, at the close of the chapter, argue that the sensible conclusion is that some authors and some texts benefit from deconstructive methods and some from reader response, but that neither is universally rewarding as a critical technique.

Monroe Beardsley (Beardsley, 1970), the house philosopher of the text-centred movement, fought a long losing battle in favour of treating the object of literary analysis as the text, an object which stood alone, divorced from any intentions on the part of the author or any play in interpretation. On this view the critic's task is to establish the meaning of the text, a meaning which is independent of any authorial intention. Save where a text is ambiguous, which is not that common, the meaning of the text is single and discoverable. The task of the critic is to determine it. There are clearly elements of positivism in this approach and it seems to me to fail at three points. First it elides any distinction between describing and interpreting. For all we are expected to do is to determine the meaning of the text by a process of finding out what the elements mean. But interpretation is, by nature, a process which permits a variety of alternatives. The point about interpretation is that it begins where the text leaves off; it is an activity of free imaginative play within constraints set by the text. The second problem is that Beardsley found it very hard to account for those quintessentially literary devices, irony and understatement. These, by definition, involve a distinction between what the text means and what the author meant by it. The point is that a distinction is required between the textual surface and the meaning and this holds whether or not the writer tells us or whether or not we guess. Third it is hard to see what can be the point of establishing a 'correct' text on this view. If the text is all there can be why should we endeavour to correct it in the light of authorial preference? We ought simply to admit the existence of a plurality of versions, no one of which is privileged.

Although the starting point of deconstruction is apparently indistinguishable from this in as much as the existence of the unauthored text is a sort of *donnée*, there is a marked difference. For deconstructionalists do not accept the assumption of a single textual meaning which is a target of enquiry. Rather, in the liberal spirit of 'Let a thousand flowers bloom', which Paul Feyerabend incorporated into his philosophy of science, the view is that interpretation is the activity which characterizes criticism and that, furthermore, there are no limits upon interpretation. It is unrestricted. It is a free and untrammelled activity. The reason for this excessively liberal view of the range of interpretation lies in the view they take of language. It is their philosophy of language which permits complete license in interpretation.

The claim is that language has an inertia which stems primarily from the origin of common words in tropes, an inertia which constantly opposes its use in direct statement making. Any attempt to exclude or repress, neutralize or marginalize rhetorical figures from texts fails to appreciate their buried or covert workings. This leads to an 'undecidability' which affects all texts. Language is a recalcitrant beast which we cannot control, strive as we may.

De Man offers a strong form of this thesis. I cannot express what I intend since the language I use has a counterweight which prevents me from formulating what I mean. De Man argues that neither author nor reader can read his own or anybody else's texts; texts are unreadable. 'Language always intervenes to deflect, defer or differentially complicate the relation between manifest sense and expressive intent' (Norris, 1983, 102). The philosophical error embodied in what Derrida calls the 'metaphysics of presence' is the belief that the speaker can ensure a perfect fit between intention and utterance, an accord between meaning and expression. De Man says explicitly of literary and critical texts, that sign and meaning can never coincide and that 'the discrepancy between meaning and assertion is a constitutive part of their logic' (De Man, 1971, 110). Now the denial of this metaphysics of presence leads to the demotion of speech. It is no longer privileged; writing, erected in its place, does not depend upon a speaking mind and we may take the text to mean what we choose. '*Il n'y a pas de hors-texte*'! It was this that led me to suggest that there is a certain similarity in the relation of both textualists and deconstructionalists to the written source. If textualists reduce interpretation to description then deconstructionalists reduce description to interpretation.

Any strong form of the deconstructionalist thesis leads immediately to scepticism and is, as a result, open to a killing rejoinder; if this is a universal feature of language, then it applies to the deconstructionalist thesis itself. What it says cannot be what the author intended it to say. But then, we will ask, what does it say? For whatever deconstruction I make of the thesis itself is couched in words, verbally or in writing, and is itself subject to the same criticism. The act of deconstruction is itself equally at risk since this can be described. Any act of understanding is potentially an act represented in language and any representation distorts. So any attempt to represent a deconstructing thought invariably fails.

How will the deconstructionalist react? Delighting in paradox he claims that, of course, deconstruction is self-deconstructing. Nothing pleases a deconstructionalist more than a little of what he calls 'self-reflection'; what we have sketched is nirvana. I think we must be brutal here. This is self contradiction, no less and no more; the protagonist is advocating the unassertability of what he is asserting; on his own arguments what he says cannot be said or thought. De Man proposes that the critic can by fiat stop the endless spiralling of the deconstructive process. The rejoinder to this must be, of course, that we have not been shown that the process is bound to begin nor that, if it is necessary, it can be stopped. And if it can be stopped here by the critic's 'will-to-power', why not earlier?

We can, of course, adopt a more spirited rejoinder, playful or even ludic. Since, on his case, the text can be given any significance we choose, I choose to take the deconstructionalist as asserting, on those occasions on which he deviates into sense, the opposite to that which I and other readers usually understand him to be saying. Let us assume that he is advocating universal transparency of meaning or the metaphysics of presence or any other doctrine anathema to the new barbarians.

'Truth', said Nietzsche, 'is a mobile army of metaphors, metonymies, and anthropomorphisms.' 'Truths are illusions of which one has forgotten that they are illusions, coins which have their obverse effaced and are no longer of account as coins but merely as metals.' Kierkegaard wrote in his journal, 'the concepts are gradually changed, they become like false coinage whilst all the time transactions happily continue to be carried out in them' (Norris, 1983, 103–4).

Unfortunately for them, this celebrated metaphor works in precisely the opposite way to that imagined by the writers. It is the confidence we have in the coinage which gives it its value. Aside from that, chunks of metal have no value in exchange. Equally it is the mutual confidence we have in words and their meaning which allows communication. If any sense could be attached to the idea that we are deluded then we should conclude that the meaning of these words is not illusory precisely because we have forgotten that they are illusions. It is the conventional understanding of words that permits us to jump from what is being said to what the speaker intends to say.

There are occasions when the attempt to say something is undermined by the terms used, but a case must always be made for thinking this so. Certainly the conventions of understanding verse are sufficiently different from those of prose to suppose that what is marginalized is relevant, though, as I have argued, it depends upon context. But elsewhere what we deem to be irrelevant is dictated by convention and the convention is enshrined in what philosophers call 'the principle of charity'. We assume that something is intendedly expressed and we interpret the utterance appropriately. Indeed it is a fact of phenomenology that when we listen to or speak language, we do not pay attention to the words except on rare occasions. They are a transparent medium.

Our problem disappears if we take the more reasonable position, hinted at by Culler (1975) in *A Structuralist Poetics*, that what deconstructionalists have identified is one sort of critical device and one which is peculiarly interesting when used on some kinds of text rather than others. Certainly the thesis cannot, for reasons we have just reviewed, be a general truth about language. It is a matter of practice rather than truth. What reasons then have we for using deconstructive techniques upon a text?

It would not be enough to say that the text looks better as a result. Peter Lamarque pointed out in a review (Lamarque 1986,

291) that the practice makes texts incoherent rather than coherent and this is not to present them in the best light. In any case, I do not think that the task of the critic is to find an interpretation which makes a text look more interesting. What we need is something more, a hint that the context of writing suggests that the culture in which the text originated encourages this form of reading. A deconstructionalist is not going to be happy at the resurrection of the author and his intentions this assumes but his misgivings will have to be ignored. In any case if he has dethroned the author it is hard to understand his attachment to the writers of the canon; if interpretation is free and unfettered we could arrive at the same set of interpretative statements from any starting point so we might as well begin with the soaraway *Sun* as with Shakespeare. Critics of a more radical persuasion will, of course, not object.

When the critics and philosophers of a culture are precursors of deconstruction like Nietzsche, or possibly Coleridge, they authorize a deconstructive reading of their literary contemporaries. This places literary understanding in the context of a history of ideas. But we can justify deconstructive criticism only upon assumptions like that of authorial prerogative and historical provenance, assumptions which are inconsistent with a general deconstructive approach.

The thesis I propose in the final part of this essay is that similar arguments hold for reader-reception theory, so let us now turn to our main target.

A neat way of setting up this latest fad of literary theorists is to use an equally fashionable philosophical nostrum, the idea of possible worlds. Originally this concept was used to distinguish mathematical and logical statements from others. Thus whilst every even number is the sum of two primes is, if true, true in all possible worlds, that Mrs Thatcher is prime minister is true in only one of a number of possible worlds, a possible world which contrives to coincide with the actual world.

It is the mode to define what a novelist does by saying that he creates a possible world. A poet or dramatist may equally well create a possible world so there is a possible world of *Hedda Gabler* as well as of *David Copperfield*. The world of *Great Expectations* contains such stalwarts as Pip, Miss Haversham and Estella and it is a world in which a young man grows up to something approaching wisdom. But, and this is where reception theory inserts itself, it is never a world which is completely specified. It is certainly more completely specified than the appearance of Kubla Khan of whom Coleridge only speaks of his 'flashing eyes, his floating hair'. But we do not know how often Pip cut his toe nails nor whether Estella had a mole on her back. Much more is unspecified. Any descriptions of landscape are partial.

This is where reception theory comes in. We each partially complete an imaginary picture of the world of the fiction or poem and we do so from our background and experience. Now I have noticed that when I am talking about a novel I have read to a friend, I recall it in terms of an imagined picture of the landscape or cityscape of the fiction. It is a sort of imagined geography; it is not a map for I recall what I thought the places looked like. But I do not usually remember the characters. I remember the setting when I can recall nothing of the plot, of the psychology of the characters or even of their names. If I were to ask you now how you remember books you have read, the men might indeed remember books in the same way; it is less likely that the women will. When I read a novel I project material into the fictional world in this way so that the world is a composite, a task jointly encompassed by the writer and myself. It is because of this that filmed versions of novels one has read sometimes shock. I always imagined Sophia in *Tom Jones* one way, whereas in the film she looks different. Perhaps I always thought that Squire Western ought to look like William Whitelaw and he does not. Note that this sort of issue does not arise with performed drama, film or music. It is specifically a literary matter. Just how much detail is involved in this picture is, of course, difficult to define. It must vary.

The roots of this sort of approach to literature lie in the aesthetics of Roman Ingarden. A literary work of art is, in his view, characterized by what he calls 'spots of indeterminacy'; it is for us, the listener, reader or viewer, to fill in his or her experience of the work with our interpretative act. Thus each encounter with the work produces what Ingarden called a 'concretization'. So we arrive at a view of art which stresses the role of interpretation. But it needs perhaps to be said that interpretation bears a slightly different sense from the more familiar. We might think of interpretation as the eliciting of themes in a work. We might recall some of the generalizations which critics make. The infamous epitaph which begins Olivier's film of *Hamlet* is a good example. Now this common sense of interpretation is not what is involved here; perhaps a better analogy is in the way that, in the performing arts, the bare essentials of the notation are filled out by the performer. For what we have in literature is the creation of a detailed world. It is in the nature of all forms of art to leave to the reader, listener or performer, space to add his contribution. Ingarden is the spiritual father of reception theory (Ingarden, 1973). The essential feature of our experience of art is that we supplement what we see.

D. W. Harding and I. A. Richards are also sometimes cited as founding fathers of the movement (Tompkin, 1980); Richards, of course, wrote of the emotive impact of literary language and this suggests an attention to the effect of literature. Jane Tompkins, to whose brief historical survey this present discussion is indebted, quotes Walker Gibson's witty piece on the mock reader, the reader not as he or she is but as he or she is postulated by an author who, whether or not he begins 'Dear reader', has some concepion of what the reader shares with him in terms of preconceptions. It is a role we play as we read. Some readers may be friends of the author and share not only his world view but a knowledge of his peculiarities; they may even know the people on whom he bases his characters; writers are usually without conscience in the way they use their friends as fiction fodder.

I have said that the movement flourished as a response to the New Criticism. It is also worth noting that the idea that the reader is on centre stage would have been hard to understand for most pre-twentieth-century criticism simply because it requires conceiving the opposite possibility of the literary work as standing on its own, independent of author and reader, a conception enshrined in textualism. Mary Mothersill quotes George Watson as arguing that the reader came to the forefront in the 1700s (Mothersill, 1984). But poetry and prose were from classical times regarded as primarily didactic. The art of writing was the art of communication, and the idea of a text independent of author or the idea that interpretation is largely free would probably have been unintelligible.

The proposal, then, is that we should not just consider relations between author and author or between reader and reader but consider the relation between reader and work as a sort of dialogue. When a work is first published it is read against a background, a pre-understanding, which is different from the background of subsequent readers. The understanding of the first reader commences a chain which is enriched as subsequent readers add their contribution. So there is a constantly varying background against which it is read. Books which were familiar when they were written will no longer be. What is conventional about the fiction will no longer be obvious; the work may satisfy or disappoint expectations; the more it surprises the greater its artistic merit. Once it is canonized, then it becomes particularly difficult to imagine it as new and unfamiliar, and it is equally difficult to read it as its original readership would have done. Jauss suggests we risk misunderstanding if we fail to reconstruct the paradigms against which the work was originally seen. This being so, literary education must be seen as an attempt at guiding us when we fill in the lacunae of the concretization. The value and meaning of the work can only become clear if we can reconstruct in this way. The task of the history of reception, in his view, is to reconstruct the horizon of expectations which existed when the text was written and how this has changed. Then we may see what was fashionable, what outmoded and what ahead of its time. This task is essential if you believe, with Jauss, that really good works exhibit negativity; they are underdetermined, open to supplementation. We need then to supplement in an appropriate way.

One crux is the extent to which we read against a background. Do we read Shakespeare or Pope against a background of other writers? Are we conscious of the way in which they vary a tradition, the way in which they depart from the quotidian style? We need to know what the words they use mean, of course; somebody may have to tell us and it may be somebody saturated in the contemporary style who knows what the Elizabethans meant by 'honour' or 'kind'. Certainly the determination of what words mean shades away into the much more interpretative issues of what a word means in this particular context. But it would be an error to suppose that no sense can be attached to the first step, the settling of the sense of these words in their customary usage. It is a fallacy to suppose that because there is no sharp distinction there is no distinction at all. I imagine that the thesis of the ubiquity of interpretation has percolated into literary aesthetics from philosophy of science where it has become a commonplace that all observations are impregnated with concepts.

En passant, I have followed standard practice here in making no distinction between work of art and text. Actually I think it would probably be more sensible to distinguish the marks on the page, the inscription, from the work to which the text is the clue. Then we can allow for the existence of corrupt texts which are inadequate guides to the nature of the literary work. However, the elements of the literary work have a meaning and we may distinguish those meanings from the more subjective affair of ascribing meaning in interpretation. But, as I say, I have not attempted to make these discriminations here. They require another essay.

Now, to return to the main argument, it is important for us to know when the text was written because this enables us to gauge the diction and also the originality. There is a certain frisson given us by the recognition that something is unique or ahead of its time but I doubt whether much part is played by the identification of the way the work might have surprised or horrified its contemporaries, though we may deduce that from its individuality. It may be more important to locate the work in the ouevre. The concept of an '*ouevre*' may be less important in literature than in music and the visual arts. English literature in particular is full of minor figures who produced one or two enduring works amongst a good deal of fustian. However, it is important to know the chronology of a great writer's productions. It is how he or she stands with respect to his own earlier work that is more important than how he stands with respect to others. Charles Rosen makes a parallel point about music. People were not that surprised by Haydn's differences from his contemporaries. Most London concertgoers of the 1790s knew enough Haydn to expect his style and not somebody else's (Rosen, 1980).

Of course, a novel may encourage expectations, only to surprise them; indeed the fiction may surprise the author. I have quoted elsewhere Pushkin's letter to a friend. 'Do you know what that Tatania of mine has done; she has shown Onegin the door; I would not have believed it of her.' The twists and turns of a plot may frustrate our expectations or fulfil them in a satisfying way, and for both Riffaterre and Jauss therein lies literary significance. Theorists about music have analysed the same phenomenon whereby music depends upon the fact that sequences which we expect to move in certain ways offer an opportunity for the composer to play games with us. Indeed much of what, in music, has been couched in the concepts of information theory is applied by these writers to literature (Iser in Tompkin, 1980).

Jauss is also, I would have thought, wrong in suggesting that great art surprises by its distance from the norm. Often it presents, and this is one definition of a classic, the perfection of a quotidian style. Pope, Spenser, Bach, Mozart and Palestrina are good examples. What they have in common is the supreme mastery of a style. Jauss, on the contrary, is drawn to those works which shock. He is a romantic. Those works which make no demands on the receiving consciousness to change he calls light or 'culinary' reading.

Most writers of this school proclaim the indeterminacy of texts and their inexhaustible potential for interpreters (Iser in Tompkin, 1980). This, again, raises the general question of the universal applicability of these techniques. It is by no means clear that pre-Romantic writers would have thought that their literary efforts could be interpreted in very various ways. Rosamund Tuve's classic study (Tuve, 1961) showed that didacticism was central to their conception of literature and that the literary work was thought of as an act of communication whose specifically literary virtues lay in its power to convince and enlighten. Now it may be argued that the modern conception of a work of art involves the assumption of the indeterminacy of interpretation. Works of art are precisely those artefacts which can be read in multifarious ways, some of which, admittedly, but not all, may be ruled out as illicit. Our conception of art differs from the conceptions of our predecessors in licensing such a free approach to interpretation; the point is that this is a consequence of our conception of art rather than a feature of the literary work *an sich*. However, this does not seem to me to justify reading it in ways other than those which would have been thought to be appropriate by the original readership. The position taken by reception theorists like Jauss whose approach is historically orientated is here at odds with theorists like Iser or Fish.

I have yet to comment upon the wealth of reception criticism which derives from psychoanalysis. Roy Shafer has recently emphasized the narrative role in analysis (Shafer, 1980), showing how the analyst tells a story which is then available to the analysand as a reinterpretation of his past, an alternative story which may or may not be convincing. Alcorn and Bracher (1985) suggest that a work of literature may offer a parallel; it may offer a narrative within which there may be characters with whom the reader can identify consciously or unconsciously, and so work through his conflicts. What we read draws on our personality and the process of identification with a figure in a text involves a rapprochement between this alien within me and the real me from whom, he has in part, been created. The possibility of interpretations depends upon the possibility of alter egos within me and reading may assist me, as Iser puts it, to formulate myself. In deciphering I formulate my capacity to decipher. So Iser memorably captures the moral effect of literature. It is by a sort of imaginary role-playing that we broaden our sympathies.

Great works, since they are inexhaustible, offer an indefinite variety of interpretative possibilities during which the reader moves from gestalt to fresh gestalt. Though he does not go as far as Fish in identifying the work with the reader's response, Iser does suggest that the literary work is somehow midway between text and response, whatever that means. The position of Fish is untenable, for we cannot hold without inconsistency that the reader realizes only one of the potential meanings the text implies, and yet claim that the text is identical with the reader's response. The problems, after all, of identifying the work or the meaning of the work with the reader's response are very evident and are, indeed, repeatedly emphasized by Ingarden. The theory precludes any possibility of our saying that one response is illegitimate or invalid. There are silly readings but Fish has denied us any way of picking them out. For what we cannot now say is that this response is invalid because it is inconsistent with the meaning of the text. But surely we wish to say that somebody who took Wordsworth's line 'heavens look down on this poor sod' as a request for forgiveness of an act of buggery had responded in the wrong way. Fish, of course, is known for his emphasis on the interpretative communities whose differing response to texts defines them. Certainly it would then be possible to make a judgement of the non-validity of a response community-relative. It is ruled out in terms of the approach of that community. But this, I fear, is not enough. We cannot intelligently interpret *Hamlet* as a study of the pros and cons of monetarism even though, given enough ingenuity, no doubt the text can be twisted into such a reading. If, then, there was such a community of economist interpreters of Shakespeare, they would have to be placed beyond the pale.

Fish focuses attention on the way in which attention to response slows down the reading experience, turning it into a series of anticipations and denials or fulfilments. This does raise the question as to whether it is a technique which applies universally and, as I have suggested, I believe this to be a crucial issue. Some texts are more suited to be read at speed. I have heard it argued that the way to read Thackeray is to skim, and I certainly find it impossible to read Antony Burgess without a steady acceleration which ends with my flicking over the pages of the last half of the book. Fish's methodology does not find a place for skimming. There are two distinct points here. It is often thought that great literature demands slow reading and much reading. I am not concerned with that here, though I presume that works which it is proper to read rapidly are works which we think to be of less stature. But certainly there may be fictions which are generally thought to be of high quality which require fast reading. Sometimes the temptation to skim is irresistible; for example, if I approach the end of an absorbing narrative and wish to see how it ends. A gripping yarn may be virtually impossible to read at a speed which is fair to its prose. More seriously, does anyone else feel that any production of Shakespeare inevitably takes the verse too fast for it to be properly savoured?

I have at last reached the question of interpretation and it is here that the important questions arise. It seems to me that the crucial question is this – is the supplementation involved in reading a work of any critical interest?

The point about criticism and about the interpretation of a work of art of any sort is that is is premised upon community. We can grant to Fish that it is what my response has in common with yours and what it could have in common that matters. The sort of geography which is involved in my response is too idiosyncratic to be of much interest to others. You may find it endearing or foolish, as the case may be. The problem is to steer between those requirements which complete a work and which count as its interpretation and those which are irrelevant to any common understanding. One critic of reception theory, Macherey, argues that the spaces in literary works are themselves to be valued and that some works are injured if we 'close them up'. But it may be that the sense of space in the text is what matters and that the overall impression of the work remains constant. Now certainly there might seem to be something inappropriate in supplementing Beckett into a world of Victorian clutter. Indeed what Umberto Eco in 'L'opera aperta' (1962, Milan, Bompiani) calls 'open' works may resist closing in this way. But it may well be that the process of supplementation is unavoidable or even unconscious. We may not want it to happen but it will nevertheless. However, our consciousness of the spareness of the text is what matters as far as the character of Beckett is concerned and this does not alter. If I am right about this, the implications for reader response theory are important, even, I think, devastating. For what I am arguing is that we experience a concretization based on the text which we, nonetheless, regard as extraneous to the text and of no critical concern. At the same time we can certainly allow that this is one of the factors which makes literary art so valuable to us. It is this capacity to make our own world from the bare bones of the text which is one of the things which makes us cherish literature. But it does not follow from this that what we do is of critical interest. Poor works, too, can offer this scope without offering us the moral direction we get, say, from *Middlemarch*. So it may be just those works which circumscribe the interpretation a little more tightly (though not too much) which we value. What is crucial is our capacity to distinguish between our response and the properties of the work. This is inconsistent with the conflation of the two by both Iser and Fish.

The crux, is evidently, that what is artistically relevant in a response can be defended by the text. An interpretation which is viable is one which goes beyond the text, certainly, but which can be defended by being shown to be present in prominent episodes in the work. (Interpretations can be wrong but they cannot be shown to be right.) The geography which is part of my response is not justified by the citing of foregrounded episodes in the same way. The basis for this is that interpretation is circumscribed, not by the author's intention, but by what he could have intended. If an interpretation is fair then the author could have intended that interpretation, though whether he did or not we may not be able to tell. Much of my supplementation is beyond authorial control. If an Australian reader thinks of *The Tempest* as being set on a Barrier Reef island, what he imagines could not possibly have been anticipated by Shakespeare; these details of authorial response are non-interpretative and irrelevant to criticism. On the other hand, the supplementation involved in recognizing Oswald's syphilis in *Ghosts* is so crucial to understanding the work, even though it is not mentioned in the text, that not to see it is not to understand.

My second and final question derives from a piece by Richard Wollheim on the visual arts. In it he considers paintings in which the viewer is in the space of the painting, though he may be off picture, as opposed to paintings in which the viewer stands outside the logical space of the picture altogether. There is a parallel for literature. In *Paradise Lost*, for example, the reader is one of the souls over which war is being waged, so he is both a reader and an actor in the drama. Gerald Prince (Tompkin, 1980) quotes Marcel Proust in *A la recherche*; 'Undoubtedly, in these coincidences which are so perfect, when reality withdraws and applies itself to what we have dreamt about for so long a time, it hides it from us entirely.' Prince suggests that the 'we' includes the narratee. It seems to me that all the general truths which we find stated or implied in literature include the narratee. In this way one of the really big questions in literary and aesthetic theory, the issue of 'truth in literature', is illuminated.

Equally, and better known, Fish's remarks about Milton's verse being destined for a Christian with circumcised ears whose faith had grown cold shows response theory at its most illuminating (Fish, 1967). These are genuine insights and reception theory directs us towards them. As in the case of deconstructive techniques, the question is whether all types of literature are illuminated by these methods. A partisan of the text like Beardsley would argue that nothing that Prince or Fish say could not be defended by the text. We would not have reason to cite any empirical evidence on audience response in its favour.

It is, indeed, not always clear what reader response theory thinks we should be addressing. Do I write about how I respond, or how a qualified reader responds, or how the hypothesized informed reader conceived by the author responds? It is significant that Jauss takes the final alternative, Norman Holland the first, and Fish, I think, the second. Reception theory is a broad church. More to the point perhaps, is that many of these analyses collapse into descriptions of the literary work rather than descriptions of response. Much of Norman Holland's reading of 'A slumber did my spirit seal' (Holland, 1976) differs only grammatically from a great deal of literary criticism not motivated by any special theory. But, to return to Fish on Milton, there we have the presumption by an author of a certain informed readership which it is our task to reconstruct. The more integrated the target culture, the more appropriate is attention to the implied reader for here shared assumptions control what the author writes.

What I suspect is that reader response theory, like deconstructionist theory, stands to literary criticism much as the aesthetics of practitioners, like Stravinski or Tolstoi, stands to their creative practice. Look for an illumination of their conception of what they are doing, certainly, which may not be the same as their actual practice, but do not look for general truths about the arts because they will not be found here. These are manifestos. What is interesting is that criticism has so far taken over the mantle of creativity as to think itself entitled to manifestos. Indeed this is perhaps just what distinguishes literary theory from aesthetics; the first produces recommendations for practitioners; the second aims at a true general theory about the arts. At least one conclusion seems unavoidable; there is a deal of bad philosophy in modern literary theory.

Notes

1. My thanks are due to Pia Salmela and Stein Haugam Olsen who read the penultimate draft. This chapter has been improved as a consequence.

References

Alcorn, M.W. and Bracher, M. (1985) 'Literature, Psychoanalysis and the Reformation of the Self; A New Direction for Reader-Response theory', *Publications of the Modern Language Association* 100, 342–54.
Beardsley, M.C. (1970) *The Possibility of Criticism*, Detroit.
Culler, J. (1975) *A Structuralist Poetics*, London, Routledge & Kegan Paul.
De Man, P. (1971) *Blindness and Insight*, Oxford, Oxford University Press.
Fish, S. (1980) 'Literature in the Reader', in J. Tompkin (ed.) *Reader-Response: From Formalism to Post-Structuralism*, Baltimore, Johns Hopkins.
Fish, S. (1967) *Surprised by Sin: The Reader in Paradise Lost*, London, University of California Press.
Holland, N. (1976) 'Literature and the Three Phases of Psychoanalysis', *Critical Inquiry*, 2, 221–33.
Ingarden, R. (1973) *The Literary Work of Art*, Evanston, Northwestern University Press.
Iser, W. (1980) 'The Reading Process: A Phenomenological Approach' in J. Tompkin (ed.), *Reader-Response Criticism: From Formalism to Post-Structuralism*, Baltimore, Johns Hopkins.
Jauss, H.R. (1982) *Towards an Aesthetics of Reception*, New York, Harvester.
Lamarque, P. (1986) Review of Floyd Merrill, 'Deconstruction Reframed', *British Journal of Aesthetics*, 26, 290–2.
Mothersill, M. (1984) *Beauty Restored*, Oxford, Oxford University Press.
Norris, C. (1983) *The Deconstructive Turn*, London, Methuen.
Prince, G. (1980) 'Introduction to the Study of the Narratee' in J. Tompkin (ed.), *Reader-Response Criticism: From Formalism to Post-Structuralism*, Baltimore, Johns Hopkins.
Rosen, C. (1980) *Sonata Forms*, New York, Norton.
Shafer, R. (1980) 'Narration in the Psychoanalytic Dialogue', *Critical Inquiry*, 6.
Tompkin, J. (1980) (ed.) *Reader-Response Criticism: From Formalism to Post-Structuralism*, Baltimore, Johns Hopkins.
Tuve, R. (1961) *Elizabethan and Metaphysical Imagery*, Chicago.
Wollheim, R. (1986) '*Imagination and Pictorial Understanding*', *Proceedings of the Aristotelian Society*, supp. vol. LX.

Chapter ten

'You will use my words to make your own meaning': listening to Nadine Gordimer's *Burger's Daughter*[1]

Christine Devonshire and Susan Cordwell

This essay grew out of a concern about our own teaching as feminists and a disturbance at the assumption, voiced during a discussion of teaching practice among women involved mainly in Higher Education, that feminism was 'a hat' that one chose to wear on particular courses with particular groups but which was 'inappropriate' elsewhere. Our immediate feeling was that what we understood by feminism was not a 'detachable' approach, but one which informs all teaching, regardless of group or course. While creating space for other approaches, we felt that it necessarily affects their 'placing', the ways in which they are presented and received.

We wanted to try to establish whether/how far the listening process – our sense of the accessibility of our own responses and our capacity to 'hear' student response – was determined by expectations on both sides, by assumptions about roles, 'appropriate' levels of discourse, areas of experience and interest, and anticipated capabilities. We decided to discuss one text, *Burger's Daughter* by the South African writer Nadine Gordimer (chosen because it fitted the criteria of classes already in progress), and listen to the responses, the readings of both the novel itself and of individual responses to it, with four different groups: postgraduate, undergraduate, school sixth-form and Adult Education. They were each involved in very different courses: Women's Studies, Twentieth-century Literature, GCE Advanced Level Literature and Contemporary Women Writers respectively.

We were not primarily concerned with specific teaching aims. Assuming the discussion of literature to be very little to do with imparting factual information and very much to do with quite literally 'playing it by ear' and allowing the discussion to be affected by the response, we approached each group with a similar range of issues, points of focus in and about the text which we felt were important. However, we anticipated that some points would be more easily heard, or would need to be introduced, elucidated differently with different groups. To a certain extent we predicted response both about areas of interest and problematic areas according to our expectations of the group.

We wanted to try to hear (or more accurately re-hear through recording the discussions) what affected the movement and range of response. What we actually began to hear, behind the attempts to articulate readings of the novel and 'hear' Rosa, Burger's daughter, were the ways in which assumptions, predictions of the other's place, prevent hearing and produce mis-readings. Ironically the discussions about this novel, a novel full of mirrors, centring on how a young woman in a particular context is 'seen' and not heard and how she attempts to speak herself and respond to what she is and what she hears, reflect the dilemmas of reading oneself and one another's meaning.

Because we had the opportunity to re-listen to the discussions, we were made more aware of areas of 'non-hearing' both of the text and of each other's responses which occurred within all the groups. When we began to explore this, the shared responses (rather than group differences) felt more revelatory of the reading/listening process.

A central common area of difficulty which emerged with all four groups was that of hearing, knowing how to read the narrator. Often Rosa is talking in the first person but her voice is disturbingly 'unplaceable'. She is looking back, 'considering only ways of trying to take hold' (p. 171)[2] but we do not know (and even by the end of the novel there is some ambiguity) where she is, who she is. This in itself is constructive because it means we have to listen to her version, her story, more attentively. She is attempting to concoct a reading out of her own confusion about her past, knowing that what she says will not be understood.

> My version and theirs. And if this were being written down, both would seem equally concocted when read over (p. 16).

The bulk of the narrative alternates between the first-person internal voice, directed at different times to three people, each addressed as 'You', and a third-person 'external' narrative in which Rosa is referred to as 'She'. Though the different versions allow us to know more about Rosa than she discovers about herself, confusion is compounded because we are not always sure who is speaking and who is being addressed:

> One is never talking to oneself, always one is addressed to

> someone. Suddenly, without knowing the reason, at different stages in one's life, one is addressing this person or that all the time, even dreams are performed before an audience (p. 16).

Rosa is talking to a 'You' in her mind which initially refers to her South African lover, Conrad, but in fact she knows that the yacht in which he attempted to sail away (from his proposed bourgeois fate) was never found: 'I may have been talking to a dead man: only to myself' (p. 210). There is almost a sense of Rosa needing to hear how her concoction sounds – certainly when the 'You' refers to her father towards the end of the novel she knows she is addressing a dead man – and because her version *is* written down it is as though she is talking to herself out loud, and the reader, if not an addressee, becomes an auditor.

The notion of speech necessarily involving an addressee is significant for Gordimer as writer, Rosa as narrator, and the reader as listener since, inevitably, they are involved in a dialogue which is always informed by the 'someone' who is being addressed. What disturbed all the groups, to different degrees, was the fact that they could confuse Rosa's and Conrad's voices – underlined by Rosa's admission that 'When we spoke to each other there was the clandestine quality of talking to oneself; the taunting and tempting of mutual culpability' (p. 69). In their 'paradis invente' 'safe and cosy as a child's playhouse and sexually arousing as a lover's hideout' (p. 21), there was a dissolving from identity to identity, 'accepting each other's encroachments as the law of the litter' (p. 69). Yet there is a solipsistic quality to the dialogue between Rosa and Conrad as Rosa says, 'If you knew I was talking to you I wouldn't be able to talk' (p. 16). Her speech with Conrad is only made possible by his absence but their relationship is crucial to her capacity to speak.

Conrad is a space into which she can physically move when she lives with him on the 'island' of the cottage, a physical space with no address to locate it within the strictures and structures contingent on place: 'the cottage was let without official tenure at an address that no longer existed. . . . It was nowhere' (p. 21). He gives her the emotional space of lover but he, like the cottage, is nameless, he remains 'Conrad something-or-other' (p. 17). He is 'someone who had no importance in their (the Burger's) life, someone who stood quite outside it, peripheral' (p. 17). Unlike all the others who 'knew' her he sees her without the assumption of her inevitable place and role. Primarily he sees her as a woman with the dilemmas of being the daughter of a particular man. This perception of her relationship with Lionel Burger and her role in the 'family' as being problematic sometimes allows and often pushes Rosa to face and finally speak her 'untellable secrets'.

Whilst Rosa is able to release, analyse and begin to shape her sense of difference and non-being as Lionel Burger's daughter into the beginnings of a positive sense of self via her relationship with Conrad, the nature of this relationship is as elusive as Conrad himself. Despite the references to their 'love-nest' many people in the groups were surprised when they discovered it was a sexual relationship, that it had a physical dimension. Rosa's use of Conrad as a mirror (or screen) in which she sees herself, turning herself slowly round, examining and touching herself in a way that is possible only in a private mirror, puts Conrad in positions that are contradictory to the normal place of lover. He is often cast almost as an observer who adjusts the angle of himself as mirror and Rosa as reflected image and subject, to facilitate her seeing.

The space Conrad provides is, in some respects, the space normally occupied in childhood. When Rosa leaves the cottage she refers to it as 'the children's tree-house we were living in, in an intimacy of self-engrossment without the reserve of adult accountability' (p. 70). It represents a time of physical and emotional self-discovery, a voyage fuelled and navigated by Conrad, but again there is ambiguity in that the voyage is not necessarily undertaken during the course of their relationship. The space that Conrad provides is one that Rosa carries with her thoughout the text. She talks to him/herself using Conrad as a context, outside the context of her perceived place, which lights situations and events in a way which allows these moments to be revelatory of herself. The growing sense in Rosa of the time with Conrad as being one akin to childhood and his closeness becoming increasingly a closeness to herself, creates an incestuous quality. This causes her to compare it to her earlier relationship with her other quasi-brother, Baasie, with whom she also 'huddled for warmth in the same bed' (p. 70).

Rosa's relationship with her adopted black brother and, more importantly, their joint relationship with Lionel Burger, is related in fragments throughout the first section of the novel. Odd sentences referring to Baasie pepper the narrative. In this section they are present to affirm the warm sensual moments, perhaps the only such moments for Rosa, with her family. As in the swimming pool, 'I was his (Lionel Burger's) little girl, dog-paddling to him with my black brother Baasie, the two of us reaching for him as a place where no fear, hurt or pain existed' (p. 115).

Whilst painfully and painstakingly re-seeing her relationship with Lionel Burger, Rosa clings tenaciously to her image of Baasie, frozen in childhood by his early removal from the Burger household, a sibling relationship which overrode, blotted out colour. Struggling to be seen herself, Rosa determinedly fails to see Baasie. It is only when Baasie names himself to her as Zwelinzima, refuting Lionel Burger, claiming his own father and his father's name, Vulindlela, and angrily denying the particularity of Lionel Burger's suffering, that Rosa is forced to perceive Baasie's difference. He is not her brother, their places are inevitably distinct one from the other. Their seeing of Lionel Burger is not a shared experience. It is one differentiated by colour, context and sex. Whilst their circumstances as children in South Africa are in many ways parallel, both their fathers dying in prison cells in the struggle against apartheid, both named by their father, for Baasie the taking of the father's name is non-problematic. His feet fit easily and naturally into his father's footsteps. The hearing of Baasie is the final revelatory moment for Rosa and it is after 're-seeing' him that she returns to South Africa.

With all of the groups (two entirely composed of women, two in which women formed a large majority) discussion focused on Conrad and Baasie. It felt important to explore how Rosa associates with her 'brothers' in her need to disassociate herself from her father. Yet even when it was agreed that their rejection, their responses to their assumed place were different, less complicated than hers can be, there was almost a reluctance to listen to the specifically female voice, the text's insistence on daughter, not merely child, of a famous father. Rosa is ambiguous about the 'sins of the fathers' because she is involved in the suffering they cause. It is an inheritance she both resents and acknowledges some part in. Despite the attraction of complete separation and the necessity to free herself from her father, she cannot 'place' him as Baasie does because of his colour, nor sail away like Conrad.

> At sea, at sea; to circumnavigate is to end up no farther than you started. The world round as your navel. Your contemplation of it in the cottage doesn't serve me any more. I am like my father – the way they say my father was. I discover I can take from people what I need. But I am aware I don't have his justification; only the facility's my inheritance – my dowry, if any man is interested (p. 192).

Discussion of the 'brothers' recognized that the pressure on Rosa was intensified by the fact that her real brother, Tony, drowned in the family swimming pool when they were young. Yet even in their childhood she had a sense of his capacity for separation, of a confidence, a weight given to his senses which is denied her, and a feeling that he could define his own place, shape his world, whereas her place is a given, her 'I' is absorbed in, defined by, 'we':

> The five-year-old boy was being allowed to help make bricks: if he had lived to be a man perhaps he would never have outgrown – given up? – this happy seclusion of what he himself was seeing, touching, feeling, from anything outside it (p. 54).

Rosa, as girl child, appears to grow up entirely through other people and what they tell her is appropriate to feel and do. 'You go through the motions . . . what's expected of you. What you've come to rely on' (p. 46). And she is very good at the performance. She learns the necessary language.

When required to act out the role of a detainee's fiancee in order to convey messages to him in prison she can remember and reproduce word for word his exact turn of phrase, his cadence, and knows she can 'be relied upon', relied upon to conceal, to place as relatively unimportant her own growing feelings of attraction, to use her sexuality while denying it:

> I did – as you say – what was expected. I was not a fake. Once a month I sat as they had sent me to take their messages and receive his, a female presented to him with the smiling mouth, the gazing yet evasive eyes, the breasts drooping a little as she hunched forward, a flower standing for what lies in her lap (p. 68).

She is used by her parents, subordinated to the cause. However they might justify this, she knows how it makes her feel: 'We didn't despise prostitutes in that house – our house – we saw them as victims of necessity, while certain social orders lasted' (p. 68). The analogy is only possible because she is female, yet she cannot verbally separate 'I' from 'we' even in her resentment until she can voice her accusation of both her mother – 'If she saw, realized – and at least she might have considered the possibility – she didn't choose to see' (that Rosa felt in reality the emotions appropriate to the role she was acting out) – and of him, 'Lionel Burger, knowing as he did, without question, I would do what had to be done' (p. 66).

Rosa is placed, in every sense, by her father. Her acceptance is assumed, she is unheard. Her access to and any spontaneous expression of self is blocked by her competence in the role of dutiful daughter. When she wants to send a message to her mother in prison she finds she does not know how to address her. As Rosa struggles to find an appropriate voice her 'innocently unsuitable tone' becomes 'the perfect vehicle' for the important thing she needs to convey, the fact that her father has not been arrested too. She chooses a hot water bottle in which to conceal the message precisely because it has no association of personal comfort for her mother (who never used one) – 'she would realise there must be some special reason for it having been sent' (p. 16). A use of language she has consciously learnt to perfection by the time she is considered old enough to marry is seen in embryo to be unconsciously adopted by the young adolescent girl. When she speculates later about what 'they' saw when they saw her outside the prison Rosa knows she was defined as 'the daughter of Lionel Burger', ironically 'little Rosa Burger', a dry-eyed and composed child who already 'had taken on her mother's role in the household giving loving support to her father' (p. 12).

She knows what assumption will be made: 'she must have somebody inside' (p. 9). While her real awareness is all focused on 'the lower part of her pelvis, in the leaden, dragging, wringing pain there', on the 'irrelevant' 'peculiar fierce concentration of the body's forces in the menstruation of early puberty' (p. 15), the 'relevant' interpretation of the schoolgirl has nothing to do with her personal or sexual identity, with her pain and confusion, but the fact that she must be visiting a relative in prison. For the faithful she is 'an example to us all of the way a detainee's family ought to behave'. For her father she is his schoolgirl daughter who 'could be counted on'. Rosa's sense of what she is remains private, unknown. Her crucial personal feelings have no place, no space 'in this family totally united in and dedicated to the struggle' (p. 12):

> Outside the prison the internal landscape of my mysterious body turns me inside out, so that in that public place on that public occasion . . . I am within that monthly crisis of destruction, the purging, tearing, draining of my own structure. I am my womb, and a year ago I wasn't aware – physically – I had one (p. 15).

Rosa's sexual identity is used, ignored, denied in a way that it is inconceivable her brothers' would have been. She has an awareness of suffering that begins with her own female body. In spite of most of the people in the discussion groups being similarly aware because they were also women, there was much more willingness to 'hear', respond to the public context rather than the private female place, the personal sexual identity which determines political meaning. It was possible to ignore, or not to hear Rosa's statement that her sex defines her struggle more than the fact that she is a survivor, alone and disconnected:

> everything that child, that girl did was out of what is between daughter and mother, daughter and brother, daughter and father. . . . I was struggling with a monstrous resentment against the claim – not of the Communist Party! – of blood, shared genes, the semen from which I had issued and the body in which I had grown. I stand outside the prison with an eiderdown and hidden messages for my mother. Tony is dead and there is no other child but me, for her. Two hundred and seventeen days with the paisley scarf in my pocket, while witnesses come in and out of the dock condemning my father. My mother is dead and there is only me, for him. Only me. My studies, my work, my love affairs must fit in with the twice-monthly visits to the prison, for life, as long as he lives – if he had lived. My professors, my employers, my men must accept this overruling. I have no passport because I am my father's daughter. People who associate with me must be prepared to be suspect because I am my father's daughter. . . . And now he is dead! Dead! . . . I knew I must have wished him to die; that to exult and to sorrow were the same thing for me (p. 62).

Rosa, like the unicorn in the tapestries described towards the end of the book, is a 'creature that has never been'. Only in the 'paradis invente' with Conrad has she been able to share the terrible secrets – 'you can fuck your mother and wish your father dead' – but ironically her father's death does not allow her to be, does not release her from other people's assumptions about her place. The co-conspirators Ivy and Dick Terblanche believe that she talked of trying to get into the Transkei because she was under orders to find a cover job there, and that she must have taken advantage of her period of 'convalescence' to say no. These two people for whom she feels affection and who 'represent an intimacy with my father greater than mine' (p. 113) cannot believe she is not waiting with them for the future when the governments of Angola, Mozambique and eventually South Africa itself will be overthrown: 'Too late for Lionel, but you're here Rosa' (p. 108). This is a misreading, an assumption of Rosa's place which quite literally leaves her speechless. 'He thought I was overcome at the thought of my father. But I was filled with the need to get away as from something obscene – and afraid to wound him – them – by showing it' (p. 111).

She is reduced to dumbness and later, when confronted with suffering, to immobility: 'I don't know how to live in Lionel's country' (p. 210). She does not know her place – 'I have lost connection' (p. 172) – and has only an overwhelming sense of being misplaced, unheard, so that it becomes imperative to re-place herself, to manoeuvre for personal space and areas of experience which are being denied – 'I want to know somewhere else' (p. 185). Rosa's need to jettison an imposed identity, an adopted language, an assumed response begins to feel like a precondition for any genuine communication, particularly so in the 'formal' discussions in which we were engaged, where assumptions about the speaker's place and anticipated response, the use of 'appropriate' language diminished the capacity to hear. For women, and especially for feminists, Rosa's misplacing and her initial complicity in this becomes almost symbolic of a condition they know personally, a common (though not exclusively) female position. Some distancing from assumed place feels necessary in order to be heard.

The different place Rosa chooses is the French home of another woman who has defected from Lionel Burger, his first wife Katya. Katya has acknowledged he was a great man and yet decided ' "there's a whole world" outside what he lived for, what life with him would have been' (p. 264). The community in the south of France is a world of people with 'nothing to hide from, no one to elude, careless of privacy, in their abundance: letting be' (p. 224). It is a framed paradise into which Rosa enters, joyously intoxicated, yet she knows from the beginning that here too she is mis-placed, unseen: 'If I'd been black that would at least have given the information I was from Africa. Even at a three hundred year remove, a black American. But nobody could see me, there, for what I am back where I come from' (p. 231).

Placing and place itself (which is more than context) are vital not only in hearing *Burger's Daughter*, both novel and character, but also – we began to discover – in hearing one another's responses in the teaching situation. Rosa is forced into the realization (through being unable to remain silent at theoretical, essentially ignorant, misreading) that 'there's no indemnity' (p. 296). She feels then very close to Gordimer's position that 'you can't opt out altogether. You are either running away from your inevitable place, or you are taking it on. By place I don't mean a predetermined place: your place depends on the role you take in society. But the fact is that you *have* a role; there's no such thing as an ivory tower – that's a place in itself. You are consciously or unconsciously creating a position in your society' (Dembo, 1983, 343).

Rosa is aware that she is 'the place in which something has occurred' and when she moves out of the place where concealment is part of the way of life she begins to uncover, to trace her own placing, both in terms of individuals and society and in her sense of self. Initially she is 'in place, outside the prison' and it is important that her mother knows 'that I had been outside; we were connected' (p. 15). However confused she becomes, she does not deny that her parents were involved in a human conspiracy, above all other kinds, a connection with blacks that was completely personal. 'They had the connection because they believed it possible' (p. 172). Yet ironically 'in that house people didn't know each other'. Conrad sees this, just as he foresees her return and imprisonment, and Rosa admits, 'you've proved it to me in what I have found since in places you haven't been, although you are exploring the world' (p. 171).

In the south of France, through a woman who has also 'defected' and been involved with a sailor, a boat builder, Rosa explores her sensuality, something owed her youth. She enters the frames of the 'paradis invente', enjoying the capacities of each of the senses and becomes

> A girl, a creature whose sense of existence would be in her nose buried in flowers, peace juice running down her chin, face tended at mirrors, mind dreamily diverted, body seeking pleasure (p. 229).

She inhabits the Present 'completely as everything in place around her, there and then. In the bar where she had sat seeing others living in the mirror, there was no threshold between her reflection and herself' (p. 272). No past, no future. She becomes enchanted by Bernard Chabalier, whom she feels can make everything possible for her, and she comes to believe it is possible to live 'out of time' within the ambit of a person, not a country:

> Bernard Chabalier's mistress isn't Lionel Burger's daughter; she's certainly not accountable to the Future, she can go off and do good works in the Cameroun or contemplate the unicorn in the tapestry forest (p. 304).

Later when she imagines a woman returning day after day to gaze at the tapestry in the museum, she recognizes the anomaly of its harmony and sensual peace in the age of the thumbscrew and the dungeon.

Rosa does not have any illusions about happiness being moral or productive. She knows 'it's possible to feel very much alive when terrible things – dread and pain and threatening courage – are also in the air' (p. 349) but she also knows because of her place, because of her South African experience, that 'there isn't the possibility of happiness without the institutions to protect it' (p. 295). She must speak, interrupt a theoretical discussion of freedom (which, for Europeans, livens up a party), to declare that 'institutions must evolve that will make it possible in practice' (p. 296). She knows suffering and, she admits later, she knows fear. A black township is a 'place'; 'a position whose contradictions those who impose them don't see, and from which will come a resolution they haven't provided for' (p. 150). No one need live dangerously in Europe, and this creates the gap, the difference in experience, place, which makes explanation impossible:

> The man in France was the one I could talk to; and when it came to the point, this was the one subject I couldn't open with him. Not that he lacks the ability to imagine – what? This place, all of us here (p. 349).

When she states that she has done nothing, he can only ask, 'What could you have done?' and that she cannot explain.

After the start of her affair with Chabalier, Rosa imagines a discussion among Katya and her friends of 'the prospects for me, you all know so well' (p. 280). They are prospects, a place, she must reject because she is a foreigner just as she was among the blacks at Fats' place where 'the vanity of being loved by and belonging with them offered itself'. But she knows it cannot be taken for nothing: 'Offered freely – yet it has its price, that I would have to settle upon for myself' (p. 169). She realizes, like the photographer Orde Greer at his trial in South Africa, that her actions have nothing to do with conscience: 'no, no – that was just a phrase, what he meant was according to "necessity"' (p. 338). They spring from a growing awareness of place appropriately in the sense used by the blacks as 'somewhere to belong, but also something that establishes one's lot and sets aside much to which one doesn't belong' (p. 149).

The more closely we listened to responses in discussion of predictability and assumed place, the more our hearing of Rosa and of the novel as a whole became relevant to our hearing of one another. What was operating within the novel was mirrored in our interaction with it and beyond this in our interaction with each other. To be misplaced is to be misread. If place is predictable then what is heard is what is expected and much is unheard, in effect silenced. (Many people, for example, confessed to having 'skimmed' the political speech Lionel Burger makes at his trial.) If as teachers we placed ourselves too defiantly as feminists (protesting, 'Here I stand. I can do no other'), though we were at least defining our own place as opposed to demonstrating our competence at learned language, there was a danger of being placeable and therefore unheard. It began to feel important to resist appropriation both of our own 'meanings' and others' because predictability and placing closed down the possibility of really listening to articulated response (both conscious and unconscious), and to silences. Rosa's rueful statement felt as though it was bound to be true, 'You will use my words to make your own meaning', but it became increasingly clear that it was important to reveal uncertainties, ambiguities, contradictions in meanings, even though the 'place' from which they were uttered felt known.

This is paralleled by Gordimer's own position. She has stated that

> The only thing I'm one hundred per cent sure of – and I have been since I could formulate what was wrong with our life here, with this country – I just know that any form of racism is wrong. I don't see how one can see both sides of this ugly question: there aren't two sides – there are people who have the right to be human. That's the only thing I can say that I'm sure of. Nothing else. (Dembo, 1983, 347)

Around this core place she is aware that her consciousness has changed and expects, hopes, that it will keep on changing. The style she chooses to convey 'this constant shifting along, on very uncertain and uneven ground' (Dembo, 1983, 341) is very personal and allusive, producing uncertainty and demanding close reading. It feels an appropriate female style and one which if adopted in discussion would necessitate a recognition of the weight of the personal and an attentive listening and engagement to understand 'what she means'.

In the novel the central character is defined to a certain extent, like any of us, by her sex, her colour and her context but she can choose how she places herself (even though the recognition of this freedom to choose is much more frightening than being placed – 'What does one do with such knowledge?' (p. 62)). She can run away. She is confused by her fear but she comes to recognize that 'No one can defect' (p. 332). What is undeniable is the suffering. What is unavoidable is a response to it. Her awareness is initiated by the painful bleeding of her own body – 'blood; the reminder of vulnerability, life always under the threat of being spilled' (p. 240). She is unable to dismiss this, to escape as the European gigolo, Didier, does into sexual games with the comment, 'It's not our affair. I'm not my father, eh?' Her experience of love is that 'it doesn't cast out fear but it makes it possible to weep, howl at least' (p. 324).

Significantly, discussion of Rosa's awareness of suffering focused on her response to the unpredictable. All the groups discussed at length two such events occurring before she left South Africa and commonly cited them as shaking Rosa's sense of place. One was when Ronald Ferguson, 46, ex-miner, died on the park bench while she was busy minding her own business. This 'first' death, 'the mystery itself', defined real loneliness for her as living without social responsibility. The second incident, when she watched an old black man brutally whipping a donkey (and behind him in the cart a woman and child were bundled under sacks), was shocking in the sense that she saw agony and drove on because as a white woman she did not know at what point intercession made sense. She confesses to Conrad,

> The real reason why I went is something only you would believe. In fact, only if you believe it will it become believable, to me. I recognize it as part of the way my life has been coded, since you forced me to read such things in the cottage; but the code is my own, not yours, not theirs. . . . A donkey. A matter for the SPCA. . . . A meths drinker dead on a park bench. A matter for the Social Welfare Department. These are the things that move me now – when I say 'move' I don't mean tears or anger. I mean a sudden shift, a tumultuous upheaval, an uncontrollable displacement, concepts whose surface has been insignificant heaving over, up-ended, raised as huge boulders smelling of the earth that still clings to them. A shift that comes to me physically. . . . Earth, guts – I don't know what metaphors to use to describe the process by which I'm making my own metaphors for suffering (p. 196).

By the end of the novel Rosa, whose work it is to help children to walk again, putting one foot before the other, accepts that 'No one knows where the end of suffering will begin' (p. 356) but she places herself in relation to the unavoidable:

> I don't know the ideology:
> It's about suffering.
> How to end suffering.
> And it ends in suffering. Yes, it's strange to live in a country

> where there are still heroes. Like anyone else, I do what I can (p. 332).

There was, however, little discussion of one other crucial incident which Rosa herself cites as shaping her decision to return. It occurs when she is most sure of her capacity to feel, most sure of her own abundance, in Europe, the place in the novel familiar and 'easiest' for most of us discussing the book: 'I had met a woman in her nightdress wandering in the street. She was like anyone else: Katya, Gaby, Donna; poor thing, a hamster turning her female treadmill. . . . My sense of sorority was clear' (p. 332). The silence, the lack of discussion of the relationship between Rosa and the women in the novel was strikingly apparent, a gap heard much more clearly on re-listening. There was some wish to read Rosa's final place, inside the prison where the women are brought together, optimistically, but there was almost no attention given to the woman outside, Katya, the woman Rosa addresses again at the close of the novel but who was 'never able to make it out' (p. 361).

Rosa responds to the cry for help from the disorientated woman wandering in the street, 'What time is it?' and realizes 'that was what was wrong – that she didn't know, couldn't remember what it was that was wrong' (p. 300). Potentially the woman could be any of the women 'isolated' in the southern French community, for whom the future means only ageing, disease and personal suffering. She is threatening because she might easily be Katya, what Katya becomes when Rosa has gone. Katya and Rosa are linked by the 'fact' of Lionel Burger between them as rejected husband and father: 'It changed them, each for the other, at different times and in different contexts. . . . That fact – the fact of Lionel – when the passing of daily life thinned or shifted to reveal it, made, like a change of light transforming the landscape, the two women into something else for each other' (p. 247). They are very close, almost parallel at times, so Rosa can consider their prospects jointly and recognize that she talks with Katya 'incontinently, femininely' as she has never talked with anyone else: 'You tell me anecdotes of your youth that could transform my own' (p. 363). The affection, the caring of Rosa for Katya feels unique too:

> When I saw you plucking the cruel beard from your soft chin, I should have come to you and kissed you and put my arms around you against the prospect of decay and death (p. 304).

Katya almost represents for Rosa the choice she might have

made. Rosa knows why Katya opted out of the South African struggle, understands her feelings that,

> If you live in Europe . . . things change . . . but continuity never seems to break. You don't have to throw the past away . . . here you never really have to start from scratch. . . . Ah no, it's too much to take on. That's what I love – nobody expects you to be more than you are, you know. That kind of tolerance, I didn't even know it existed – I mean, there; if you're not equal to facing *everything*, there . . . you're a traitor. To the human cause – justice, humanity, the lot – there's nothing else (p. 250).

Rosa too, likes the European inheritance but feels eventually that it is not hers to choose.

Perhaps the general sense of the absence, the lack of weight of Rosa's natural mother (though there are several details about Cathy Jensen given in the text) is caused by the lack of emotional bond which in contrast is undeniable between Rosa and her father's first wife. Similarly, of the other two women brought together with Rosa in prison at the end of the novel, Clare Terblanche (the only character in a parallel position because of her age, colour and context) is eclipsed by Marisa Kgosana, wife of an imprisoned black leader. Again Rosa's emotional attachment, her awareness and pleasure in 'the element of sensuality' in Marisa's presence is clear:

> For Marisa it seems easy. She doesn't have to find a solemn face, acknowledge the distance between the prison and the cosmetic counter. She doesn't close away, go to cover, dead still, as I do. She doesn't have recourse to putting things delicately or explaining herself for fear of being misunderstood or misjudged. Defiance and confidence don't mourn; her beauty and the way she assumes it are stronger than any declaration (p. 136).

In a book dominated by brothers, Clare Terblanche has a place as significant as Baasie's as the 'sister' of Rosa. Clare's mother, Ivy Terblanche, acted as a second mother to Rosa: 'In the enveloping acceptance of Ivy's motherly arms she feels as if I were her own child – there is expectance, even authority. To her warm breast one can come home again . . .' (p. 114) Their, Clare and Rosa's, situations are closely parallel. They are both children denied the normal central role in a family. Their parents are engaged in and frequently imprisoned for the struggle against apartheid. Clare in her only extended conversation with Rosa in the text is placed as 'the other': 'the other had come', 'the other girl' (p. 118), 'So the other – Clare – knew' (p. 120). She is Rosa's other, a shadow on the other side of Rosa's door, a shadow which 'had no identity' (p. 118). Clare has acceded to her role as the child of Dick Terblanche, plunging into the political struggle. She is compared to, identified with her father: 'At the inner starting-point of each eyebrow a few hairs, like Dick's her father's stood up' (p. 120). Of Clare's political statements Rosa exclaims, 'Exactly what your father says' (p. 125). Unlike Baasie, however, her father's footsteps do not fit her with ease. Her struggle is written across her body, breaking out in peeling eczema which leaves, 'tormenting patches of inflamed and shedding skin, stripped of familiar context' (p. 124).

Despite the obvious significance of Clare as a 'sister' to Rosa and her image as a daughter who has taken on the role which Rosa is refusing, it is interesting that none of the groups 'heard' Clare or gave her much space in their discussions. The likelihood of this non-seeing is perceived by Rosa. She describes Clare as a female who 'has no vision of herself to divert others from her physical defects' (p. 123). Indeed the main response to, memory of, Clare in the groups was of her dandruff and eczema. For Rosa she had 'a body that had no signals; it would grow larger and at once more self-effacing. Few men would find their way, seek her through it' (p. 122). More significantly, few women in the groups found their way to her. Yet the conversation with Clare feels 'real' in a way that stands out in stark relief to the other conversations in the first section. Rosa responds to Clare emotionally, physically and with a driving need to make contact: 'We were suddenly plunged, reckless of confession, pooling the forbidden facts of life' (p. 125).

The meeting/talking of Clare and Rosa is initiated by Clare who seeks out Rosa to ask her to steal the key of the photocopier in her office so the machine may be used to produce political leaflets. Rosa masks their speech with the radio whose bland family messages punctuate the dialogue. Rosa's refusal both of Clare's request and her own assumed role spawns a tension of resistance which, because of their closeness, becomes a struggle between Rosa and Clare with each other and with themselves. 'Resistance brought them closer and closer to one another although they had not moved' (p. 121). Their resistance is played out through their bodies and the difference of their responses is placed in the context of female sensuality, 'they were aware of each other for a moment as females' (p. 121). Rosa's body is described as 'a body with the assurance of embraces, as cultivated intelligence forms a mind' (p. 121), whilst Clare's flesh is dumb. Even when their differences as women are stressed their paradoxical sameness underlines tension. Clare is not dismissable. She, to some extent, is Rosa: 'I watched her as if she were myself' (p. 127). The political confrontation between Clare and Rosa over the possibility of action in South Africa is played out in the language of Marxist polemics but Clare's horrified response to Rosa's persistent questioning is jarringly compared to Rosa's response when Conrad describes watching his 'mother and her lover fucking in the spare bedroom. She would deal with what was put before her without allowing herself to see it, just as I did' (p. 126). The ambiguity of voice in *Burger's Daughter* compounds the weaving of the personal and political when Rosa's comment, 'It's part of the strategy of the struggle' (p. 126) is tacked on to this image of non-seeing. The struggles, political and personal, are thus intertwined.

The further element of this episode is the discovery of a used sanitary towel in a cupboard. Their joint disgusted response is deemed by Rosa to be essentially white and middle-class. As the discussion progresses Rosa becomes increasingly aware of her sexuality as being different from and in opposition to Clare's lack of sensual and sexual knowledge: 'I was aware of an unpleasant strength bearing upon her from me. She's something sad rather than ugly, a woman without sexual pride' (p. 123). Thus when Clare disposes of the sanitary towel as she leaves the flat, Rosa sees it as an act not of white hygiene but as a refusal of the female sensual body. She 'stalked ahead of me as if she had successfully disposed of a body' (p. 129).

In the women's prison where Rosa is detained after the children's revolt in Soweto she is involved in a community based on communication, connection across race and culture in whatever way feels appropriate. The small precious gifts of prison economy (cigarettes, a peach, a tube of hand-cream, a minute electric torch) are exchanged and tiny scrolled messages conveyed by black common-law prisoners and cleaning women. Marisa announces her presence, from her solitary confinement to Rosa's and Clare's, through hymns, ANC freedom songs in Xhosa, a pop song, and 'the voices of other black women took up and harmonised whatever she sang' (p. 355). Rosa's contact is through touch, through therapeutic exercises and laughter, her communication visual. She manages to obtain sketching materials – a children's drawing book and a box of pastels – and paints a naive imaginary landscape with a failure of perspective appropriate to it 'that could rouse no suspicions that she might be incorporating plans of the layout of the prison etc.' (p. 355). Even her Christmas card depicting a group of carol-singers in which Marisa, Rosa and Clare, and an Indian associate of them all were unmistakably recognizable was used to communicate to those outside that, though isolated, 'these women were in touch with each other' (p. 356).

At the end of the novel Rosa is, literally, in a similar place to her father. She refers to 'a watermark of light that came into the cell at sundown every evening . . . something that Lionel Burger once mentioned' (p. 361) and like his, her communication is censored. Apart from the bonds and the multi-sensual means of communication among the women, a major difference is that Rosa is writing to a 'foreign' woman. Even though some of what she says will never be understood, her caring is clear, their contact is possible through known reference, shared experience.

Gordimer as a contemporary woman writer (and particularly in this text where the central narrator and protagonist is a young woman) insists on the reader listening to the personal detail of female experience. This experience must be acknowledged and, for women at least, offers a way in through a 'known' place to the particular place of South Africa. The woman inside seems to be insisting on the duality of public and private in the sense that the political can only have meaning, can only begin to be understood, through the personal. We began to feel the crucial relevance of this in the experience and re-hearing of the group discussions. Rosa's dilemma, because of the denial of her personal voice and potential, began to reflect our own – the need to find ways of speaking and hearing others' speech which allows acknowledgement of ourselves and the other(s) not just as places but as places in which something has occurred.

Through discussion of a novel where the writer refuses to allow the reader the authority, that clarity of place (both reader's and character's), to which she is normally given access, we were made aware of the reliance on authority in the teaching situation and the 'deafening' effect of assumptions associated with place. It is very difficult, in different ways, for both teachers and students to 're-place' themselves, not least because it makes us all more vulnerable, more unpredictable. It was evident from the groups we taught that this was more likely to happen the more familiar the participants were with the tutor. Ironically, the better we knew one another, the less was assumed, the more real listening seemed to be taking place.

We came to the conclusion that in order to disrupt the

structures of expected response, action in three main areas would be productive:

(1) It feels necessary not only to create a context for discussion in which the personal voice is given space, but also to give authority to individual experience, which in turn should shift the weight of authority away from the teacher.

(2) To balance this it would be useful to undermine the assumed authority of 'appropriate' language. There was a tendency in all the groups, present in embryo with the younger students and most apparent with the most 'academic', to couch their responses in the formal registers of political or literary critical terminology. This effectively blocked access to personal response, allowed individuals to shed their particular identities and sail away to the safe charted regions of 'objective' analysis with little recognition that they were neither 'hearing' nor 'being heard'. If we accept, like Rosa, that it is a denial of ourselves as women to 'sail away', then we need to try to ensure that our feminism remains personal, not predictable.

(3) The most shocking area of this exercise was being faced, undeniably, through recording the discussions, with our own incapacities to listen effectively to the text and to other people's responses to it. Our preconceptions about important areas of discussion/investigation meant that we were reluctant to allow authority to move away from our own responses to the extent that we often did not hear or misread student response. We assumed the likely movement of the discussion, predicted connection and placing, which meant that not only did we fail to respond to alternative directions but were largely unaware – until we listened more carefully – of the 'gaps', the significant areas of silence. We only began to really hear the text when we re-listened to what was not said about it.

The practice of recording discussions, and possibly building up a bank of tapes accessible to other tutors/groups who might want to cover similar material, could be extremely productive in preparation, assessment and improvement of our own teaching. It would also be useful, occasionally, to give students the opportunity to re-hear and analyse discussions in which they have been involved. As a way of refining our capacity to listen and – what feels vital to feminists – our ability to hear silences, we found recording the seminar discussions a revelatory and valuable exercise. It is one which we think should be more widely adopted.

Notes

1. We would like to thank the following groups for their co-operation in the discussions: Women's Literature group, Department of Continuing Education, University of Sheffield; 2nd year Combined Honours students, University of Newcastle-upon-Tyne; A level Literature group, High Storrs Comprehensive School, Sheffield; MA Women's Studies students, Sheffield Polytechnic.
2. This and all subsequent references following quotations in parentheses refer to Gordimer (1979).

Bibliography

Dembo, L.S. (1983) (ed.) *Interviews with Contemporary Writers*, Madison, University of Wisconsin Press, 339–47.

Gordimer, N. (1979) *Burger's Daughter*, London, Jonathan Cape.

Chapter eleven

Responding to the Word: problems and pitfalls in interpreting the Bible

Mark Corner

Scripture has a wax nose
(*A proverb often quoted by Martin Luther*)

Appreciation of the problems inherent in understanding the Bible is not merely a product of the Enlightenment or of modern 'scientific' thought. Arguments over methods of biblical interpretation have been a constant theme in the history of Christian thought. Indeed, they were already apparent whilst the canon of Scripture itself was being formed, since differing views of what a text meant and how it should be read often determined an attitude towards whether it should be included in the canon. Christians may always have agreed about the importance of the Bible, whether or not they regard it as the supreme authority in determining their faith. But they have always been ready to disagree with one another over its meaning. Indeed extreme sceptics would argue that the Bible can be made to mean virtually anything.

Martin Luther himself appreciated these difficulties of interpretation. His theology was built up out of his biblical teaching. To understand his thinking on justification by faith alone, the nature of Christ, the Church or the Sacraments, all those pillars around which the edifice of the Protestant Reformation was to be constructed, one has to understand his years as a Professor of Biblical Theology at the University of Wittenberg, lecturing day by day on the Psalms or the Epistles of Paul to the Romans, Galatians and Hebrews. Yet despite the function of Scripture as the primary source of his ideas, it was Luther himself who echoed the idea of its being 'a wax nose'. Like a face whose plasticity gives it a range of different expressions and makes ambiguous the thoughts which it harbours, the Bible is capable of being read and interpreted in a number of different ways.

Thus it is said that Luther, exasperated with his fellow

Reformer Huldrych Zwingli, wrote in chalk on the table across which they were swapping arguments '*Hoc est corpus meum*' – 'this is my body'. Luther was reminding himself of the words attributed to Jesus at the Last Supper, when he broke bread and distributed it to his disciples. The words proved, to Luther's satisfaction, the doctrine of the 'Real Presence', namely that at the celebration of the eucharist Christ is 'really' – and not merely symbolically – present in the bread and wine.

To Zwingli, however, the phrase was being wrongly interpreted. He did not question that Jesus spoke those words, or that the text of the Bible was true. The issue was: what truth? Zwingli recalled another passage of the New Testament, from St John's gospel, where Jesus says: 'I am the true vine'. Does this mean to say, Zwingli asked rhetorically, that there is a 'real presence' of Christ in vineyards? Of course not. The passage is to be understood symbolically. Indeed the whole passage reads: 'I am the true vine, and my Father is the vinedresser' (John 15:1). One could hardly understand the idea of the Father as 'vinedresser' in anything other than symbolic terms, similar to words like 'Judge', 'Shepherd' and 'King' which the New Testament uses of God. 'This is my body' therefore becomes 'This stands for my body', and a symbolic rather than real presence is affirmed.

Luther and Zwingli, in common with the other Protestant Reformers, affirmed the supreme authority of the Bible for Christians, and argued the corrupt institution of the medieval church on the basis of comparison with the simple early Christian communities described in the New Testament. Indeed, the claim of the Protestant Reformers to be the 'true' church, despite their precarious foothold on power in the early sixteenth century, was based upon a biblical theme, that of the 'true remnant' which God chooses as a faithful and pure residue when the rest of Israel has fallen into idolatry and corruption. The Protestant minority in Europe, like the minority within Israel described in the Old Testament, was the 'true' people of God. The Reformers needed the Bible as a weapon with which to challenge the all-consuming power of the church to be its own interpreter and its own justification, and resist an ecclesiastical totalitarianism which (at that time) had a monopoly of history and could describe the origins of Christianity in such a way as to suit what it had become.

The Luther-Zwingli debate over the eucharist, however, pointed to the other side of the coin. Luther might have owed everything (in one sense) to the Bible – his theological ideas, the ideological means for his escape from the church and its claim to interpret the whole of reality, a means to communicate with others and share his own quest for freedom. But the Bible was still 'a wax nose'. It was open to numerous interpretations, and once the break with Rome had begun, a fissiparous tendency came to the fore among those who were to become known as Protestants, with Lutherans, Zwinglians, Calvinists, Anabaptists, all dividing from one another over how to interpret crucial passages of the Bible. Having taken the Bible out of the hands of the church which had claimed to possess the sole authority for its interpretation, they found that there were a thousand authorities for its interpretation, that every man or woman with access to the text (and these numbers increased exponentially through the development of printing in the late fifteenth century) could claim authority for understanding its meaning. There were as many interpretations as there were interpreters, and every reader was an interpreter.

Of course the Reformers themselves couldn't succumb to such a pessimistic view of their reliance upon Scripture. They pointed to the role of the Holy Spirit in understanding the Bible. The Spirit became a kind of supernatural guarantor that a faithful Christian's reading of Scripture would be the correct one. 'Let it therefore be held as fixed', wrote Calvin in his *Institutes of the Christian Religion*, 'that those who are inwardly taught by the Holy Spirit acquiesce implicitly in Scripture; that Scripture, carrying its own evidence along with it, deigns not to submit to proofs and arguments, but owes the full conviction with which we ought to receive it to the testimony of the Spirit' (Calvin, 1975, I, Ch. VII, 72). Far from taking the view that they were rejecting the church's interpretation of the Bible for a mass of individual opinions, the Reformers took the view that they were rejecting a human interpretation of Scripture for a 'divine' one, the understanding mediated directly into the mind by the Spirit of God. They were avoiding a form of 'idolatry' which placed a human view of the truth above God's own truth.

In reality, the attempt to reach for the doctrine of the Holy Spirit in order to spread a holy calm upon the waters of individual interpretation did nothing to solve the problem. 'Proofs and arguments' remained in abundance, divisions among the Reformers over biblical exegesis refused to go away, and whilst each interpreter might lay claim to the Holy Spirit as his or her guide, such divine assistance did little to bring one interpretation closer to another.

Since the Reformation, Protestantism has continued to wrestle with the central problem raised by its espousal of a 'biblical theology'. On the one hand, it points up the Scriptures as critic and even judge over the church, refusing to allow the church to 'possess' the Bible by manufacturing interpretation to suit its own ecclesiastical values. But then it faces its own problem of how to interpret a set of books which, once free of the magisterium of the church to determine their meaning, appear vulnerable to an endless number of individual and perhaps eccentric analyses. This dilemma has contributed to the recent history of the churches since the Reformation, which has often seemed to consist of a conflict between Catholic authoritarianism on the one hand and Protestant sectarianism on the other.

Nowhere has the dilemma of interpretation for Protestants been more clearly revealed than in the case of Fundamentalism. This movement is now a powerful social and political as well as religious force in the United States, whilst fundamentalist or 'evangelical' groups have a considerable backing in Britain too. Although in origin the term refers to a series of tracts written in the 1910s on a whole range of doctrines, *The Fundamentals* (see Barr, 1981, 2), the term 'Fundamentalism' is commonly associated with a particular attitude towards Scripture, one which believes in its infallibility and inerrancy. The fundamentalist regards the Bible as the inspired Word of God and the absolute authority which determines the faith of individual Christians.

Yet among fundamentalists the fissiparous tendency of Protestantism is if anything more evident than among other groups of Protestants. It is on this 'sectarian edge' of the Protestant faith that one finds countless divisions and sub-divisions among clusters of different interpreters, all united in their view of the Bible as their supreme authority but less united in their view of what it is actually saying.[1]

The various forms of Millenarian belief, for instance, or the various forms of Charismatic and Pentecostalist Christianity, represent a set of religious groupings whose commitment to the authority of Scripture is absolute but whose reading of it is clearly relative. Whether it is the Book of Daniel or of Revelation pointing to the coming thousand year reign of Christ on earth, or the speaking with tongues spoken of in Paul's Letter to the Corinthians, the use of key texts by Millenarian or Pentecostalist writers is open to the charges of selectivity and misinterpretation, not only from those outside these loose groupings but from those within them too. The conglomeration of views on the sectarian edge of Protestantism is the clearest expression of a tendency which characterizes the denomination as a whole, namely a vacuum in interpretation. Taken out of the hands of the church, but unable to be entrusted to individuals, Scripture has to be controlled by some other method (at least for those who feel that they cannot rely upon supernatural intervention by the Holy Spirit).

The drive towards a systematic theology in Protestantism arises in part out of this need for regulation. The early confessions, like the Confession of Augsburg of 1530 expressing the kernel of Lutheranism, tried to provide a summary of the main doctrines of the faith, which might function as a kind of 'written magisterium' governing the interpretation of the Bible. But these confessions had certain disadvantages when compared to the 'living' magisterium of the church. They were themselves open to misunderstanding and arguments over meaning, as when Cardinal Newman in the nineteenth century shocked the Anglican establishment with his claim that the Thirty-Nine Articles were consistent with a view of the Church of England as an example of reformed Catholicism. And the confessions were themselves, like the biblical texts, locked into a particular time and culture, unable to respond to social change. Protestantism appeared to be locked into an infinite regression. The biblical texts were regulated by the text of the confessions, but the confessions, too, required textual analysis and commentary.

One response to the 'Protestant dilemma' is to return to a strict view of the church as arbiter of Scripture. Support for this view can be found from the process of the formation of the biblical canon, a selection which took centuries to accomplish throughout the church. Since the Bible was put together by the early Christian communities in response to their needs, it could be argued, it is clearly a product of the church, and can perform no other purpose than to reflect and assist the interests of the church.

At the same time, the commitment of the Protestant Reformers to 'free' the Bible from the church evokes sympathy. Unless the scriptural text can act as a source of criticism for the church, it cannot be '*ecclesia semper reformanda*' (a church constantly reforming itself). Instead it becomes a fossilized religious community, a petrifying forest of ecclesiastically-sanctioned interpretations which do nothing to challenge the church from within. The Greek Orthodox community, with its strong belief in the Bible as a treasure kept exclusively by the church and understood in terms laid down by the ancient church fathers of the first few centuries CE, could be seen as an illustration of a religious culture decaying through the lack of such a challenge as that which Protestantism has undoubtedly posed to the Roman Catholic church.

The general problems of interpretation which we have tried to set out here go back further than the rise of 'biblical criticism' in the eighteenth and nineteenth centuries. Certainly the development of modern techniques of historical, literary, and scientific enquiry poses particular problems for the biblical exegete. However, long before the Scriptures were ever analysed along the paths of 'source' or 'form' criticism, they were being read and interpreted in a variety of different ways, whether it be the use of rabbinic forms of exegesis, medieval types of allegory, or the more literal approach of the Protestant Reformers. Modern criticism may have sharpened and widened the tools of analysis. It has not, however, altered the nature of the basic quest for understanding the texts.

Our survey so far has examined some of the reasons why understanding the Bible is such an important and difficult issue for Christians. But in order to progress further we have to look more closely at those developments of the last hundred and fifty years, the era of so-called 'scientific criticism' of the Bible.

Modern biblical criticism has proceeded in two stages, which we will outline briefly in this section. Our claim is that only with the advent of the second stage in contemporary biblical hermeneutics has the work of scriptural interpretation achieved a satisfactory approach to the text.

In the first stage of modern criticism, attention was focused upon the circumstances in which the Bible was originally written. Partly, this involved recognition that the Christian Scriptures are not a single book but a collection of texts, written (if one includes the Old Testament) in different languages over the space of a millenium. Modern printing represents as a book what is in reality more a library of Judaeo-Christian thought, a thousand years of selected reading from a particular religious tradition. This recognition reminds the interpreter that the unity of the biblical message has to be established by criticism and cannot be presumed in advance. For instance: the most famous passage of 2 Timothy remarks that 'All Scripture is inspired of God. . .' But can one take this to be 'The Bible's view of itself', or merely the view of a writer whom scholars by common consensus deny to be Paul himself and place somewhere in the early second century? In other words, might other biblical writers disagree with the author of 2 Timothy?

It is, of course, this possibility of internal disagreement between the biblical authors that makes the charge of selectivity against various interpreters of Scripture such a potent one. If one could be sure, once one had found one part of the Bible stating a view on, for instance, Jesus' attitude towards divorce, that this must be the view of the whole Bible, then 'selectivity' would be less of a problem. But when one recognizes that it is possible that Mark represents Jesus refusing to allow divorce in any circumstances, whilst Matthew makes an exception in the case of adultery, the question becomes much more complicated. Moreover, once one tries to consider Jewish teaching in general on the subject, including the views to be found in the Old Testament (which Christians have a habit of alternately treating as Holy Writ and as a 'primitive understanding' that has been altogether superseded by the New Testament) then the picture becomes more complicated still. It ceases to be clear that the Bible speaks with one voice, and the possibility arises that it speaks with several voices. In this context, the art of listening to Scripture must constitute attentiveness to the harmony (or even discord) of different sounds, rather than the simplicity of attending to a single repeated note.

The main forms of criticism which constituted this first stage of modern biblical criticism were 'source', 'form' and 'redaction' criticism.[2] All of them deepened understanding of the circumstances within which Scripture was originally composed. The student of the New Testament, for instance, is now equipped with a 'genealogical tree' for the Synoptic Gospels, suggesting both the role of Mark as a source for Matthew and Luke, and the common use made by these two latter gospels of a collection of Jesus' teachings and sayings known as Q (from the German *quelle* = source). An attempt is thereby made, with as accurate a system of dating as possible, to identify the sources of the biblical material, both those within the canon and those outside it.

Analysing the biblical material according to 'form' had also been very significant at this stage of criticism. Thus certain passages of Scripture might be identified as reflecting certain liturgical forms in the early christian communities, such as hymns, blessings or confessions. Other passages reflected literary forms, not so much as they existed in the 'churches' but as they might be found in other religious or philosophical movements of the time which were clearly influencing the nascent christian self-consciousness. Such 'form criticism' helped to build up a picture of the social and cultural context of the composition of Scripture, by looking at the '*Sitz im Leben*' of different patterns within the text.

As with source criticism, form criticism reinforces the view that the biblical material was not composed in a vacuum but in a particular social and intellectual context. It emphasizes the fact that whilst traditionally many Christians have seen the Scriptures as 'given to' the communities which adopted them by God, rather as the tablets of stone were given to Moses on Mount Sinai, in reality it would be more accurate to say that those texts 'emerged from' those early Christian or Jewish communities.

A third and more recent approach to interpretation, but still one very much within the first stage of biblical hermeneutics, is that of 'redaction criticism'. Here the focus of attention is upon the intention of the author in 'creating' a text. The notion of 'redaction', however, makes clear that there is no idea of scriptural writings being composed entirely as the work of individuals. The concept of 'redaction' is closer to that of editor than author. It is the notion of an individual who uses pre-existent material, but in such a way as to impose upon it a particular editorial slant.

Put together, these three forms of criticism – source, form and redaction – enable the biblical scholar to understand more precisely how the Bible came to be written, both in terms of the resources available to the writers in terms of traditional literary and religious forms and sources, and in terms of the input of their own particular and possibly original editorial influence.

However, these methods reflect a limitation. They concentrate upon the circumstances in which the texts were originally put together, but they ignore the circumstances in which they have subsequently been – and are subsequently being – read and understood. They build up a '*Sitz im Leben*' of the writers of Scripture, but not one for its readers. They are therefore inadequate and one-sided if taken to constitute the whole work of interpretation.

At the second stage of biblical criticism, that which has generated so much interest in the question of hermeneutics in contemporary biblical studies, the exegete is encouraged to remember that his or her own '*Sitz im Leben*' is as important to the understanding of Scripture as is that of the biblical writers themselves. The social and cultural constraints of the reader are as significant for the work of exegesis as are those of the writer.[3]

Source, form and redaction criticism all helped to place the biblical texts within history, rather than 'above' it as 'sacred' rather than secular literature. The picture emerged of texts built up slowly in response to the needs of particular communities, using tools of analysis and forms of thought available at the time. But now biblical criticism increasingly recognizes that it must place the readers as well as the writers of Scripture in *their* historical context. The interpreters of the text, like the 'sacred literature' which they are interpreting, cannot lift themselves any more than their object of study out of the flow of history, and regard the past from a standpoint that is somehow 'above' the present.

From this recognition of the 'two horizons' of interpretation, that of the reader of Scripture as well as that of the writer, biblical interpretation in recent years has come to work in a number of disciplines. It has traditionally worked in those disciplines which open up the past. Every exegete has tried to train himself or herself to be a reasonable classicist, historian and archaeologist. But now it increasingly adds to its task the study of those disciplines which open up the present, studying the context within which the Bible is read rather than that in which it was written. The exegete has to understand a far wider range of disciplines in the light of this necessity, including sociology, linguistics and politics. It may be a daunting task, but it represents a new stage in awareness on the part of exegesis. It is no longer simply listening to the past, but also hearing itself as it listens. The development raises profound questions concerning truth and objectivity which cannot be discussed at length in the course of this chapter, but it undoubtedly represents a deeper understanding of the problems involved than did the work of earlier interpreters.

Because much of the literature on contemporary biblical interpretation is extremely technical, and certainly beyond my capacity for understanding, this chapter will offer a few examples of exegesis designed to illustrate some of the insights gleaned from a study of the Bible which recognizes the 'two' horizons rather than one.

To begin with, we may consider the following passage from Paul's letter to the Romans (all quotations are from the Revised Standard Version unless otherwise stated):

> Greet Andronicus and Junias, my kinsmen and my fellow prisoners; they are men of note among the apostles, and they were in Christ before me (Romans 16:7).

The interesting point about this (apparently rather uncontroversial!) passage concerns the name 'Junias'. For some commentators it is a woman 'Junia' who is being referred to, an alternative version which some translations, for instance the New English Bible, draw attention to.

The question of whether Paul is referring to a man, Junias, or a woman, Junia, in this passage becomes significant when we go on to read that he refers to them as 'of note among the apostles'. For it raises the possibility that a woman might be an apostle, something that has important implications for the churches today when they consider the role of women in contemporary Christianity, particularly in the context of the ordination of women. Contemporary arguments on this issue concentrate much of their attention upon 'what Scripture says' about the place of women in the Christian community. But the debate over Romans 16:7 demonstrates that a lot of work has to be done to ensure that we know the text of Scripture in the first place. In this case, the possibility arises that in the course of translation the text has been interpreted away.[4]

To look more closely at the text of Romans 16:7, it is necessary to look at what has been written about it in commentaries and in lexica. Too much detail clearly cannot be entered into here, but I should like to set out what one particular lexicon has to say on the subject of the Greek word *Ἰουνιᾶς* (translated usually by the name Junias).

The tome in question is the *Greek-English Lexicon of the New Testament and other Early Christian Literature*, edited by Arndt and Gingrich. Published in 1957, the book is a translation of the fourth edition of Professor Walter Bauer's pre-eminent work of lexicography, which undertook a systematic search in Greek literature down to Byzantine times for parallels to the language of the New Testament. It remains the definitive lexicon for consideration of New Testament words, although scholars would clearly also consult commentaries and dictionaries of the Bible in considering any text.

This is what the lexicon has to say on the subject of 'Junias':

> *Ἰουνιᾶς, ᾶ, ὁ* Junias (not found elsewh., prob. short form of the common Junianus; cf. Bl-D. {125,2; Rob. 172) a Jewish convert to Christianity, who was imprisoned w. Paul Ro 16:7; s. on *Ανδρόνικος*. – The possibility, fr. a purely lexical point of view, that this is a woman's name *Ἰουνια, ας*, *Junia* (mlt-H. 155; ancient commentators took Andr. and Junia as a married couple, S. *Ἰουλία*) is prob. ruled out by the context (s. Ltzm., Hdb. ad loc.). M-M.*

From Bauer's comments we can glean the following:

1. The text may either be taken as referring to a woman or to a man. In the Greek New Testament the accusative singular *Ἰουνιᾶν* appears, which may derive either from the man's name

'Ιουνιᾶς or the woman's name *'Ιουνιά*. The only difference is one of accent (*'Ιουνιᾶν* or *'Ιουνιάν*).

2. From what Bauer calls a 'purely lexical' point of view, the balance of probability is slightly in favour of a woman's name, since Junia was a common Roman name, whereas Junias is not found elsewhere at all, and would have to be interpreted as a contraction of the name Junianus. On the other hand, such contractions did occur (for instance Olympas as a shortening of Olympianus), so that the possibility of a male name cannot be excluded.

3. However, Bauer favours the view that a man is being spoken of on the grounds of what he calls 'the context'. The suggestion has been made, for instance, that a man and a woman would not be 'fellow-prisoners', although, as Dodd points out in his commentary on Romans, the passage does not necessarily imply that they were in the same prison (Dodd, 1932, 238–9). Probably the most important consideration of 'context', however, is the reference to Andronicus and Junia(s) as 'of note among the apostles'.

Gingrich makes clear that this is an important consideration for him when he writes about 'Junias' in the *Interpreter's Dictionary of the Bible*:

> Grammatically it might be a feminine, though this seems inherently less probable, partly because the person is referred to as an apostle (1962, ii, 1026–7).

The term 'apostle' does not always have the specific sense of 'one of the twelve appointed by Christ himself' in the New Testament. It is also used of a wider body, including delegates of churches (see 2 Corinthians 8:23) or travelling evangelists. Dodd himself is quite prepared to countenance the idea of Andronicus and Junia as a husband and wife team of apostles in this broader sense, like Aquila and Prisca referred to in Romans 16:3. Even the earlier commentary by Sanday and Headlam, although itself inclined to believe that a man is being referred to by the text, quotes the following remark from the early church father St Chrysostom:

> how great is the devotion of this woman, that she should be even counted worthy of the appellation of apostle! (Sanday and Headlam, 1908)

Moreover, although there may not be other references in the

New Testament to women as apostles, there are references to women performing tasks or having responsibilities within the early Christian communities which bear comparison with the role of apostles. A number of women are referred to as leaders of house churches. Indeed, of the six passages in the Pauline epistles where greetings are sent to a house-church, five include a woman's name among the leaders. In the list of greetings which ends the letter to the Romans which we have been considering, eight of the twenty-six to whom Paul sends greetings are women (Foster, 1950–1, 378). Such numerical listing has its limitations, but it is sufficient evidence of the important part which women played in the early church, a role which would not be inconsistent with that of apostle in the broader sense described above.

It would seem, then, that Gingrich and others, including quite possibly Bauer himself, may be wrong to set the balance of probability against rather than for the reading 'Junia'. They would have done better to follow what Bauer calls 'a purely lexical point of view', rather than adopt the lexicographically less likely translation on grounds of vaguely-defined contextuality.

The examination of Romans 16:7, however, raises important issues of biblical interpretation which can be divided into three areas:

First, questions of textual reading. The availability of different manuscripts from which to piece together an authoritative version of the text (and of course the textual critic has to work with copies of the putative 'original' works of Scripture – nowhere, for instance, can one find a letter written by St Paul himself, only copies of copies of such letters) makes the task of producing a standard version very difficult. A number of Bibles are careful to offer alternative readings in their margins, but none can avoid the choice of which reading to include in the main body of their text. The work of translation then compounds the difficulties even further as the text is 'reproduced' in another language. Translation inevitably brings with it interpretation – as A. J. Arberry recognized in his definitive translation of the *Qur'an* which he chose to entitle *The Koran Interpreted*. Such difficulties make clear that the biblical scholar doesn't first 'have' the text and then interpret it. The work of interpretation informs the very process of establishing the text. Hence the nature of our discussion over Junia(s), which is not a discussion of what the text means but of what the text actually is.

Second, questions are raised of historical judgment. This is what Bauer attempts to do by his mammoth survey of parallels to the language of the New Testament in contemporary and later

Greek language. His painstaking research into the past yields the result that Junia was a common name but Junias an unknown one, although shortenings of longer names were not uncommon and Junias might be an abbreviation of Junianus. This allows us to see a balance of probability in favour of a woman's name. Historical research into the role of women in the early christian communities also allows us to ask whether there is evidence of their taking the sort of responsibility in the church which the term 'apostle' designates. This is also of significance.

Third, however, questions are raised which belong to the 'second stage' of biblical criticism which we have tried to outline, questions which in this case would be more sociological and political. What of the context of the interpreter? These questions are often raised by modern feminist readings of the Bible, which point out that the overwhelming majority of biblical interpreters have been male, and that their commentaries have been written in patriarchal societies. What contribution has this made to their capacity to listen without distortion? How far does Bauer's preference for a reading of Junias, rather than Junia, despite the balance of lexicographical probability, because of the 'context of the verse', reflect the fact that mid-twentieth-century Germany was an example of a patriarchal society? How far does Bauer's reluctance to think of a woman around Jesus as an apostle have to do with the sort of roles which the women around Bauer played, or were excluded from?

The study of Romans 16:7 and the history of its exegesis illustrates the importance of attending to both 'horizons' of interpretation. By drawing attention to the patriarchal context of textual analysis, feminist studies of the Bible have shown a perceptive regard for the 'double' *Sitz im Leben* of writer and interpreter.[5]

Such studies have also been more alive than many to the fact that Scripture has not remained unaltered since the texts were first written. Nor has it simply been 'preserved' by the church, as if the role of the church was an entirely passive one. In two important ways the church has done much more than 'preserve' the Bible – it has determined the Bible.

The first way is that of formation of the canon. Over a period of several centuries, the early church developed a list of texts which were eventually standardized into the twenty-seven books of the New Testament. In the process a large number of texts were excluded from the canon, some of them works that were very popular in the patristic period. The criteria of inclusion and exclusion from the canon were complicated, but what is undoubted is the consequent marginalization of those texts which didn't 'make it'. Most Christians today know the texts of the New Testament relatively well – after all, to obtain them they only have to purchase or consult one of the millions of Bibles sold world-wide, and since the canon is fixed they can consult any version. But texts which have not been included in the canon they hardly know at all, since they exist only in what are seen to be scholars' reference works hidden in the bowels of libraries.

In the period from the second to the fourth century, however, all these works, both those later to be included in the canon and those which came to be excluded, would have been relatively well known. What has interested feminist criticism is the possibility that some of the works that came to be excluded described the role of women within the Christian community in a far more positive and active light than those works which came to be included in the canon. Feminist theologians argue that the patriarchal nature of Roman society, which eventually affected the nature of the church itself, influenced the christian community to marginalize texts which described a relatively independent role for women as followers of Jesus. An interesting illustration of this viewpoint is Bernadette Brooten's comparison of the canonical 1 and 2 Timothy with the extra-canonical Acts of Paul and Thecla (Brooten, 1980, 55–61).

Whatever the strength of this feminist critique of the formation of the canon, it is bound to make the interpreter more aware of the role of the church in fashioning – not simply preserving – Scripture. He or she will not fail to be aware of the circular nature of appeals by traditionalists in the church to the Bible when the role of women in today's church is discussed. The feminist criticism that women did in fact have a central and important role, including a leadership role, in the beginnings of the Jesus movement, but that the church gradually suffocated it and marginalized some of the texts in which it was most clearly expressed, forces the interpreter to recognize the dynamic and ideologically sustained process by which the Bible came into existence, let alone that by which it has to be understood.

The second way in which feminist criticism makes clear that the church had done more than merely preserve Scripture concerns those texts which have been included within the canon. As we have seen from our study of Romans 16:7, important decisions affecting interpretation have to be made in the editing and translating of the biblical corpus. Here again, it is impossible to see the church in an entirely passive role. Both in selecting and editing the text of scripture, the presuppositions of the ecclesiastical or academic interpreter are at work. As a library of works which have served the purposes of the Christian community in different ways at different points in its history, the Bible has to be seen as a product of its time – not only the time when the texts themselves were written, but the later times in which they were brought together into a canon, edited and translated. As James Barr has pointed out, the New Testament era, as biblical exegetes usually understand it, was an era in which there was as yet no New Testament. The texts were written, but the sense of their being brought together into an authoritative 'Christian' canon was not yet established. The anachronism of the idea of a 'New Testament era' illustrates the ease with which many biblical scholars slip into the habit of excluding from consideration the history of Christian thought after 200 CE It is in this manner that the horizon of the interpreter so easily disappears from sight, even when the work of 'interpretation' consists not so much in making sense of the biblical corpus as in establishing it in the first place! The work of feminist theologians has helped considerably in broadening biblical scholarship to appreciate the necessary '*Horizontvershmelzung*' that provides the key to sound exegesis.

The second biblical passage to be considered is rather more familiar, one that is regarded as central to the theology of Judaeo-Christianity:

> You shall not make for yourself a graven image, or any likeness of anything that is in heaven above, or that is in the earth beneath, or that is in the water under the earth; you shall not bow down to them or serve them; for I the Lord your God am a jealous God. . . . (Exodus 20:4–5).

This is the second of the ten commandments. Since the first commandment is concerned with the prohibition of other gods, the ban on images here is taken to refer to images of the true God:

> The second commandment intends to say that Yahweh is the kind of deity who cannot properly manifest himself in any kind of image; Yahweh was to the Israelite a God manifesting himself in his word and in history. (Hyatt, 1971, 211)

The question then arises as to *why* images of God are prohibited. For Hyatt the point of the ban is to make clear that God cannot be manipulated by humanity. Those who made images, he claims, 'sought to control the gods for their own purposes, but Yahweh could not be used. . .'. In his study of the theology of the Old Testament, Edmond Jacob wrote that the prohibition on the making of images of the Deity and adoring them 'represents the main trend of Israelite religion', and commented, 'To make a representation of God means to desire to imprison him within certain limits. . .'. (Jacob, 1958, 42)

This notion that making images of God represents an intention to control the divine being has established itself very strongly within Christian theology. At one level the source of the prohibition might be thought to be a 'primitive' idea that making an image gives one power over the object represented, much as the witchdoctor destroys his enemies by sticking pins in wax effigies of them. But in Christian tradition it has acquired a wider significance. It has, of course, been a passage often quoted in support of iconoclastic movements within Christianity. In his *Institutes of the Christian Religion* Calvin uses Exodus 20:4 as the lynchpin of his argument against what he calls the 'papist' belief that images in churches are 'the books of the unlearned' (Calvin, I, Ch. XI, 91). But beyond this lies a deeper concern with what Calvin calls the nature of the human mind as a 'perpetual forge of idols'.

For Exodus 20:4 has been interpreted as much as a prohibition upon mental images of God as upon material ones. The concept of God, like the material idol, seeks to 'contain' and 'control' God, to reduce the divine being to something comprehensible by the human mind, to catch God within the net of human understanding. The mind fashions its idols too, when it claims to be able to 'know' God in terms of human concepts. It is forging an idol as truly as do those who forge idols of iron and bronze.

In his *Church Dogmatics*, Karl Barth places the prohibition of images in the context of other Old Testament passages which point to the incomprehensibility and majesty of God. Quoting from the books of Job and Isaiah, Barth recalls the Hebrew poetry that exults in God's otherness to humanity. The question, 'To whom, then, will ye liken God?', is interspersed with the images of nations as a drop in a bucket, and God sitting upon the circle of the earth, whose inhabitants are laid out beneath him like grasshoppers. Idolatry, Barth argues, is 'sinful' in that it is 'folly' – it is a pathetic attempt to do the impossible, to contain the uncontainable. It must not be done, because what it attempts to do simply cannot be done (Barth, 1936–73, Vol. 2, part 1, 431).

Certainly Barth's approach, despite his dominance of twentieth-century theology, is a recognizably Protestant one, in the Reformed tradition. Yet his interpretation of the prohibition upon images in terms of the recognition that God's transcendence excludes human attempts to define God mentally (as much as efforts to 'represent' the divine being materially) has been received by many Catholic theologians too, including critics of Barth like von Balthasar, Henri Bouillard and Hans Kung.[6] The second commandment reminds humanity of the 'Godness of God', and in that light what Barth calls the sheer folly of attempting to represent the divine being mentally or physically.

The emphasis upon God's unknowability receives a further and interesting development in the work of one of the theologians of liberation who has taken a particular interest in biblical exegesis – Jose Porfirio Miranda. In his *Marx and the Bible*, Miranda interprets the prohibition upon images, similarly to Barth, as an insistence upon the unknowability and 'non-objectifiability' of God, but he adds the further claim that the desire to define and objectify God is itself a reflection of Western academic traditions. He sees the search for knowledge of God as a distraction from the practical objective of obedience to God's commands. In the prohibition of images, Miranda sees the Bible as stating something very similar to Karl Marx when he made the famous remark about philosophers only having interpreted the world, when the point was to change it (Miranda, 1977a, esp. 36ff).

According to the broad sweep of Miranda's analysis, the whole of Greco-Roman culture, and the western philosophical tradition that developed out of it, constitutes a kind of academic diversion from the gospel. It has transformed the biblical God who commands and is obeyed, into the 'God of the Philosophers' who exists as an object of thought only. The process of communicating the gospel to the Greco-Roman world and the succeeding cultures of feudal and capitalist Europe has robbed the Christian faith of its essence, according to Miranda's argument. It has turned a way of life into a way of thought.

The contrast between the 'God of the Bible' and the 'God of the Philosophers' is one that has been played upon many times in the course of church history. Tertullian asked the rhetorical question: 'What has Athens to do with Jerusalem?' in the third century; Blaise Pascal turned from the God of philosophy to the God of 'Abraham, Isaac and Jacob' in the course of a vision which he wrote down and kept in his breast pocket, to be the foundation of his famous *Pensées*. Some of the Protestant Reformers were also prone to making this distinction. But in all such cases the contrast is between reason and faith, between knowledge of God based upon human intelligence and knowledge of God based upon revelation. In effect, the contrast was between two forms of knowledge. Miranda, on the other hand, views the biblical God as one who rejects 'knowledge' of any kind as the path to salvation, whether it be knowledge based upon the reasoning powers of the human mind or upon the direct receipt of understanding through faith in God's self-revelation. The God of the Bible, Miranda insists, is interested only in just action, not in a correct understanding. Just as the Gentiles were able to fulfil the law without knowing it (Romans 2:14–15), so also we are able to do God's will without any knowledge or even experience of the divine being.

In an intriguing commentary on St John's gospel, *Being and the Messiah* (Miranda, 1977b), Miranda sets out to make this, traditionally regarded as the most 'esoteric', 'other-worldly' and 'spiritual' of the four canonical gospels, a work firmly committed to the principle that God is 'known' only through the practical commitment of just action. Miranda believes that this principle is expressed through St John's treatment of 'works', and it is worth briefly examining a particular set of verses in order to elucidate Miranda's approach.

In John 14:8–11, Jesus is presented by the disciple Philip with the demand: 'Show us the Father'. He responds by telling him that none of those who had been with him should need to make that request. They should know that 'I am in the Father and the Father in me'. Jesus then expands upon his relationship with the Father:

> The Father who dwells in me does his works. Believe me that I am in the Father or the Father in me; or else believe me for the sake of the works themselves.

Philip, in Miranda's presentation, typifies an 'academic' approach to Christianity. 'Show us the Father' reflects the intellectual's quest for a proof, a demonstration or an argument for God's existence. It is an approach rejected by Jesus in the way that he rejects the Pharisees when they ask for a 'sign'. But against this approach Jesus sets, not the demand to 'have faith' as an inner act of commitment or as an inner experience, but the demand to act justly. He points to the works of the Father, and speaks of a belief which is 'for the sake of the works themselves'. Christianity, Miranda's exegesis seems to be suggesting, is a way of living and acting rather than a way of thinking.

Miranda's commentary on John is problematic, controversial and question-begging. Indeed Miranda's exegesis has been heavily criticized by other liberation theologians, for instance Alfredo Fierro in *The Militant Gospel*.[7] But it remains a revealing exercise in biblical interpretation. The passage of John 14 mentioned above has been a focus of many traditional Christian debates about Christology (the person of Christ). Controversy has raged about the 'status' of Christ, particularly the notion that he is 'in' the Father and the Father 'in' him. Does this mean that he is a human being, a divine being, a being both human and divine, or something in between the two, a semi-divine quasi-angelic being? If he has two natures, one human and the other (by virtue of being 'in' the Father) divine, how does he maintain his identity as one person? In the terms often used by theologians, what 'ontological' value do prepositions like 'in' have, when they talk of Jesus as 'in' the Father?[8]

Miranda sidesteps the whole debate. He sees it as part of a Western philosophical and theological tradition which has distorted the biblical message. The interpretation of John 14 in terms of an argument about the nature of Christ is itself the product of a particular culture, one that has been developing through certain set social forms – imperialism in the ancient period, feudalism in the mediaeval period and capitalism in the modern. It is in the interest of these societies that Christianity should be perceived as a way of thought, an intellectual argument about issues like Christology. The Christian religion has satisfied that social interest by presenting itself in intellectual terms. The debate between Philip and Jesus is interpreted as an academic one, in which two men discuss the proper way to conceive of Christ in relation to God.

Miranda, by contrast, claims that the real point of the passage is to reject all academic theological reflection in the traditional way that it has been conducted in western churches and universities. Such reflection has only served to distract from the real function of Christianity, which is to act as a movement of social transformation. But since that transformation would effectively subvert the forms of social organization that have characterized the West since ancient times, it comes as no surprise to Miranda that this 'intellectualization' of the faith has occurred. It is simply a reflection of the sort of society within which the faith has come to be expressed. Miranda's solution to all that head-scratching which characterizes the 'liberal' Bishop of Durham on the one hand and his 'conservative' critics on the other hand is a simple one. A plague on both your houses! You are both playing the same academic game, trying to find the right formula to express some article of belief like the Virgin Birth or the Resurrection. Therefore you are both contributing to a false but appropriate misconception of Christianity as a way of thinking. You are both distracting it from its true function as an agent of social change, one that would in effect revolutionize the society you live in. The problems of theology as they have been addressed through the centuries are thus all relativized and rejected by Miranda as a 'bourgeois' distraction, a form of idolatry that is clearly rejected by a biblical tradition that refuses to tolerate idols!

Miranda's sweeping approach is commonly regarded, even from within the Theology of Liberation, as overwhelmingly simplistic. However, its inclusion here as an example of that 'second stage' of biblical criticism which examines the *Sitz im Leben* of interpreter as well as text interpreted is for a particular reason. Its simple audacity demonstrates the power of new forms of exegesis to challenge current ways of thinking and to generate new ideas about Christianity. Moreover, Miranda's exegesis demonstrates the way in which the ideological criticism of religion associated with Marx might be brought to bear upon the work of biblical interpretation, and yield fresh if controversial insights into the meaning of Scripture.[9]

The examples of exegesis which we have looked at in connection with Feminist and Liberation Theology, however, raise a number of difficult questions concerning truth and meaning. In our concluding section, we shall consider some of the issues arising from contemporary hermeneutics concerning the possibility of objective interpretation.

Before concluding, I should like to set out in summary form the main points of this chapter.

1. From its formation, and not simply from the rise of 'scientific' biblical criticism, Christianity has been concerned with problems of how to interpret Scripture.
2. The importance of interpretation is demonstrated by the key part that disagreement over the meaning of texts has played in church history.
3. Such disagreement, even or perhaps especially among those for whom the Bible is supremely authoritative, demonstrates that 'The Word of God' carries little weight without a knowledge of what that 'Word' means. This 'dilemma' may encourage a 'Catholic' view of Scripture interpreted through tradition and the church; but the place of Scripture as a focus for criticism of the church remains a lasting legacy of the Protestant Reformation.
4. Against this background of conflict over Scripture and its interpretation may be seen the later rise of 'biblical criticism'. In

its first stage such criticism brought out the social and cultural setting of the Bible's composition; in its second and more recent stage it has brought out the *Sitz im Leben* of the reader/interpreter of Scripture too. Hence the 'two horizons' of interpretation.

5. The example of Junia(s) illustrates that interpretation begins with the process of formation of the text, rather than being an activity directed to a text already 'neutrally' formed. The influence of the reader's *Sitz im Leben* is brought out by the reluctance of 'patriarchal' Western society to countenance a significant role for women in the origins of Christianity – a reluctance which reflects hesitation about their receiving such a role in contemporary Christian institutions. That is the claim of modern feminist theologians and some of the evidence can be assessed from this section.

The impact of feminist criticism is to revise the 'passive' metaphors of the church as 'preserver' and 'keeper' of Scripture, and to suggest a more 'active' role as determining Scripture, both through the selection of the canon and through the editing and translation of texts. This 'active' role reinforces the importance of the reader/interpreter's (or editor/translator's) *Sitz im Leben*.

6. Miranda's exegesis, from a liberationist perspective, provides a radical re-interpretation of the Bible which attempts to challenge the whole tradition of Western theology and biblical criticism with 'the biblical message'. His Marxist critique highlights the setting-in-life of the interpreter, because of its commitment to the view that ideologies are generated 'appropriate' to the socio-economic context of their formation. Miranda's work shows how contemporary biblical interpretation can receive new insights from the sociology of knowledge, although the Marxist critique Miranda offers may not itself be convincing.

Where do these comments leave us on the central issue of 'truth' and 'objectivity' in interpretation? For many people, reminded of the history of conflict in Christian thought over the meaning of Scripture, the possibility of 'true' exegesis will seem remote. Much of the attraction of Fundamentalist views about the Bible in the modern world derives from contemporary insecurity and doubt born of a lack of confidence in the churches' ability to reach conclusions about 'what the Bible teaches' (although paradoxically, as we have seen, Fundamentalists themselves have great difficulty on this question). The latest trends in biblical interpretation may seem to convert what once seemed a remote possibility into an absolute impossibility. By its emphasis upon the way in which the reader of Scripture, as much as the writer, is determined by his or her context of reading, modern hermeneutics may seem to have sunk all efforts to understand the Bible as an authority in an acid bath of relativism. A commentary on John's Gospel will be seen to have the truth-value of a colour preference.

Such pessimism is the product of some very muddled philosophy. In the first place, it should not be forgotten that this sort of 'relativism' directed at the meaning of Scripture is not new. Pick up Schweitzer's *The Quest of the Historical Jesus*, and you will read of how every significant nineteenth century life of Jesus reflected the society of its author much more than the real society of Jesus himself. When Schweitzer accused Renan of writing a sentimental life of Jesus suggestive of 'an ecclesiastical art emporium in the Place St Sulpice', he was doing to nineteenth century biblical exegesis (in the form of biography rather than commentary), what modern feminist or liberationist criticism does to Bauer, Gingrich, Hyatt and so on. At the end of the day, however, neither gives up the idea of 'objective' interpretation. Both convey the impression that they are clearing away dross rather than demonstrating that there is no such thing as 'truth' in exegesis. For all his romantic rhetoric about Jesus coming to us as 'one unknown', Schweitzer asks us to believe in an 'objective' description of him as a charismatic Jewish figure with apocalyptic dreams and a firm confidence that he can bring about the end of history by forcing God's hand with his act of self-sacrifice on the cross (Schweitzer, 1910). Similarly, modern feminist criticism may point up the way in which biblical interpretation has traditionally been carried out by male scholars in a patriarchal environment; but the feminist theologian still seeks to establish the objective reality of the important role played by women within the earliest Christian communities (Fiorenza, 1983).

Second, the word 'relativism' requires very careful handling. Contemporary biblical hermeneutics is, certainly, 'relativist' in the sense that it emphasizes the relation of the interpreter, as well as the author, of Scripture to his or her social environment. But this form of relativism is not reductionist. Compare the idea that concepts are 'relative' to the particular languages in which they are expressed. Everyone learns to speak and communicate in a particular language, and the language may well limit and determine the possibilities of expression – in German or French I cannot distinguish between 'mind' and 'spirit' without difficulty, since the words 'esprit' and 'Geist' cover both, and this fact about language influences my powers of thought. But this is *not* to say that I cannot say anything 'true' or 'objective' because I must use the medium of language, or because all my ideas are 'related to' and dependent upon a particular linguistic medium. The sorts of criticism which we have discussed in this chapter may be 'relativist' in the sense that they are alive to the social context within which the interpreter works, and dismissive of the idea that he or she can write or think from within an ivory (or ecclesiastical) tower outside and above contemporary history. But that is not to deny the interpreter the power to make true or false judgments. Indeed, it ought to enhance that power. Modern biblical criticism insists that responsive listening to texts must be self-responsive. It can be conscious of the past only by being self-conscious in the present.

The Jesuit, Father Tyrrell, once accused the Protestant theologian von Harnack of seeing only the reflection of his face at the bottom of a deep well when he sought to interpret the Bible. But it is only when one is unconscious of the influences upon one's own thinking that the Bible acts as a mirror rather than a gateway. Of course the enormous problems in interpreting texts must never be overlooked, and the issues surrounding meaning or meanings are far more complicated than this chapter could possibly do justice to. All I would say in conclusion is that some of the recent developments in biblical criticism may be working for, rather than against, that effort to understand the biblical texts which, whilst it may be tempted to take endless short-cuts on the way to truth, must always have truth as its goal.[10]

Notes

1. An excellent account of Fundamentalist hermeneutics is offered by James Barr (1981) especially chapter 7, 'Variations and Conflicts'.
2. Fortress Press of Philadelphia has produced a useful series, 'Guides to Biblical Scholarship', on different forms of biblical interpretation. For methods appropriate to the 'first stage' of hermeneutics, see Krentz (1975 – this has been published separately in Britain by SPCK), McKnight (1969), and Perrin (1970). For methods appropriate to the 'second stage' see Patte (1976) and Beardslee (1970). It has, however, to be pointed out that literary and structuralist criticism, which we do not discuss in this chapter, straddle in some respects the two 'stages' of criticism as we have defined them, and need much further discussion before they can be categorized. For examples of feminist and liberationist criticism, see the notes below. Christopher Tuckett (1987) has a useful summary of different forms of criticism, but the most comprehensive and magisterial account of developments in biblical criticism remains Thistleton (1980).

3. A very good illustration of this 'second stage' is given in J. L. Segundo (1979), Chapter 1.
4. Many discussions of feminist hermeneutics have been produced in recent years. One of the most impressive is Fiorenza (1983). Letty Russell (1983) gives examples of exegesis. For an interesting illustration of the way in which a new understanding of Scripture can have profound effects upon church doctrine, see the Report produced by the Church of Scotland Woman's Guild and Panel on Doctrine Study Group, *The Motherhood of God* (1984), which examines the biblical foundations for female as well as male imagery of the divine being.
5. This has been brought out particularly by studies of the way in which female 'characters' in the Bible have been presented and understood in Christian tradition through the centuries. See, for instance, Moltmann-Wendel's study (1982), and the development of those ideas in the first part of Jürgen Moltmann and Moltmann-Wendel (1984, 1–51). The issue of *Concilium* devoted to 'Mary in the Churches' (No. 168) contains interesting discussion of the 'Mother of God' in Christian tradition. See also Reuther (1974).
6. The most comprehensive study of Barth in historical perspective is unfortunately untranslated, whilst the best study is translated very badly. For the former, see Henri Bouillard's three-volume *Karl Barth* (1957). For the latter, see Hans Urs von Balthasar (1967).
7. Fierro (1977). He 'dismisses' Miranda without much discussion on pp. 372ff.
8. There is an exhaustive list of books asking these unanswerable questions, and concluding either with a plainly incredible solution or making a virtue of necessity and claiming that their inability to solve the 'Christological problem' reflects a form of humility in the face of the mystery of God. For a recent and entirely orthodox study of the debate, see Gunton (1983).
9. A widening interest among theologians in the sociology of knowledge, and the opening up to theological consideration of the 'Frankfurt School', is proving very fruitful in the field of biblical interpretation (consider, for instance, the value of the concept of 'ideological suspicion' – Habermas – in the study of texts). For an introduction to this important and valuable reflection, the writings of Paul Ricoeur are a good beginning (e.g. 1974), whilst the translation of Hans-Georg Gadamer's magisterial *Wahrheit und Methode* (Truth and Method) makes that work accessible to the English reader. These writings, however, all make for difficult reading. The best one can often hope for is flashes in the fog. John B. Thompson's *Critical Hermeneutics* (1981) which provides an introduction to Ricoeur, is perhaps the best starting-place.
10. This might seem like a naively triumphalist, objectivist way of concluding. But it is difficult to see how the ideal of arriving at the truth can be jettisoned, however much difficulties in the way of reaching that truth – or even recognition of the impossibility of

arriving at it – require to be affirmed. But this raises questions that have not been within the range of this chapter, not least those surrounding Pilate's unanswered question: 'What is Truth?'

References

von Balthasar, H.U. (1967) *Karl Barth: Darstelling und Deutung seiner Theologie*, Cologne.
Barr, J. (1981) *Fundamentalism*, London, SCM.
Barth, K. (1936–73), *Church Dogmatics*, Edinburgh, T. and T. Clark.
Beardslee, W. (1970) *Literary Criticism of the New Testament*, Philadelphia, Fortress Press.
Bouillard, H. (1957) *Karl Barth*, Paris, Aubier.
Brooten, B. (1980) 'Feminist Perspectives on New Testament Exegesis', *Concilium*, 138.
Calvin, J. (1975) *Institutes of the Christian Religion*, Eerdman's, Grand Rapids, Eerdmans Publishing.
Dodd, C.H. (1932) *The Epistle of Paul to the Romans*, London, Hodder & Stoughton.
Fierro, A. (1977) *The Militant Gospel*, London, SCM.
Fiorenza, E.S. (1983) *In Memory of Her*, London, SCM.
Foster, J. (1950–1) 'St. Paul and Women', *Expository Times*, 62.
Gingrich, F.W. (1962) *Interpreter's Dictionary of the Bible*, Chicago.
Gunton, C. (1983) *Yesterday and Today: A Study of Continuities in Christology*, London, Darton, Longman & Todd.
Hyatt, J.P. (1971) *Exodus*, London, Marshall, Morgan & Scott. (1962)
Hyatt, J.P. (1962) *Interpreter's Dictionary of the Bible*, New York, Abingdon.
Jacob, E. (1958) *Theology of the Old Testament*, London, Hodder & Stoughton.
Krentz, Edgar (1975) *The Historical-Critical Method*, Philadelphia, Fortress.
Kung, H. and Moltmann, J. (eds) (1968) 'Mary in the Churches', *Concilium* 168.
McKnight, E. (1969) *What is Form Criticism?*, Philadelphia, Fortress.
Miranda, J.P. (1977a) *Marx and the Bible*, London, SCM.
Miranda, J.P. (1977b) *Being and the Messiah*, New York, Orbis.
Moltmann, J. and Moltmann-Wendel, E. (1984) *Humanity in God*, London, SCM.
Moltmann-Wendel, E. (1982) *The Women Around Jesus*, New York, Crossroads.
Patte, D. (1976) *What is Structural Exegesis?*, Philadelphia, Fortress.
Perrin, N. (1970) *What is Redaction Criticism?*, London, SPCK.
Report of the Church of Scotland Study Group (1984) *The Motherhood of God*, Edinburgh, St Andrew's Press.
Ricoeur, P. (1974) *The Conflict of Interpretations: Essays in Hermeneutics*, Evanston, Northwestern University Press.
Ruether, R.R. (ed.) (1974) *Religion and Sexism*, New York, Simon & Schuster.

Russell, L. (1983) *Feminist Interpretation of the Bible*, Oxford, Blackwell.
Sanday and Headlam (1908) *The Epistle to the Romans*, Edinburgh, T. & T. Clark.
Schweitzer, A. (1910) *The Quest of the Historical Jesus*, London, A. & C. Black.
Segundo, J.L. (1979) *The Liberation of Theology*, New York, Orbis.
Thistleton, A. (1980) *The Two Horizons*, Exeter, Paternoster Press.
Thompson, J.B. (1981) *Critical Hermeneutics*, 34, Cambridge, Cambridge University Press.
Tuckett, C. (1987) *Reading the New Testament*, London, SPCK.

Chapter twelve

The birth of the reader

R.S. White

> . . . we know that in order to restore writing to its future, we must reverse the myth: the birth of the reader must be requited by the death of the Author (Barthes, 1986).

'. . . I make sure the dish is in the oven really early. The long slow cooking makes all the difference, it's the secret of its success. I cook', Mrs Castle said happily, 'the potatoes and the peas separately and I make the potatoes into creamed whirls. At the last minute I put some very finely chopped mint and parsley into the delicious gravy.'

'Oh yummy, yum!' Christobel swallowed, 'you're making me so hungry. Do you have sweets as well?' she asked.

'Yes.' Mrs Castle's well-shaped smile, if allowed, would have reached her ears. 'For dessert with this dinner I usually make Banana Boats.' She waited still looking round as if about to hand little dishes of Banana Boats.

Miss Porch, again in her mind, saw Mrs Castle bending even lower over the table, for hours, decorating carefully sliced whole bananas with little strips of angelica and tiny chocolate wafers held in place with minute drops of a perfectly made caramel.

* * *

The symposium, having deteriorated, was declared over and Miss Porch began an explanation about reading being a creative process and that it was not necessary for the writer to write absolutely every detail belonging to the characters – for example, their living arrangements and their meals need not be described unless they were an essential part of the story or the novel. Readers, she told them, can piece things together in rapid retrospect. Imagination, she said, in the reader must not be overlooked as endless pictures can fill the reader's mind from what the writer offers. A great deal, Miss Porch went on to say, of understanding comes from the reader, or in the case of a play, from the audience (Elizabeth Jolley, *Foxybaby*).

The death of The Author

The Author, of course, is not the author. We still want our authors in all their human facets, needing money, needing praise, being interviewed on television (if they are photogenic and articulate), getting drunk with their friends, laughing about rivals' books. The Author is a considerably more abstract, metaphysical being, defined as 'the intention behind the work'. The author is a presence, The Author is an absence, once as potent but as insubstantial as a myth. Its death was predicted in the 1920s with T. S. Eliot's insistence on the 'impersonality' of the work, James Joyce's image of the writer disappearing behind the work, retiring to pare his fingernails. Behind them, of course, stood others such as Baudelaire, Mallarmé, Wilde, who wished the work to be read, rather than its writer psychoanalysed. What began as an apparently suicidal act by these practising writers was in fact a desire, comparable and parallel to the desire of painters who turned to abstract, non-representational forms, to escape what they regarded as an unhealthy scrutiny into their own psyches. It was in response to the increasing tyranny of critics clutching their volumes of Freud that writers could say, with Eliot, that 'honest criticism and sensitive appreciation is directed not upon the poet but upon the poetry' (Eliot, 1932, 17). For very different reasons (mainly to justify their place alongside scientists as 'rigorous' and 'objective') critics themselves took up the campaign to kill off The Author. In the 1950s, people like Wimsatt and Brooks, 'New Critics', the 'Chicago School', ridiculed notions of The Author as Presence in the Work, derided 'the intentionalist fallacy' and 'the biographical fallacy'. This left them free to chase up ambiguities (their special preoccupation) with the fastidiousness of the scientist splitting atoms, knowing that no Voice would come from The Author inconveniently complaining, 'That is not it, at all. That is not what I meant, at all.' And now, in the wake, come linguists, philosophers, semioticians, such as Jakobson, Derrida and Barthes, dancing on the grave of The Author, proclaiming that He never existed, that all we have is 'the free play of the signifier'. All we are left with is The Text.

The text is alive

There are considerable advantages in all this. Once The Text is made our sole *datum*, then we are free to 'discover' (the reason for those inverted commas will become clear) patterns in the Text that are 'there' whether or not The Author intended them – indeed, they may flatly contradict what The Author may have wanted to say. Semiotics – the science of signs – is an attempt to 'decipher' works of art and literature, to find underlying structures, 'collective representations' (Saussure), shared 'mythologies' and 'conventions' through which the Text represents and speaks to the society which created it. Roland Barthes in *Mythologies* (Barthes, 1957, 1972) attempts to 'unmask', to 'decode', 'demystify' the forms of common representational events (wrestling, toys, the face of Garbo, striptease, cookery in magazines) as part of an attempt to de-universalize western petit-bourgeois cultural assumptions. There may be an infinite number of 'signifiers' for one underlying structure or value-system, a 'signified'. In Barthes' case, the Text is not a written artefact (necessarily) but any carrier of significance, anything which is said to convey 'meaning'. For linguists, meanwhile, the Text can be language in any form, spoken or written, and the Speaker suffers a fate similar to the Author's when we find books and articles with titles such as *Must We Mean What We Say?* (Cavell, 1976). Language too is seen as merely a set of signifiers which can be inspected for conventional forms generating other predictable forms – neither more nor less than signs that can be decoded. In literary criticism the Text-centred movement equally inspects works for their underlying structures, taking direct inspiration from Saussurian linguistics and the philosophies of, mainly, Derrida. There are many splinter-groups – cultural anthropologists (Frye), generic critics or formalists (Todorov and Bakhtin), orthodox structuralists (mainly to be found among film critics), deconstructionists (Hartman) – but they are linked by a common desire to look not at imputed or intended meaning but at the forms which carry what some call meaning. The purists would say that the form *is* the meaning, no more and no less – 'the medium is the message' as McLuhan said in those olden days. The whole movement, which can loosely be called Structuralist, has made it much easier for other groups which *are* concerned with 'meaning' to operate. Marxists and feminists have been around for much longer than the Structuralists, but until a form of analysis arrived which made it legitimate to focus on the 'deep structure' of underlying conventions, rendering irrelevant appeals to 'universality' by killing off the Author as Authority, their claims for discovering class or gender-based biases in respected works of literature was ignored as in itself partisan. Even a work such as *Hamlet* has been seen, in its underlying value-system, as a work biased against women (Rose, 1986), or (for the sake of argument) as a dangerous cultural influence since it underwrites selfish individualism. Nothing, it seems, is sacred, after The Death of the Author. And a corollary is that Shakespeare's plays are no more intrinsically significant or mysterious than a television soap-opera, a Beethoven symphony no more valuable than an advertising jingle. Each can be decoded, reduced to its basic structures, and each can be just as revealing about underlying attitudes held by the society and the historical context in which it was born.

Once the argument reaches this level, however, problems begin to reveal themselves, and they are ones not easily solved within the hermeneutics of an Authorless system based on decoding signifiers and identifying structures in a Text. Most of the problems can be reduced to two leading questions. The first is how can one critic claim to have found and adequately described (demystified) the underlying set of structures of a work (*Hamlet* is misoginistic) if another critic also claims to have found the (different) underlying set of structures (*Hamlet* is about bourgeois individualism; or revenge; or superstition and rationality . . .)? In other words, if the methodology at its most basic is so scientifically and coolly devised, should we not all come to the same conclusion? The answer given to this problem is that if 'the text is a fabric of quotations, resulting from a thousand sources of culture' (Barthes, 1968, 53), then the Text is plural in its nature, and a decoder may be focusing on a particular structure while ignoring others. But if this is so, then the second question can be posed. *Where* are the structures, waiting to be 'discovered' (here the inverted commas raise their heads), if one 'discoverer' might 'find' one set while another 'finds' a different set? If there were, to retrace our steps, an imputed Author, then we could say s/he put all the structures there, in a bewildering but finite series, knowing that any one critic's investigations will be too limited to find them all; more or less in the way that Bacon's God gave us a complicated but eventually knowable world if each investigator can pool resources with others. Without an Author, this argument cannot be sustained within the system of thought, and so a different one has been devised: although there is no motivating force behind the work, no 'individual genius' leaving us patterns to 'discover' or uncover, yet the work of art is constituted of 'textual strategies' (Eco, 1981, 11). The Text, in other words, is its own creator, with all the properties and capacities in the past that have been associated with an Author. But if the notion of 'intentions' has been covertly reintroduced by devising a self-creating Text, have we not come full circle and embraced in a different guise the very element (prior intention, whether Author's or Text's) which we tried to exclude from the system?

Other problems, associated with the two discussed above, lead to equally contradictory positions. If two different analysts 'discover' quite different structures, how can these structures be said to 'inhere' in the Text as distinct from in the critic's mind? Semioticians may say they have developed a 'meta-discipline' from which to view the work of art from the outside, just as linguists who believe in the primacy of 'Speech-Acts' may claim a meta-language in order to speak analytically about language from the outside. At the very least, this cannot be proved to be satisfactory, and at the most it can be attacked as loose thinking. If the critic speaks of a narrative in a novel s/he must at some point refer to the events in the terms in which the Text presents them; if the linguist is to speak of language used around him or her, then the words used, in order to be intelligible, must be in collusion with those of the 'sample' Speaker at some point. The dyer's hand is subdued to what it works in (Shakespeare, *Sonnet 111*) and there is no way that the critic or linguist can even know, let alone prove, that the chosen analytical form of discourse lies 'outside' the Text or Speech-Act under consideration. Even if a highly complicated and unfamiliar set of technical terms is created to carry on 'meta-discourse', surely these terms are subject to the same kind of demystification, reduction to underlying systems, even revelation of ambiguities, plural understandings and biases, among the group of semioticians who initially think they are understanding each other?

The next sub-problem may result from a failure of nerve even amongst the structuralists of strongest fibre. Though they wish to exclude the notion that one form of Text is better than another, to assert that a soap opera is as worthy of critical attention as Shakespeare, they cannot avoid implicitly making value judgements in the very act of saying that the one is as important as the other. Here we find some squirming and some infighting among practitioners. One group will boldly accept the notion of value-judgement, and argue that a contemporary soap-opera is in fact more worthy of close analysis than Shakespeare, because the former is culturally located in a social context which is immediate, relevant and accessible to us, while the other is remote and less 'significant'. Others, while claiming to be impartial, can be driven by a *reductio ad absurdum* to admit that there comes a point where some documents simply do not have enough content to merit as lengthy an analysis as another. To compare and contrast a poem by Seamus Heaney with the same number of words in the telephone directory may smack of perversity (though this does not logically matter since discoveries have come from equally unpromising projects), but more important, few would confess to finding the same degree of analytical interest in the second project as in the first. By admitting this, the analyst is acknowledging (or rather creating: see below) some factor of significance in the Heaney poem, some 'value' – perhaps complexity or expressiveness – not shared by the telephone directory. Finally, the fainthearted, who admit they do exercise some judgement about what they choose to analyse and yet still do not want to jettison the whole system of sign-reading and decoding that they have built up with such care, will defend a distinction between what sounds ominously like something they have fought to reject: 'high' culture and 'popular' art are metamorphosed into the scientific-sounding distinction between 'open' (or 'free') and 'closed' texts, the former being measured in 'the flexibility of the *text* in *validating* (or at least in not contradicting) the widest possible range of interpretative *proposals*' (Eco, 1981, 33; my italics). In the book from which this quotation comes, Umberto Eco shows that the distinction is not nearly so clear as it may seem, that Superman comics may provide as 'open' a text as Dante – but the point I wish to emphasize is that the terms of the statement quoted, highlighted by my italics, emphasize still the primacy of a Text which *author*izes (validates, does not contradict) certain 'proposals', even if, just before these words, he mentions 'the reader' who is being 'requested' by the Text to exercise a certain 'type of cooperation'. The last question, resulting from all the others, is this. If the Text is so self-generating, has so many requests or demands to make, has interest for sophisticated interpreters only insofar as it reaffirms or contradicts the complicated theories of these analysts, then what on earth is the Text *for*?

The birth of the Reader

Emphatically, if the Author is dead and the Text, treated as sacred repository of structures, leads us into contradictions and absurdities, then the Text is *for* the Reader. Books are written to be *read*. And if the semiotician can simply, humbly, accept his or her own status as just another reader whose access to 'truth' is exactly equivalent to any other reader's, and whose activity of 'making sense' of the text is as worthy of scrutiny as the Text itself, then most of the problems melt away. The structures do not reside in the Text, awaiting discovery. They lie in the mind of the reader (semiotician or otherwise), awaiting discovery in the *con*text of the text, in a moment of apparent meshing of the reader's preoccupations, centres of attention and leading ideas, with a set of neutral words on the page in front of that reader. Readers create structures. Readers place their own meanings in texts. Each reader will place a meaning, a structural overlay, upon a text, and it is inevitably different from meanings placed upon the text by another reader.

By my Reader I do not mean Umberto Eco's abstract 'Model Reader':

> The reader is strictly defined by the lexical and the syntactical organisation of the text: the text is nothing else but the semantic production of its own Model Reader. (Eco, 1981, 10)

I mean any reader encountering any text under any circumstances. (Although I should be inclined to specify a person who is literate, encountering a text whose vocabulary is in a language which the reader understands, although it is probable that these constraints are not necessary in strict logic.) Let us take as examples two texts mentioned by Eco, one which analysts have described as Open, the other as Closed (or relatively Closed) and let us personify five readers for each:

Finnegans Wake by James Joyce

A. I scanned it in the bookshop and found it weird but funny.
B. I read it from cover to cover but couldn't make head or tail of it.
C. I found it deficient in plot, but a profound comment on the fragmented quality of society and language in this century.
D. I found the plot gripping, but it didn't say anything important.
E. A load of rubbish. Why do people write so only their friends can understand them?

Casino Royale by Ian Fleming

A. It was so exciting I couldn't put it down; I wanted to see how it ended.
B. I enjoyed the beginning, the scene-setting, but the end was predictable.
C. I found James Bond a really witty character.
D. Politically dangerous – violent, racist, anti-communist – all black and white.
E. So badly written I didn't get past page two.

Of course, I could have done some fieldwork and gathered 'real' comments by 'real' readers, but my potential readers seem plausible enough in their reactions, and all that would have been gained by the research would have been to gather another ten (or fifty) different comments – sometimes only subtly different, sometimes dramatically – but all different nonetheless. Any of the comments above could have been made by either a sophisticated, trained literary critic (listen, for example, to 'The Critics' on radio), or by somebody completely without training. The conclusion is a paradox: on the one hand, each response constitutes a valid critical statement which tells us something about the text; and on the other hand, each response is solipsistic, tells us something about the reader but nothing about the text. My argument is that no matter how many comments we were to gather, from no matter how many professors of literature or 'people in the street', the paradox would still hold for every single one. There are no 'good' or 'bad' readers, educated or ignorant in such a republic. There are simply infinite numbers of readers. The resolution to the paradox is that each Reader creates a unique Text. Each reader creates the 'meaning' which s/he finds.

Before returning to the phrase 'wants to find', the question of the reader's intentions, let us change the example, taking five people who read *Great Expectations* five years ago, and have just re-read it:

A. I loved it then, it seemed so lifelike; but now that I've studied literature I see it as a myth about bourgeois guilt about money.
B. I didn't like it then, but I've seen the film since, and that made me more interested because I could visualize the scenes.
C. I once found it really funny, full of macabre jokes – now it seems a complete tragedy.

D. I can see more in it now – Miss Havisham is just like my aunty.
E. I hated it then and I hate it now – no difference.

How do we account for such responses? Have the first four developed, 'matured', changed, while the fifth has not? Or did the first four just get it wrong on both occasions of reading, while the fifth got it right first time? Theoretically, either conclusion (and many more) is possible, except that such a mode of analysing returns us to the position which led to contradictions and perhaps fallacies – the assumption that the Text is stable, has plural 'textual strategies' waiting to be 'discovered' and that it holds a finite set of 'meanings'. It seems much easier, prevents the need for endless reworking of a Text-centred theory, simply to conclude that on each occasion of reading, a person is a different reader bringing to the work a new set of (in the words above) ' "meanings" which s/he wants to find'. Even the response of E does not of necessity cancel out this possibility. In short, rather than Texts being plural, an individual Reader is plural. A theory based on such an assumption explains the evidence much more simply and elegantly than a Text-centred analysis, and it preserves what I take to be the axiomatic recognition that Texts exist for Readers, not Readers for Texts.

To emphasize some of the points I have made, I should create 'readers' responses' which appear to make no sense at all in order to test the theory, but instead I shall descend to the truth (so far as memory can be taken as licence for distortions). I once taught a group of four keen students. When I asked the teacherly inane question, 'What is *The Nigger of the Narcissus* about?' I received these four answers:

A. It is about the effect of death in an environment controlled by the writer.
B. It is about the causes and effects of racist attitudes in society.
C. It is about trade union solidarity facing threats from malingerers, authority and scabs.
D. It is about the naval skill of the captain (I consulted the official almanac and apparently, as Conrad says on page 50, the Cape was almost unpassable in that year), and hence it's about the moral authority of the man in command. (This appears to contradict C.)

As a teacher, I see it as my job not to 'discover' but help to 'create' a meaning from whatever is given to me by way of honest responses to literature. In this case it was not too difficult to help each student develop his or her respective argument by asking for textual evidence and more detail. But I must admit to a complete bewilderment throughout the hour, in trying to 'create a meaning' for myself about what was happening in the tutorial. It was impossible to say that any of these ideas was 'wrong', 'uninformed', 'fundamentally unsound', and it was impossible to say that any of the readings was 'better' than the others, still less 'correct'. Nor could the readings be dismissed as 'subjective' since each person was able to convince the rest of us that the pattern s/he was seeing could be confirmed by close scrutiny of the text. The hour was, from my point of view, a practical demonstration of the creativity of individual readers, the nebulous nature of a text which, like a spider's web, could catch so many different flies. It was equally clear that each of the readers had created a meaning to suit his or her own current preoccupation in the wider, social context in which we were all living. The same, I realized, could be said of my own 'response' or created meaning of *The Nigger of the Narcissus*. The lesson was a salutary and humbling one, for it made me realize that there is no point at which an honest reader can say something completely absurd about a text (even '*Hamlet* proves that the world is made of green cheese', is potentially capable of holding a definable meaning if it is explained or offered in good faith, perhaps as a metaphor), and also that no matter how 'trained' or knowledgable a teacher is in a subject, it is difficult to defend an inherent superiority of one's own reading over others. The only situational constraint (in a tutorial, at least) is that the meaning should potentially be sharable by cooperative listeners who are prepared in good faith and in honest engagement, to create their own meanings out of what is given.

Readers' needs

Having (I hope) given birth to the Reader, I can begin to investigate the contentious statement that the Reader will create meaning from the text by finding what s/he wants to find. Of course, the phrase 'wants to find' is wrong. It is patronizing, it leads into fruitless psychological speculation (Platz, 1986, 98) and excludes the possibility of genuine change in a reader's structure of ideas. It can, however, be refined and glossed in an attempt at least to suggest the unfathomable complexity of the process. For a start, 'wants' holds a fruitful semantic ambiguity, pointing towards a lack and a desire. We 'want' to find something we have not yet found, we desire to fill the gap. We also 'want' or wish to reaffirm something we already have, some burning sense that a particular subject is 'significant' above all others. In the first sense we yearn towards a completer understanding, in the second we are predisposed to hang onto what understanding we already have, knowing that change may be painful (Marris, 1974, 1986). Reading is the filament that glows between the two conductors, the negative and the positive staying the same, and changing.

In order to be cryptic, I shall suggest in summary a calculus, a method of calculating, how the reader's needs or wants operate. Given the infinite plurality of our subject, it would be impossible to achieve a logarithm, a finished tabulation of all possible calculations. (Nor is this in any way desirable.) Analysis of the reader's response could perhaps focus upon and incorporate three fields:

The field of availability.[1]

There must be some knowledge already in the reader's experience which is capable of generating meaning. If a person has not heard of trade unionism, s/he will not, at least in so many words, create a structure of trade union solidarity in *The Nigger of the Narcissus*. There may be some prior awareness that groups of people have behavioural properties which include cooperative action, and a comparable reading may emerge, but it will not be the same. It is tempting to say also that the text (as at least a set of words) must hold something which is capable of being available to the reader who has a specific kind of knowledge available in his or her own context. I suspect that this may be so, but it might also give more credit to the text than it is due, and also there is a mysterious area where what we call neurosis, obsession, can create sharable meanings out of the most unlikely material. At the very least, however, we should be able to say that the reader must find something within his or her *own* available resources (which include the text which is being read) that can lead to a new creation. Within the individual reader, as knowledge changes through experience, so the availability field will change and allow new creations of meaning. This field is the area in which we seek reaffirmation of something already known, or extension of the known.

Close analysis of the field of availability in any one reader encountering a specified text would reveal the richness of the field, and the curious complexity of a kind of self-control. The richness comes in the diversity of individual experience. It will be related to the reader's previous experience of reading: an Elizabethan scholar will bring to a Shakespearean sonnet some knowledge acquired from reading other Elizabethan sonnets, and these understandings may not automatically be available to somebody who has read only westerns. Conversely, the reader of westerns will have a confident grasp on certain conventions of this genre which will not be shared by our cloistered academic. In both cases, it should be added, apparent knowledge is not necessarily a help, apparent ignorance will not necessarily be a hindrance, in creating a text. Specialist knowledge may be a constraint, a diminution of the field of desiring new knowledge (see next category), while absence of this kind of knowledge might well free the reader to create new structures of meaning or value, even to create a text which is definably 'bad' in the reader's terms even though the experts say it is 'good'.[2] In the second instance, the field of desiring may be opened up by the lack of specialist knowledge. And then there are important areas of non-specific, non-specified knowledge. People are inclined to read books with the same analytical equipment that they have devised to 'read' life: a socialist will have different assumptions, a different field of availability, from a fascist, or a person who claims to be politically independent or indifferent (all will have equally strong political assumptions, if political is defined as attitudes to power, but each will be different).

In the case of reading imaginative literature in particular, the individual field of availability will include settled or confused ideas about human relationships. The reading of *Jude the Obscure* created by a man embittered by failed relationships with women will be different from that created by a lesbian seeking a new social context in which sexuality can be expressed. Both will be different from that of a person excluded from a university because of the lack of 'appropriate' qualifications. A host of other factors enter the field of availability, such as age, socio-economic interests, place in the family, and much more. Consider how differently *King Lear* will be created by imagined readers placed on these scales. Where self-control comes is in the capacity of the mind to ignore or suppress areas of available knowledge if the reader decides, probably subliminally, that they are not appropriate. An expert in stamps may have little trouble suppressing this knowledge when s/he is reading a medieval lyric, but more mysteriously it seems quite possible for a policeman to forget his assumptions about law and order when reading about the slaughter of American Indians or Australian aboriginals in earlier times. But if we accept the possibility of the suppression of available attitudes and assumptions, we are really shading into a different field, the one where the reader seeks to reach beyond availability into new territories.

The field of desiring

This is the area where we reach beyond our immediately available contexts. Whether we call it curiosity, wonder or desire, there is a faculty that is entranced by the unknown and the alien and strives to comprehend and personally accommodate it. Words, or sets of words, may hold for readers an alluring incomprehensibility that makes them build up a context in which they take on meaning.

> And there, indeed, is one of the great and marvelous characters of beautiful books (and one which will make us understand the role, at once essential and limited, that reading can play in our spiritual life) which for the author could be called 'Conclusions' and for the reader 'Incitements'. We feel quite truly that our wisdom begins where that of the author ends, and we would like to have him give us answers, while all he can do is give us desires. (Proust, 1971, 35)

If this field is to exist in the individual reader, there must be a desire in the positive sense – a wish to expand consciousness. It is probably rare for such a field to be in operation all the time, and this may account for the common experience of finding ourselves virtually obsessed with a poem or song on one day, quite indifferent to it the next. The effort to sustain desire of any kind, even when the object does not allow total fulfilment, is rare. However, it should be noted that the absence of such a field of desiring is in itself a part of the creation of meaning – it operates even if what is created is, to the reader, boring or predictable. The notion of the field of desiring is relevant, even when it is not activated. The mood of this field may well be totally negative – the reader may be bringing scepticism, cynicism; in the case of professional critics the desire to demystify – but it remains, for all that, a need to reach beyond the known, ostensibly to investigate the work of literature, but more pertinently to create within oneself new regions of consciousness. The field of desiring can be the most magically creative of all, or it can be most creatively destructive of old modes of thought. What this means is that it comes most naturally to the 'naive' reader, who is inclined to be 'swept away' by the language, the ideas or the imputed feeling-states with which that reader will fill the open cavity of the text;

and it is the field from which the professional or 'trained' reader will often back away, perhaps fearful of the embarrassment of self-indulgence, perhaps just afraid of straying beyond the other two relatively familiar fields, the already known and the useful.

The field of usefulness

Plato said that we do not go to imaginative literature in order to be able to do something practical like building a table or waging a war. Instead, we go to a carpenter or a general. And yet there is a sense in which his own enterprise of writing a *Republic* can be interpreted as going to the mode of fiction precisely in order to carry out a project which he was predisposed to think was useful – the creation of an ideal state. Many writers (to let the author creep back into a debate which, after all, has been fuelled by his or her efforts), are most urgently ambitious to 'do the world some good'.[3]

> Because I praised the useful, which
> In my day was considered base
> Because I battled against all religions
> Because I fought oppression or
> For another reason.
>
> Because I was for people and
> Entrusted everything to them, thereby honouring them
> Because I wrote verses and enriched the language
> Because I taught practical behaviour or
> For some other reason.
>
> Therefore I thought my name would still be
> Mentioned. . .
>
> (Brecht, 1976, 264)

This may be the statement of an author expressing a hope, or the manipulation of a textual strategy, but it also defines one of the potential fields of the reader. We may, more often than we think, go to imaginative literature to find the useful praised, to be taught practical behaviour. The limitation, but also the creative strength of the reader's role, however, is that we are already aware of what will be 'useful' to us, and in what area we are looking for tips on 'practical behaviour'. Proust has said eloquently that if we go to literature for lessons in living we are doomed to disappointment, and if our demands are too specific we may even be in a state bordering on the psychotic. But he equally acknowledges that the need itself is human. Nor need our activity of creating what is useful to us (by fastening upon words in a poem or events in a novel) be particularly mysterious or unhealthy. Critics look in literary works for what is useful to them in writing their book or article; students ransack a text for thematic consistency to fuel an essay due on Friday; others come to the literature of love in order to cope with the chaos in which they live, by creating structures of feeling that may be appropriate in their own circumstances. One aware of the necessity to confront death may read *Lycidas* for what is most useful, a form of philosophical consolation or a voice of anger. The field of usefulness is the most primitive, and the most morally based of all, for it is the one that links us all together. Tolstoy, through his notion of the 'infectiousness' of art, was to acknowledge this value of reading most directly.

By now some of my own readers may be very exasperated (although, incidentally, if they are then they are conveniently exercising the availability field, the desiring and the usefulness fields – they are creatively engaged with the argument). They throw up their hands and cry, 'But surely it is commonsense that the text imposes some constraints? Why would the text exist as a single, unique entity if it did not by definition preclude certain responses or understandings? A sane person surely cannot read an electrician's manual in the same way as a novel – the mode of the text itself prevents this.' The appeal to commonsense is always difficult to parry because it is an activation of the 'field of availability' without a compensating expression from the field of desiring. The answer to these problems lies in the question itself: '. . . cannot read . . . in the same way . . .'. Precisely. It is the application of initial restraints, or the flouting of restraints, that occurs in the *reader*, not in the text. Either the preconceptions (field of availability) of the reader delimits what s/he wants to find in the book . . . or the field of desiring helps him or her find (create) a meaning which other readers see as surprising . . . or the field of usefulness gives a specific impetus to the reader's activity. The example given by my angry rhetorical questioner allows us to see this in practice. An electrician reads an electrician's manual for specific advice about how to solve a technical problem (let us say), while s/he reads a novel for enjoyment or 'escape'. Those are the particular reader's needs expressing themselves. But a novelist reading an electrician's manual may find the field of desiring foremost among the responses: s/he may find the language wonderful, poetic, full of 'flowing currents', 'charges', 'filaments', 'voltage and wattage' . . . evocative and both linguistically and conceptually opening up a warm new world of words and thoughts which may filter into the next novel. In other words, it may be as enjoyable as the novel is to the electrician. (Or, our rider, it may be baffling and problematic – or tedious – but this by no means diminishes the appropriateness of my analysis). And if the same novelist reads a novel, s/he may find no enjoyment at all – the desiring field may not be activated, and all the reading produces is a technician's assessment, positive or negative, of the practical ways in which a narrative has been presented, not unlike, in fact, the electrician's response to the manual, a reading of which may or may not solve the burning problem in his or her professional life. When the text happens not to be either an electrician's manual or a novel but the Bible, then suddenly the volume of readers, each different in expertise, knowledge, desires, and demands for practical and spiritual answers, increases exponentially, and each of these multifarious readers is plural both in the instant of reading and in the changes wrought by passing time. Readings of the Bible provide perhaps the greatest evidence that the Author is dead, the Text is neutral, and that the reader is, and has always been, creative and alive.

What, finally, is the status of the 'neutral' text? Is it not possible to argue that the text is the first reading, the most complete reading (in the sense that every detail is noticed, every word equally significant)? The author, recollecting, re-collecting, projecting, reading patterns of experience that are partly implicit in his or her own mind (available), partly created and imagined (desiring knowledge), all in the service of trying to change or at least to entertain future readers (the useful), reads into reality, that is, writes a text which is then placed at the disposal of its infinity of new, creative readers.

Notes

1. I found this phrase (used with a different meaning and signification) in Geoffrey Thurley's (1983) *The Romantic Predicament.*
2. The most pernicious tendency of twentieth-century criticism (following the example of Mathew Arnold) is to see its main function as the 'discrimination' or 'judgment' of good from bad, without providing criteria, or at best providing criteria which would be disputed by many people. In art criticism, the equivalent distinction is between 'ugly' and 'beautiful', a fallacy exposed by Jean Dubuffet in

'Anticultural Positions', a lecture delivered on 20 December 1951 at the Arts Club of Chicago:

> It seems to me that the Occident will not suffer a great loss if it loses this idea of the beautiful. On the contrary, if he becomes aware that there is no ugly object nor ugly person in the world and that beauty does not exist anywhere, but that any object is able to become for any man a way of fascination and illumination, he will have made a good catch. I think such an idea will enrich life more than the common idea of beauty. (From unpublished manuscript)

Dubuffet learned English specifically in order to write this lecture. I am grateful to Suzanne Montgomery for showing it to me.

3. Among poets the phrase is virtually a commonplace (used in so many words by at least Samuel Johnson and John Keats, and in spirit by Sir Philip Sidney in his *Defence of Poetry*) although critics resolutely block the artists in their most important aim, by either trivializing or ignoring the didactic element. In doing so, critics are creating their own meaning, but their exclusions are influential.

References

Barthes, R. (1957, trans. 1972) *Mythologies*, translated A. Lavers, St Albans, Granada Publishing.

Barthes, R. (1984 trans. 1986) *The Rustle of Language*, translated R. Howard, Oxford, Blackwell.

Brecht, B. (1976) *Poems*, (eds) J. Willett and R. Manheim, London, Methuen.

Cavell, S. (1976) *Must We Mean What We Say*, Cambridge, Cambridge University Press.

Eco, U. (1981) *The Role of the Reader: Explorations in the Semiotics of Texts*, London, Hutchinson.

Eliot, T.S. (1932) *Selected Essays*, London, Faber and Faber.

Fish, S. (1980) *Is There a Text in This Class? The Authority of Interpretive Communication*, Cambridge, Massachusetts, Harvard University Press.

Flynn, E.A. and Patrocinio, P.S. (1986) *Gender and Reading: Essays on Readers, Texts and Contexts*, Baltimore, Johns Hopkins University Press.

Jolley, E. (1985) *Foxybaby*, Harmondsworth, Penguin, 67–8.

Marris, P. (1974, 1986) *Loss and Change*, London, Routledge & Kegan Paul.

Platz, N. (1986) 'Analysing the Reader: A Critical Survey of Recent Psychoanalytic Theories of Reading' in G. McGregor and R.S. White (eds) *The Art of Listening*, London, Croom Helm, 87–101.

Proust, M. (1971) *On Reading*, translated J. Autret and W. Burford, London, Souvenir Press.

Rose, J. (1986) '*Hamlet* – the *Mona Lisa* of Literature', *Critical Quarterly* 28, 35–49.

Rylance, R. (1987) *Debating Texts: A Reader in 20th. Century Literary Theory and Method*, Milton Keynes, Open University Press.
Thurley, G. (1983) *The Romantic Predicament*, London, Macmillan.
Tolstoy, L. (1898) *What is Art?*, London, Oxford University Press.
Tompkins, J.P. (1980) (ed.) *Reader-Response Criticism: From Formalism to Post-Structuralism*, Baltimore, Johns Hopkins University Press.
Wimsatt, W.K. and Beardsley, M.C. (1946) 'The Intentional Fallacy', *Sewanee Review*, 54, 468–88.
Wimsatt, W.K. Jr. and Brooks, C. (1957) *Literary Criticism*, London, Routledge and Kegan Paul.